History of Christianity in India

History of Christianity in India

History of Christianity in India

A Reader

Woba James

Christian World Imprints

First Published in 2019, **2022** by

Christian World Imprints
Christian Publishing & Books from India
A-71 Group, Wazirpur Industrial Area
Delhi-110052
cwidelhi2017@gmail.com
www.ChristianWorldImprints.com
Phone: +91 11 41526079

ISBN: 978-93-5148-394-6 (HB)
ISBN: 978-93-5148-395-3 (PB)

Printed in India.

Contents

Author's Preface

This book is a result of the long-felt need of the students especially students undergoing theological education under the Senate of Serampore College (University) and Asia Theological Association curriculum that has been often expressed to me, one of their course teachers. What my students need is a book that is designed in accordance to their course syllabus in the History of Christianity in India. Hence, I finally decided to put my efforts in bringing out a book that to some extent caters to their need. As such my gratitude goes to them for being the main motivation behind my work here and as such this book is dedicated to them – my beloved students.

This book covers the History of Christianity in India from its beginnings till the 21st century. It has twelve chapters in all. It is imperative that I admit that this work would not have been possible without the inspiration, encouragement and support of my students, friends, family and several well-wishers. Though I might not be able to mention all of them here, few of them deserve my acknowledgement. First and foremost, I thank God the Almighty for all the blessings bestowed upon me, for seeing me through the entire time and process of this work. Secondly, I express my heartfelt gratitude to the enthusiasm and encouragement I received from my students, who served as the backbone for this work. Thirdly, my teachers, who, all through my theological journey, served as the source of inspiration, especially my department teachers in different Colleges and Study Centers. Lastly (but not the least!), my gratitude goes to my wife Dr Lovely Awomi James who once again took great pains in meticulously reading through my manuscripts and our children Khoesiivio James Woba (Avi) and Rathrune James Woba (Ane) for their love and forbearance.

Woba James
Eastern Theological College
Jorhat

Introduction

Sensing the great need for a book on the *History of Christianity in India: A Reader*, this work invests a sincere effort, to bring out a single volume book that covers a major portion of the subject History of Christianity in India. The method upon which this work rests is a historical analysis. This work is heavily dependent upon those authoritative historical sources and reputed scholars who have contributed so much to the preservation and flourishing of History of Christianity in India. As the readers go through the book, they will be able to easily identify those sources as they are given in the footnotes without which, this work would not have been possible. The writer believes that this book will be of some help to the readers (especially students) in their study and understanding of the History of Christianity in India.

As mentioned in the preface, this book has twelve chapters. The first chapter **The Origin of Christianity in India** deals with the subject of the Origin of Christianity in India, taking under our critical study the various sources of the St Thomas tradition to see how far they are historically reliable. The second chapter **Indian Christianity and Its Relation with Christian of the East** takes the subject of the ecclesiastical relation that existed between the Church in India and the Church of the East in the early centuries which is supported by diverse local and outside sources of tradition. The third chapter **The Roman Catholic Christianity in India** traces the history of the Roman Catholic Church in India and the religious policy of the Portuguese in its attempt to establish the Roman Catholic Christianity in India. The fourth chapter **The First Protestant Christianity in India** analyses the history of the first two protestant missions in India – the Tranquebar Mission and the Serampore Mission. The fifth chapter **Protestant Christianity in Different Regions in India** analyses some of the important issues that accompanied the growth of protestant missionary activities and the emergence of the British power in India. The sixth chapter **Colonialism and Protestant Christianity in India** takes the subject in analyzing their religious policies towards Christian mission in India. The seventh chapter **Christianity and Nation Building in India,** deals with the rise of Christianity and National Independence movement, Bengal renaissance, social activities, empowerment of women and Christianity and caste and Christianity and communalism in India. The eighth chapter **Indigenous Missionary Movements and the Rise of Indian Church** deals with the development of quest for Indian Identity and indigenization of Indian Christianity. Chapter nine **Indian Christianity and Ecumenical Movement** gives a historical analysis on the Indian Ecumenical Movement and the various issues that come under its wings. Chapter ten **History of Christianity in North East India** traces the growth of Christianity in North East India through different missions and church traditions. The eleventh chapter **Issues of Pentecostalism in India** gives a brief history of the rise of Pentecostalism in India, which happens to be the fastest growing Church in India. And the final chapter **Post Independent Indian and Christian Movements** deals with the rise of Religious Fundamentalism, Minority Rights, and Reservation for Dalit Christians, Ashram Movements and Theological Institutions in India.

Chapter 1

The Origin of Christianity in India

1. Introduction

The origin of Christianity in India is not an easy subject to understand owing to the limitation of direct existing evidences. Traditionally, there are three views concerning the origin of Christianity in India. The most popular opinion is that Apostle Thomas brought Christianity to India. Secondly, that Apostle Thomas and Bartholomew brought Christianity to India. The third opinion is that Christianity was brought to India by a group of Christians migrating from East Syria or Persian Churches. For our study, let us take under our serious consideration the various sources of the St. Thomas tradition to see how far the information contained in them is historically acceptable.

2. Sources and Traditions Concerning Apostle Thomas Coming to India

The Tradition concerning the origin of Christianity in India had grown from both inside and outside India. The tradition that grew outside India can be termed, 'Western tradition,' and the tradition that grew from within is called 'Indian tradition.'

2.1. The Western Tradition: The Origin of Christianity in India

2.1.1. *The Acts of Judas Thomas*

The Western tradition is supposed to have originated from an apocryphal book called 'The Acts of Judas Thomas,' which represents the Syrian Edessan tradition as well as the Alexandrian tradition.[1] The Edessan tradition places powerful emphasis on India as the place of Apostle Thomas' ministry while the Alexandrian tradition places Parthia as the place of Thomas' ministry. It is believed that the Acts of Judas Thomas was written in Syriac about the beginning of the third century in Edessa by Bardesanes (between A.D. 180 and A.D. 230).[2]

According to the tradition of the Acts of Thomas, the Disciples of Christ, after the ascension of our Lord Jesus, gathered together and cast lots to locate the place of their ministry. India came upon Thomas but was unwilling to go. He said "I have not strength for this, because I am weak and I am a Hebrew: how can I teach the Indians?"[3] The same night, Jesus, appearing to him in a vision, encouraged Thomas to go to India, promising him of His presence. Still Thomas continued to show his indecision saying, "withersoever thou willst, Our Lord send me; only to India I will not go."[4] However, the following day, he met a merchant by the name Habban who was seeking for a carpenter to build a palace for the king, Gundaphorus.[5] It was with this merchant that Thomas arrived in India.

On reaching India, the king gave adequate money to him and asked him to build the palace. Instead of following the King's order, Thomas took the money and spent it on the poor. On the appointed day when the king asked for the palace, Thomas replied to him that he had built the palace for him in the heaven. On hearing this, the king was livid with anger and in his fury threw Thomas into prison. Meanwhile, Gad, the king's brother fell ill and died. Being taken to heaven, he was shown the palace built by Thomas for his brother. Gad obtained permission to get back, and on his return he told his brother about the palace and requested the release of Thomas. Thomas was released, and both Gad and Gundaphorus received baptism and he continued his ministry.

The tradition continued to says that upon the request of the neighboring king Mazdai, to heal an officer's wife and daughter who were possessed with evil spirits, Thomas went to the next kingdom and healed them. His preaching resulted in the conversion of some noble women, including the king's wife. Upon conversion some of the women declared their intention to abandon marriage.

[1] Depending more on the Acts of Judas Thomas. Cf. K. M. George, *Christianity in India throughout the Centuries* (Hyderabad: Authentic Books, 2009), 88.

[2] Cf. J.N. Farquhar, "The Apostle Thomas in North India," *Bulletin of the John Rhylands Library*, 10 (1926): 80ff. (Hereafter cited as Farquhar, *The Apostle Thomas in North India*).

[3] M.K. Kuriakose, "History of Christianity in India: Source Materials," *Indian Theological Library* No. 9 (Madras: Christian Literature Society, 1982), 2. (Hereafter cited as Kuriakose, *Source Materials*).

[4] 'Acts of Thomas,' quoted in G.M. Moraes, *A History of Christianity in India from Early Times to St. Francis Xavier: A.D. 52-1542* (Bombay: Manaktalas, 1964), 25. (Hereafter cited as Moraes, *A History of Christianity in India*).

[5] Cf. A.M. Mundadan, *History of Christianity in India, Vol. I: From the Beginning up to the Middle of the Sixteenth Century*, revised edition (Bangalore: CHAI, 2001), 25. (Hereafter cited as Mundadan, *History of Christianity in India*).

The king was infuriated by this and ordered his soldiers to kill Thomas and had him killed. After some time, the king's child was possessed by some evil spirit. Believing Thomas' bones would cure the king's child, they opened the tomb of Thomas. The tomb was found empty and it was told that the bones had been carried away to Edessa.[6] This, in brief, is an account of the Acts of Thomas.

2.1.2. *Testimony of Church Fathers*

Unfortunately the church Fathers give us very little information about Thomas. However, from the third century onwards, they make some vague allusions about Thomas's ministry. Most of the Pre-Nicene Church fathers like Origen, Clement of Alexandria, and Eusebius following the Alexandrian Tradition refer to Parthia as the place of Thomas' ministry. Hippolytus, Bishop of Portus, written in the early years of the third century mentions that Thomas did his ministry in Parthia and in many other countries and died in a Indian city called 'Calamene.'[7] A similar kind of account comes from Dorotheus, Bishop of Tyre about the end of the 3rd century. He observes that Thomas preached the Gospel to the Parthians but suffered martyrdom at Calamina, a town in India.[8]

On the other hand, the Post-Nicene Church fathers and historians like St. Ephrem, St. Gregory of Nazianzus, St. Ambrose, St. Jerome, Gregory of Tours and Martin of Tours accept the view that Thomas came to India.[9] St. Ephrem of Syria, representing the Edessan tradition gives a little more detailed account of the work of St. Thomas in India. In his hymn he says,

> The one begotten his apostle chose,
> Among them Thomas, whom he went
> To baptize people perverse, in darkness steeped.
> A dark night then India's land enveloped,
> Like the sun's ray Thomas did dark forth;
> There he dawned, and her illumined....[10]

It goes on to say,

> Blessed art thou, O Thrice-blessed city! That hast acquired this pearl, none greater doth India yield; blessed art thou worthy to possess the

---

[6] Cf. Mundadan, *History of Christianity in India*, 26.

[7] F.E. Keay, *A History of the Syrian Church in India*, third edition (Delhi: ISPCK, 1960), 4. (Hereafter cited as Keay, *A History of the Syrian Church in India*).

[8] Keay, *A History of the Syrian Church in India*, 5.

[9] C.B. Firth, *An Introduction to Indian Church History*, revised edition (Delhi: ISPCK, 2001), 4-6. Cf. also A.C. Perumalil, *The Apostles in India* (Allepy: Prakasm Publication, 1971), 23-60. (Hereafter cited as Perumalil, *The Apostles in India*).

[10] Kuriakose, *Source Materials*, 5.

> priceless gem! Praise to thee, O Gracious son, who thus thy adorers dost enrich![11]

Fifth century historians Theodore (430-458), Nicephorus, Gaudentius, and Sophronius also refer to Thomas as apostle to India.[12] St. Gregory of Tours (544-595) talked about the existence of a monastery and temple of great size and excellent structure and ornaments in that place in India where the body of St. Thomas lay long before it was transported to Edessa.[13] All these sources show that there was a continuous tradition in the west connecting Thomas with India.

2.2. Indian Tradition: the Origin of Christianity in India

The Indian tradition was in oral form till the 16th century, and it contains about the ministry and martyrdom of Thomas in India. This oral tradition had developed from Malabar Tradition, Mylapore Tradition and Chaldean Tradition. According to the Indian tradition, St. Thomas landed in Malankara, near Cranganore, (Kodangaluru) in 52 A.D. His preaching resulted in founding of seven Churches – 1. Maliankara 2. Palayur 3. Gokkamangalam 4. Niranam 5. Chayal 6. Parur and 7. Quilon. Before leaving Kerala he ordained priests from four Nambudri Brahmin families.

After some time, he came to Mylapore. His preaching, accompanied by various miracles, resulted in the founding of a church in Mylapore. Later he went up to China preaching the Gospel. He came back to Madras and the Brahmins who were jealous of him speared him to death in 72 A.D., while he was praying in the little mount and his body was found by the Christians and they buried him in the church he constructed in Mylapore. Folk songs in Kerala - Ramban Pattu, the Veeradyan Pattu and Margam kali pattu – reflect this tradition.[14] These folk songs are sung by both Christians and their Hindu neighbors even to this day, keeping alive the memory of the apostle in the minds of the people.

The Chaldean tradition is to attribute of the apostolate of Thomas all the areas where the east-Syrian church has influence at one time or the other. For instance, the Syriac Breviary, summing up the tradition, says,

> By St. Thomas has been abolished the error of idolatry from India; By St. Thomas the Chinese also with the Ethiopians have turned to the truth; By St. Thomas have shown the beams of the doctrine of life in

---

[11] Kuriakose, *Source Materials*, 5.

[12] Cf. Keay, *A History of the Syrian Church in India*, 6.

[13] Keay, *A History of the Syrian Church in India*, 5.

[14] A.M. Mundadan, *Sixteenth Century Tradition of Thomas Christians* (Bangalore: Dharmaram College, 1970), 60-67. (Hereafter cited as Mundadan, *Sixteenth Century Tradition of Thomas Christians*).

all India; By St. Thomas has flown up and gone up the kingdom of Height among the Chinese.[15]

But the Mylapore and Malabar traditions talk about Thomas' ministry only within India. The Mylapore tradition is primarily concerned about the miraculous building of the house or church by the apostle. The main difference being while Malabar tradition locates them in Kerala, the Mylapore tradition locates them in Coramandil. Common to both tradition are: the so-called 'miracle of the boy' whom the apostle brought back to life; 'the miracle of the rice according to which Thomas paid to the laborers sand which turned out to be rich treasures or coins in the hands of the recipients.[16] In spite of the discrepancy, the point to observe is that the Indian tradition talks in unrelenting terms regarding St. Thomas' apostolate and martyrdom in India.

2.2.1. *The Non-Christians Testimonies about Thomas*

The tradition about Thomas' ministry and martyrdom in India is prevalent even among the non-Christians too. For instance, a local tradition among the Brahmins holds that while Thomas was preaching in Palayur, he is believed to have wrought a miracle, suspending the water in the air in the shape of a flower and this led to the conversion of a number of Brahmins of the village. However a few hurriedly left the place saying the next bath would never be but in the neighboring Venbenad.[17] Even to this day, the Brahmins have no contact with this town, and it is considered cursed for (Chawakad) generations.[18] The prevalence of similar tradition is evident also in the writings of the non-Christians. A Brahmin writing called 'Keralopathi' seems to talk about the ministry of Thomas. Though it was written to prove the hierarchy of the Brahmins, it talked about a certain foreigner, Thomman, who is spoken of as Sarva Veda Vighahan came to Malabar and converted to his Buddha faith many prominent people of the land including the reigning Cheraman king, Bana parumal.[19] Though its historicity is doubtful, its reference to the conversion of the local ruler by a foreign religious teacher seems to reflect the widely prevalent tradition about the coming of the foreign teacher.

The Portuguese who came to India in the 16th century, were surprised to learn that the St. Thomas Christians had in their possession not only songs, but

[15] Cited in John M. Kaserow, "Christian Evaluation of Buddhism from Clement of Alexandria to the Renaissance," *Doctoral Dissertation* (University of St. Michael's College, Toronto: 1976), 49.

[16] For detail information on these stories Cf. Mundadan, *Sixteenth Century Tradition of Thomas Christians*, 44-46, 50-52.

[17] S.G. Pothen, *The Syrian Christians of Kerala*, fourth edition (Madras: K. M. Cherian, 1968), 15. (Hereafter cited as Pothen, *Syrian Christians*).

[18] Ken Newton, *Glimpses of Indian Church History*, second edition (Bombay: Living Light Publications), 1975.

[19] Cf. Pothen, *Syrian Christians*, 15.

also written record which commemorated the life, work, and death of St. Thomas. Francisco Dionysio writing in 1578 about the Apostle and the community founded by him remarked,

> What is known below is known from the information supplied by old people; it is the common and unanimous belief of all; they hold it as a well-handed down tradition; they have put these things in their books and their songs.[20]

The Portuguese collected all the information both from the Christians as well as from the non-Christians, and give written form to the tradition. These letters, survey reports, etc., are the earliest written documents for the Indian tradition.

2.2.2. *Tomb of Thomas*

The tomb and relics of Thomas received much attention in the Portuguese reports. Interestingly, the tomb of Thomas in Mylapore is referred to often as a seemingly strong argument to establish the coming of Thomas to India. Some historians have questioned the authenticity and view that the tomb of Thomas is a creation of the Portuguese who came in the 16th century. L.W. Brown reflecting this observes,

> It is clear that the identification of the Mylapore tomb…burial place of St. Thomas the apostle and the ascription of special sanctity to various places in the locality - St. Thomas mount a little mount - were entirely the work of the Portuguese….[21]

Yet from the seventh century onwards, the location of the tomb of Thomas has been expressly referred to. For instance, Gregory of Tours (544-595) wrote that he had learned from Theodore the Indian that there was a great monastery in India where Thomas' body lay before being transported to Edessa. To quote,

> His (Thomas) holy remains after a long time were removed to the city of Edessa in Syria and there entered. In that part of India where they first rested, stands a monastery church of striking dimensions… This Theodore, who had been to the place narrated to us.[22]

---

[20] F. Dionysio, "Informa ao de Christandade de Sao Thome," 395, cited in Mundadan, *History of Christianity in India*, 36.

[21] L.W. Brown, *The Indian Christians of St. Thomas* (Cambridge: Cambridge University Press, 1956), 57. (Hereafter cited as Brown, *Indian Christians of St. Thomas*).

[22] Miraculorum Liber, 1:32. Patrologei Latina, 71.733, cited in Perumalil, *The Apostles in India*, 75.

In 638 Isidore, based on Passio's account, mark the martyrdom and burial place of Thomas as 'Calamina,' an Indian town. He said,

> This Thomas preached the gospel of Christ to the...Parthians... Byrcanians and the Bactrians, and to the Indians of the Oriental region and penetrating the innermost regions and sealing his preaching by his passion he died transfixed with the lance at Calamina, a city of India, and was buried with honor.[23]

According to Mar. Solomon of Basra (1222) observes that some say "the apostle was buried in Mahluph, a city in the land of the Indians."[24] Amr, son of Mathew, in 1340 gives more definite information when he said, "Thomas' tomb is in the island of Meilan in India on the right hand side of the altar, in his monastery."[25] Finally four Mesopotamian bishops writing in 1504 talked of "the houses as well as the tomb of the apostle St. Thomas stand on a city on the sea named 'Meilapor.'[26] The identification of Calamina, Meilan, or Mahluph with Mylapore, as the burial place of Thomas though not definite, in the light of the long standing tradition, we may conclude that the tomb of Thomas is not the creation of the Portuguese and it was in existence much before their arrival.

The Latin missionaries, namely John of Monte Corvino in 1305, Oderic of Padenone in 1324, John Marignolli in 1349, and Durate Barbosa in 1504, claim to have seen the Church built on the tomb of Thomas. Medlycott writes,

> Preceding onwards the said Nicolas arrived at a maritime city, which he name Malepur, situated in the second gulf beyond the Indus. Here the body of St. Thomas lies honorably buried in a large and beautiful Church....[27]

Here, we may assume 'Malepur, the maritime city' to be Mylapore. Thus the tomb of Thomas is not at all the invention or fabrication of the Portuguese. It is also significant to note that no other part of the world laid any serious claim for the possession of the tomb of Thomas other than Mylapore.

3. The Tradition of St. Bartholomew Coming to India

The tradition concerning St. Bartholomew's apostolate in India originated from the 4th century with Eusebius of Caesarea and St. Jerome. According to them around 190 A.D. Pantaenus, a noted Christian teacher of Alexandria, visited

---

[23] "Extract from Etymol. Liber. 14.3.5.6. Patrologia Latina 82.497," cited in Perumalil, *The Apostles in India*, 37.

[24] Cf. Perumalil, *The Apostles in India*, 15.

[25] Perumalil, *The Apostles in India*, 18.

[26] Perumalil, *The Apostles in India*, 18.

[27] A.E. Medlycott, *India and the Apostle St Thomas* (London: n.p., 1905), 95, cited in Moraes, *A History of Christianity in India*, 20. (Hereafter cited as Medlycott, *India and Apostle Thomas*).

India. During his visit Pantaenus found among the Christians, a copy of the Gospel according to St. Mathew in 'Hebrew.' The Christians over there told him that it was left by St. Bartholomew, who had preached to them. Jerome affirming this adds that he preached to the Brahmins. Historians like Milne Rae, E.M. Philip, and J. N. Oglive, believe that this talks only about St. Thomas' ministry. Few others are of the opinion that Pantaenus must have visited South Arabia, and not India.

However, Fr Heras, Fr A.C. Perumalil and Dr G. M. Moraes affirm the visit of Pantaenus as well St. Bartholomew. They hold Konkan coastal region of Bombay, known as Kalyan to be the field of Bartholomew's ministry.[28] In support, they point out to the 5th century source 'Hieronyminum Martyrologium,' which says that St. Bartholomew was beheaded for Christ in India. They also point out to a Greek tradition, according to which Bartholomew went to India. Saying that the word 'Kalyan' means 'happy' they argue that it refers to Kalyan in India.[29] A.C. Perumalil thinks that the vestiges of ancient Christianity which the missionaries in the 16th century found in Konkan region are remnant of the early Christians converted by Bartholomew, and they must have later merged with the other Christians of Bombay after the arrival of Portuguese. Interestingly, Bishop Brown admits the visit of both St. Thomas and St. Bartholomew to India. Yet we have more reasons to believe in the apostolate of St. Thomas than the St. Bartholomew, as we have more local claim.

4. Evaluation of the Traditions

Since the 4th century, there is general consensus in the sources that Thomas came to India. But, in spite of this consensus, several historians like Basnage and Tillemont, James Hough, John Kayes, etc., out-rightly denied the possibility of Thomas coming to India and regarded the tradition as nothing more than a pious myth. Their main question was how is it possible for a Palestinian Jew to travel such a long distance and come to India, in those days when travel and communication facilities were very scarce? Saying this they argue that Thomas could not have come to India at all. But, those of us who live in the 21st century are well informed about the trade link between India and Roman Empire around the dawn of the Christian era. Hence, their argument doesn't stand. The trade link and communication between India and Mediterranean region seems to have started at least with the conquest of Alexander the Great. P. Thomas maintains that,

> Regular envoys were sent by the Greek kings to Indian courts, matrimonial alliances between Eastern and Western Princes become

[28] Cf. Perumalil, *The Apostles in India*, 180ff; Moraes, *A History of Christianity in India*, 43ff.

[29] Cf. Mundadan, *History of Christianity in India*, 65.

> common, and caravan laden with merchandise passed up and down the Hyber for trading centers from Bay of Bengal to Black Sea.[30]

Moreover, Starbo, who lived in the time of Augustus Caesar, observed that he had seen 120 ships sailing in India.[31] Ptolemy gives a good deal of information about the trade centers in India.[32] Pliny complaints,

> The subject (of setting forth the whole route from Egypt of India) is one worthy of our notice, seeing that in no year does India draws our empire of less than fifty millions of sesters, giving back her own wares in exchange, which are sold among us at fully one hundred times their prime cost.[33]

It was believed that the trade relationship between Roman Empire and South India resulted in regular diplomatic relations. Thus, on the occasion of the ascension of Augustus Caesar to the throne, Pandyan king (South India) is known to have sent an embassy to congratulate the Emperor.[34] The close relationship between these two parts of the world is further confirmed by thousands of gold and silver coins discovered in various parts of South India, Coimbatore in Tamil Nadu and Calicut in Kerala. A hoard found recently at Eyyal, near Cranganore, contained 46 silver coins of Claudius and Nero.[35] These numismatic[36] evidences speak for the trade link between India and Roman Empire.

Furthermore, the Tamil classics such as Puranamuru, Agananuru, Pattupattu and Sialappadigaram give vivid description about the Greeks, who were referred to as Yavanavas.[37] Agananuru says that the Yavanavvas (Greeks) came in large number carrying gold coins and returned with pepper.[38] All the evidences from Greek, Latin and Tamil literature and numismatic affirms the trade link and constant communication between India and Roman Empire.

Next the question that arises is, why the Pre-Nicene Church Father refers Parthia, as a place of Ministry for Thomas? Historians like Heras and A.C. Perumalil suggest that during the first century Parthian Empire was spread across

---

30 P. Thomas, *Christianity in India and Pakistan: A General Survey of the Progress of Christianity in India from Apostolic Times to the Present Day* (London: George Allen and Unwin Ltd., 1954), 5. (Hereafter cited as Thomas, *Christianity in India and Pakistan*).

31 Kuriakose, *Source Materials*, 1.

32 Kuriakose, *Source Materials*, 1.

33 Cf. Perumalil, *The Apostles in India*, 9.

34 Thomas, *Christianity in India and Pakistan*, 7.

35 Brown, *Indian Christians of St. Thomas*, 61.

36 Study of the collection of coins or medals.

37 Cf. Moraes, *A History of Christianity in India*, 37.

38 Meile, "Les Yavannavas dan I Inde Tamoule," *Journal of Asiatique*, 90, cited in Moraes, *A History of Christianity in India*, 37.

the North western India. Actually, the vague name 'Parthia' is used only to refer to India.[39] Based on the Acts of Thomas some historians like G. Milne Rae and Dahlmann argue that St. Thomas came to North India.[40] They argue that the 14 gold coins and 1565 copper coins discovered by Mason in Punjab and Afghanistan since 1834 bearing the name Gundaphorus in Greek on one side and Pali on other side, dated to be 1st century[41] and the stone inscription Takht-I-Bahi discovered by Bellow and now available in Lahore Museum, containing Gundaphorus' name[42] and dated to the A.D. 46 seem to support the North Indian version. It is true that Gundaphorus was an Indo-Parthian king ruling between A.D. 51 and A.D. 74. His territory stretched from Kandhas in Eastern Persia to the Punjab and probably as far North as Kabul.[43]

The circumstantial evidences are more in favor of the South Indian apostolate of Thomas. The frequent sea-traffic between South India and Roman Empire would have facilitated the coming of Thomas to Southern India than to the Northern India. The demand in Rome was mostly for spices, pepper, perfume and ivory and they were available in plenty in South India. In addition to that, the claim of the community of Syrian Christians who claim to be the descendants of the converts of Thomas stand a better claim for Thomas' ministry in Southern India. To the Syrian Christians of Kerala the belief in the apostolic origin of Christianity is almost an article of faith for generations.[44] It is significant to note that no other place other than Mylapore in India claims to have the tomb of Thomas. Moreover, the Syrian writers like, Mar. Solomon, a Nestorian Bishop, Amr affirm the apostolate of Thomas in South India. The popular name of the St. Thomas Christians in South India was 'Nazarani.' Interestingly the name given to the followers of Christ during the apostle's time was 'Nazarene.' This resemblance also supports the view that the main events must have truly taken place and that too in South India.

---

[39] Moraes, *A History of Christianity in India*, 56.

[40] K.N. Daniel, *The South Indian Apostolate of St. Thomas* (Serampore: CHAI., n.d.), 8. (Hereafter cited as Daniel, *The South Indian Apostolate of St. Thomas*).

[41] Stephen Neil, *History of Christianity in India: The Beginning to A.D. 1707*, Vol. I. (Cambridge: Cambridge University Press, 1985), 27.

[42] Cf. Moraes, *A History of Christianity in India*, 52-56.

[43] Cf. Samuel Hugh Moffet, *A History of Christianity in Asia*, Vol. 1, second edition (New York: Orbis Books, 1998).

[44] Thomas, *Christianity in India and Pakistan*, 18.

Chapter 2

Indian Christianity and Its Relation with Christians of the East

1. Introduction

This chapter is an attempt to present the relationship between the Indian Christianity and the Christianity of the East in the early centuries. Christianity in India was founded by the Apostle Thomas in the first century itself, yet Christianity in India suffered a decline in the course of time and it was revived with and through the arrival of Christians – merchants, missionaries, priests and believers from Persia especially of the 4th and 9th-10th centuries.

2. Indian Christianity in the Early Centuries

In spite of the vague picture we have, we know for sure that the Christianity in India had close connection with the Christianity in Syria and in Persia. Its ecclesiastical language was Syriac and the Christianity in India had been receiving its Bishops from East and that it was not an autonomous Church. Yet the question of attributing the origin of Christianity in India to the immigrants could not be considered seriously, because to do so would be to intentionally bypass the rich sources of tradition especially of the natives, who for centuries have held dear to their hearts, faith and culture. Besides, the immigration events come much later in the 4th and 9th-10th centuries.

2.1. Tradition Concerning the Migration from Mylapore to Malabar

When tradition had it that the Christian community of Mylapore emigrated to Malabar, the obvious question to follow would be 'why?' Why or what caused the migration? We have here also different versions – namely two[45] at that:

1. One version says that it was caused by natural calamities such as floods and earthquakes;
2. The second version says that it was due to man-made disasters such as war, persecution and the like.

M. Gomes, a Portuguese reported in 1517 that Mylapore lay ruined due to natural calamities like sea encroachment, inundations and the resultant depopulation of the town area. Abuna, an East-Syrian Bishop, reported also that the land was likewise destroyed and as a result the Christians left the place and shifted to the West Coast of India.[46] Diogo Fernandes, another Portuguese reported that, the Thomas Christians were persecuted by the non-believers and were expelled from the region altogether that they migrated to Quilon and Cranganore and to other parts of India. Besides, the Christians were told that they could still come to Mylapore on a pilgrimage but could not reside there. According to Francisco de Ros, and Barros (Portuguese), the St. Thomas Christians left Mylapore due to the effects of wars, famines and persecutions from the non-believers and Muslims.[47] Thus, they were forced to disperse into different groups and set off to different parts of Malabar.

Fr Mathew writes (local source) that not long after the passing of the Apostle Thomas, the Christian community found itself without any proper guide or leader. At this juncture, a magician entered the scene at Mylapore and began working wonders through his magic that many Christians were lured away from the true faith. Only those who stood firm in their faith sought and found refuge in Malabar among the brethren there.[48]

From the above divergent views, we conclude that the cause of Mylapore Christians' migration to Malabar was due to natural calamities as well as the persecutions and wars that forced them to fled and seek refuge from the fellow-brethren in Malabar.

3. Relation between the Indian Church and the East-Syrian Church of Persia

It is not only the Christians in India that stand strongly on the Apostolate of St. Thomas but also the Christians in Persia. The Christians in Persia hold that

[45] Cf. Mundadan, *History of Christianity in India,* 71.

[46] Cf. Mundadan, *History of Christianity in India,* 72.

[47] Cf. Mundadan, *History of Christianity in India*, 73.

[48] The Account of Fr Mathew (1730) in S. Giamil, Genninae Relationes (1902), 562-564, cited in Mundadan, *History of Christianity in India,* 74.

Apostle Thomas on his way to India visited Persia and founded the first Christian community there.[49] Christian community in Edessa and Seleucia-Ctesiphon also claim the Apostolate of Thomas – Edessa through Mar Addai, a disciple of Apostle Thomas and Seleucia-Ctesiphon through Mar Mari, a disciple of Mar Addai. Besides this the close relation between India and the East is the commercial relations that they had since the early centuries.

Although, no serious claim to the Apostolate of St. Thomas is put forward by the Persian Christianity, the Apostle is, however, considered to be intimately connected with their Church. Quoting an East-Syrian Bishop who wrote to the Portuguese in 1533, Mundadan adds:

> St. Thomas... by the command of Jesus Christ was sent to parts of Babylon.... He converted many to Christianity and built houses of prayer. St. Bartholomew proceeded to Persia and there he was buried in Tarao in a monastery across Tabris.... Apostle Thomas went to Socotora and then continued his journey to India and China.[50]

Thus, both the Christian of the East and the Christian in India share a common tradition of their origin – connecting to the apostolic tradition of the first century.

3.1. Tradition Concerning the Immigration of Persian Christians to India

According to Portuguese tradition that Thomas of Cana, a merchant by profession came to India in A.D. 345 along with a large group of 300 to 400 families, including some clergy.[51] It narrates how a Bishop saw in a vision, about the miserable condition of the Indian Christians and reported to the Catholicos who then sent Thomas of Cana, to Malabar to investigate and report back. Thomas went and then returned with a report of confirmation. He was then sent back to Malabar with a large group of Christians including the Bishop who saw the vision, priests and deacons.

There is a parallel story from a Malayalam tradition too. It says that Joseph, Bishop of Edessa, in a dream heard a call from the poor Christians of Malabar. He thus approached the Catholicos of Jerusalem with his dream and the latter requested Thomas the merchant to report on the condition of the Christians of Malabar after his next voyage to India. When Thomas came back with a report that the Christians of Malabar were in great need of help, the Catholicos

---

[49] Cf. Xavier Koodapuzha, *Christianity in India* (Kottayam: OIRS, n.d.), 49. (Hereafter cited as Koodapuzha, *Christianity in India*).

[50] Cf. Mundadan, *History of Christianity in India,* 83.

[51] Cf. Firth, *An Introduction to Indian Church History,* 28. See also A. Mingana, *The Early Spread of Christianity in India* (Manchester University: 1926), 49. (Hereafter cited as Mingana, *The Early Spread of Christianity in India*).

commissioned Thomas to go to India along with a huge group - the Bishop of Edessa, several clergy and with many families. The group was received warmly by the Indian Christian community and as well as by the local Rajah, who permitted them to settle there and also gave them certain social privileges.

3.1.1. *The Southists and Northists among the Indian Christians*

An interesting story lies behind the division among the Indian Christians that resulted after the arrival of Thomas of Cana. Thomas of Cana had two wives – one a noble woman (from his own country)[52] and the other a slave, though belonging to a good caste.[53] Scholars are of diverse views regarding the origin of the division among the Indian Christians. Some holds that the division is between those who intermarried with the Indians and those who did not. For them, those who did were called the 'Northists' (Vedakumbagar) and those who did not were called 'Southists' (Thekumbagar).[54] Mundadan seem to favor the view that the division is between the Christians of Apostle Thomas and the Christians of Thomas of Cana.[55] However, the general view is that the names 'Northists' and 'Southists' originated from the separate locations of the two groups – the ancestors of the Northists who lived in the Northern part of Mahadevarapattam and the Southists who lived in the Southern part of it.

3.2. Visit of Pantaenus in A.D. 190

Eusebius talks about early connection of the Christianity of the East with the Indian Christians by mentioning the visit of Pantaenus, the teacher of Alexandrian School, to India in A.D. 190. St. Jerome reiterating Eusebius's statement adds that he preached among the "Brahmins." However, most of the historians are of the opinion that, Pantaenus visited south Arabia, and not India.

3.3. Visit of Bishop David of Basra in about A.D. 295-300

About 295-300 A.D., David, Bishop of Basra on the Persian Gulf, an eminent doctor, seems to have visited India and preached.[56] This is the first evidence we have for the Persian Bishop visiting the Indian Christians which shows the association of Indian Christianity with the Eastern Christianity.

---

52 Keay, *History of the Syrian Church in India*, 21.

53 Keay pointed out that she is sometimes described as originally from the Nayar caste. Cf. Keay, *History of the Syrian Church in India*, 21.

54 Cf. Firth, *An Introduction to Indian Church History*, 29. He also adds that the Northists outnumber the Southists in population.

55 Cf. Mundadan, *History of Christianity in India,* 98.

56 Cf. C.V. Cheriyan, *A History of Christianity in Kerala* (Kottayam: n.p., 1973), 56. (Hereafter cited as Cheriyan, *A History of Christianity in Kerala*).

3.4. Bishop John of Persia Represents India in A.D. 325 Nicaea

One among the participants of the first ecumenical Church Council held in Nicaea in A.D. 325 was Bishop John of Persia and known as 'Metropolitan of Persia and of Great India.'[57] He signed in the council Registers as representing the Christianity in Persia and India.

3.5. Visit of Theophilus 'The Indian' in A.D. 354

According to Keay, Theophilus visited India in the year A.D. 356,[58] while for Xavier Koodapuzha, it was A.D. 354.'[59] It is said that the Roman emperor Constantius sent an embassy to certain countries bordering the Red Sea and the Arabian Sea under the leadership of an Arian Bishop Theophilus. On his visit, Theophilus found Christians in India doing several things contrary to the practices of the East Christianity, like sitting while the Gospel is being read. He is believed to have reformed them.[60]

3.6. Daniel the Indian Priest at Edessa in A.D. 425

Another written source from the 5th century talks about Indian and Syrian Christianity. A Syriac commentary on the Epistle to the Romans, produced at Edessa, translated from Greek to Syriac, by Mar Komai, with the help of Daniel the Priest, the Indian in A.D. 425.[61] We may therefore even assume that the ecclesiastical language of the Indian Church was Syriac and the Church in India had even grown to the extent of sending their candidates for theological education to the ecclesiastical centre, at Edessa.

3.7. Visit of the Alexandrian Merchant Cosmos Indicopleustes between A.D. 520 and 525

He visited India between A.D. 520 and 525, as a merchant sailor and later between 535 and 550 became a monk and wrote in his monastery a book entitled *Universal Christian Topography*. In this book, he made references to the existence of the Christianity in India. Cosmos writes:

> Even in Taprobene (Ceylon), an island in further India, where the Indian sea is, there is a Church of Christians, with clergy and a body of believers... In the country called Male (Malabar), where the pepper

---

[57] Cf. Keay, *History of the Syrian Church in India*, 18.

[58] Keay, *History of the Syrian Church in India*, 22.

[59] Koodapuzha, *Christianity in India*, 59.

[60] Cf. Koodapuzha, *Christianity in India*, 59, citing T.K. Joseph, *The Malabar Christians and their Ancient Documents* (Trivandrum: 1929), 2. See also, Keay, *History of the Syrian Church in India*, 26.

[61] Cf. Mundadan, *History of Christianity in India,* 99, citing William G. Young, *Handbook of Source-Materials for Students of Church History, Indian Theological Library*, No. 28 (Madras: 1969), 28.

> grows, there is also a Church, and at another place called Kalliana there is moreover Bishop, who is appointed from Persia.[62]

He also indicates that the Christians in India are ecclesiastically dependent on the Persian Christians and there was at least one Bishop from Persia.

3.8. Letters of Two Persian Patriarchs in the 7th, 8th/9th Centuries

We can also get a clearer idea on the relation between the East-Syria and the Indian Christians through the letters of two Persian patriarchs – Mar Ishoyahb III (A.D. 647/8 or 650/1) and Mar Timothy I (A.D. 780 or 789-823). The many letters of the Patriarch Mar Timothy I revealed about the relation of the two Christian communities especially of East Syria sending missionary monks to India. In the book of Ibn-at-Taiyib titled 'The Law of Christendom,' two letters of Mar Timothy I with their references on India have been summarized.[63] The first letter is addressed to the Christian community in India instructing them on the election of the metropolitan wherein they are to abide by the advice of the patriarch and not their king. The second letter of Mar Timothy I to the Christian community of India refers to certain canonical abuses that had entered into the issue of ordinations of metropolitans, bishops, priests and deacons. Hence, the above-mentioned letters of the two patriarchs of the Church of the East serve as evidence to the ecclesiastical relation between the two Christian communities that existed in the early Christian centuries.

3.9. Tradition Concerning Mar Sapor and Mar Prot in the 9th/10th Centuries

Sapor and Prot were two Seleucian saints who came to India in A.D. 823. An account of their arrival:

> Then in the year 823 the Syrian Fathers, Mar Sapor and Mar Prot with the illustrious Sabriso came to India and reached Kullam (Quilon). They went to the king Shakirbirti and asked him a piece of land in which they could build a church for themselves and erect a town. He gave them the land they desired and they built a church and erected a town in the district of Kullam, to which Syrian bishops and metropolitans used to come by order of the Catholicos who sent them.[64]

---

[62] Cf. Koodapuzha, *Christianity in India*, 59-60, citing M.K. Kuriakose, *History of Christianity in India: Source Materials* (Madras: CLS, 1982), 8-9.

[63] Cf. Mundadan, *History of Christianity in India,* 102.

[64] Mingana, *The Early Spread of Christianity in India*, 45. Cf. also Cheriyan, *A History of Christianity in Kerala*, 111.

Their coming to India is considered to be the second immigration of Syrian Christians from Persia. There are several copper plates that talk about the presence of this Christian community in India by that time. Three of the five plates are at the Jacobite Seminary at Kottayam and the other two are at the possession of the Mar Thoma Church at Tiruvalla.[65] They are mostly written in Tamil and Malayalam. Two pages are in Pali and Arabic. Another copper plate written in Tamil, is available with Kottayam Old Seminary. It talks of a grant made by the king called Vira Raghava Chakravarti to Iravi kortan of Mahadevarapatnam. The title "Manigrammam" is bestowed on Iravi Kottan, probably implying Christian merchants of Cranganore. He received besides this honor, two castes people to serve as slaves for him and his people, and tolls and dues on all merchandize in Cranganore harbor and town. According to local tradition, these two brothers preached, converted many to Christian faith and performed many miracles.[66] They died in Quilon and were buried there in the Church they had built.

The tradition of the Indian Christians is that during the 9th to 16th century the Christians enjoyed certain independence of the Hindu Rajas. They were fairly prosperous in trading and landowning. They were considered as high caste - low only to the Brahmins. They were privileged to travel on the elephant, Syriac as ecclesiastical language and the high social status enjoyed by them.

---

[65] Cf. Firth, *An Introduction to Indian Church History*, 3.

[66] Cf. Mundadan, *History of Christianity in India,* 105.

Chapter 3

The Roman Catholic Christianity in India

1. Introduction

The Roman Catholic Church was very active in its endeavor to spread Christianity during the 16th and 17th centuries. The experience of loss it went through in Europe due to the rise of Reformation, made them to take greater efforts to regain their power in other parts of the world. The success they had through Counter Reformation gave them more self-confidence. They used this outcome to the fullest for the Evangelism to the dominance as exhibited by the Catholic countries such as Portugal and Spain in Navigation.

2. Religious Policies of the Portuguese in India

The Portuguese term 'Padroado' refers to the right of spiritual or religious jurisdiction granted by Pope Nicholas V to the Portuguese king, Alphonse V by his famous Bull Romanus Pontifix in 1455 over all the lands discovered or to be discovered by the Portuguese in the East.[67] The rivalry between Spain and Portugal in discovering and Christianizing those lands that were discovered by them resulted in conflicts. To solve these conflicts the Pope had divided the Globe into East and West and authorized Portuguese to evangelize the East and the West to Spain. It gave to their rulers certain rights and duties. Accordingly, the kings were granted a say in the appointment of the bishops within these regions, and in

[67] Cf. S. Vanatius Fernando, "Portuguese Patronage (Padroado) and the Evangelization of the Pearl fishery Coast," *Indian Church History Review* XVIII (December, 1984), 94.

the sending of missionaries. Thus, the Portuguese came to exercise ecclesiastical patronage in India and the Padroado was strongly reaffirmed.

3. The Conversion of Paravas to Christianity

The Pearl fishery was a great source of income to the Paravas and this attracted rival regimes and middlemen. The Muslim Arabs had established a monopoly over the sea-borne trade, and total control over the Pearl fishery. The Poor Paravas were exploited and oppressed in various ways. They were reduced to slaves and day-laborers. The Portuguese took control of the Pearl fishery from the Muslims by military force in 1524.[68] The conflicts between the Paravas and Muslims led the the Paravas head-men to approach the Portuguese captain Pero Vaz of Cochin and asked for his assistance against the Muslim. The Paravas agreed to become Christians with their people if the Portuguese liberated them from the clutches of the Muslims. 85 Parava head-men were baptized at Cochin immediately in 1535. Captain Pero Vaz delivered the Paravars from the Muslims and consequently between 1535 and 1537 about 20,000 Paravas in 30 villages were baptized.[69] Thus, the Paravas mass conversion under the Portuguese Padroado took place. Therefore, one can conclude that it was the tension among the Paravas and Muslims that seems to have brought Christianity to this region. The Paravas mass-movement toward Christianity brought the Jesuit missions to India, such as St. Francis Xavier and Robert de Nobili.

4. The Missionary Methods of Francis Xavier

He was a Spaniard nobleman and from a royal family of Navarre and France. He joined with Ignatius Loyola and five others to form a brotherhood known as the 'Jesuits' or "the Society of Jesus' on 15th August, 1534,[70] which became an organized society in 1540 under the approval of the Pope. They committed their lives to totally serve the lord through a life of celibacy and poverty and to be ready to go wherever they are sent for the proclamation of the Gospel.[71] Upon the request of the Portuguese king, Francis Xavier was sent to India along with another priest, Paul de Camerino.

---

[68] One day in 1535, a Parava woman insulted by a Muslim man, for an unknown reason as she went to sell "Paniyaram" (rice-bread). The woman reported the insult to her husband, who in turn picked a quarrel with the Muslim responsible. This Muslim man, in a fury, cut off the long ear-lobe of the Parava man and carried it away together with the gold ring it bore. Considering the incident as affront to the whole community, the Paravars took weapons and attacked the Muslim quarter of Tuticorin, killing many people. In retaliation, the Muslims of the coast formed themselves into a huge army and blockaded the Parava villages, cutting off supplies and ruthlessly killing the Paravars.

[69] Cf. Firth, *An Introduction to Indian Church History*, 52.

[70] Cf. Koodapuzha, *Christianity in India*, 177.

[71] Cf. Firth, *An Introduction to Indian Church History*, 56.

It was under the Padroado that Xavier was appointed as Ambassador of the Pope and was sent to India in 1541. His voyage to India took 13 months. He spent greater part of the voyage in ministering the sick. By the time he landed at Goa on 6th May of 1542, he was already reputed as a saint. Christians were worldly and loose-living and the large number of Indo-Portuguese resulting from the mixed marriages and otherwise was ill-instructed and ill-disciplined.[72] Xavier was revolted by the immorality of many of his compatriots.[73] He approached the people mainly through the children. He went about the streets ringing the bell and calling out, "faithful Christians send your children". He began by singing the lessons he had rhymed and then made the children sing them, so that they might become better fixed in their memory. Afterwards he explained each point in the simplest way.

On October 1542 Francis Xavier landed at Manappad and the Pearl fishery coast. Till the end of 1544 taking with him 3 Indian Christian helpers from the Goa Seminary, he visited the 30 villages between Cape Comorin and Tuticorin who were Christians in name but entirely ignorant of the faith and without Church services of any kind. He began to baptize all the children who were born after the mass baptism of 1536-1537. His method was baptizing first then instructing.

He started his work with Tuticorin. He translated catechism into Tamil, with the help of his Indian seminarians. He also composed short talk on what it means to be Christian, what heaven and hell are, and who goes to the one and who goes to the other. He went through the whole village with a little bell and called together all men and the boys he could find, and began to teach them twice a day the prayers, the creeds and the commandments. He uses one of his seminarians to repeat what he had said in order to make sure that the hearers really understood what he was saying. He asks his hearers to go home and teach others likewise. Xavier was thus very thorough in his missionary work, taking every little detail into care and consideration.[74]

His evangelizing process pattern: on Sundays he would gather all the Christians of the village and ask them to repeat the prayers he taught them. Then he would recite the creed sentence-wise, which will be repeated by the people. This would be followed by the explanation of it with the help of his interpreter. He would ask them whether they firmly believed in each article, and they would reply in unison, with their arms crossed before their breast, that they did. Then he explained to them the Ten Commandments. Afterwards 'Hail Mary' is recited.[75] In this way, Xavier catechized the Christians.

He make regular tours among the Christian villages, by appointing in each place one of the intelligent members as Catechist, and leaving copies of the course

[72] Cf. Mundadan, *History of Christianity in India*, 454.

[73] Cf. Koodapuzha, *Christianity in India*, 178.

[74] Cf. Thekkedath, *History of Christianity in India*, 156f.

[75] Cf. Thekkedath, *History of Christianity in India*, 156f.

of instruction with them. The Catechist received a stipend, from funds provided by the Portuguese government and administered by their agent of Tuticorin.[76] He was instrumental in starting St. Paul's college at Goa, for the higher education of local Christians, and for the preparation of local clergy.[77]

Simple chapels of mud and thatch were built gathered the people for the daily prayers and lessons. He sent for the teacher of Catechism and examined the progress of the children. He employed harsh method to abolish immorality and idolatry. For example an idolatrous house ordered to be burned, when Xavier was told a particular house had idols. On the other hand, Xavier was a compassionate Shepherd. When the Christians suffered ill-treatment under the unscrupulous Portuguese or were raided by the troops of warring Rajahs, he always comes to their aid.

Xavier also baptized the fishery coast people of Travancore Coast, the *Mukkuvas*. It is said that within a month's time, Xavier could baptize more than 10,000 people.[78] In 1545, he went to Mylapore, Malacca and to Indonesian Islands. He returned to Goa and then to the South east coast. In 1549 he set out for Japan with the Japanese convert Anjiro and few Jesuits. After his ministry there he returned to India. After three months he went to China but on the way he died, on 2nd Dec. 1552.[79] His body was buried in Malacca temporarily and later it was taken to Goa. He was canonized as saint by Pope Gregory XV in 1622.

Like Paul he is known especially through his letters, he has been criticized for hasty and superficial methods never stopping to learn languages or really getting to know the culture of the people, trusting to memory work and verbal expressions of belief, and always ready to drop one piece of work and go in search of another.

Baptism was done in large groups. The instructions were very short and there was no period of moral probation. One of the reasons for this extra-ordinary hurry of his was probably due to the quick advance Islam was making at that time in and around India.

5. Jesuits in the Mughal Court

Akbar, came to the throne in 1556, was a man of great intelligence and considerable interest in religion. With his ascension to the throne the classic period of the Mughal Empire began. He was one among the Mughal rulers who introduced religious tolerance.[80] He invited teachers of all religions to come to his court and he listened to them. In March 1579, Fr Gil Eanes Pereira, a Jesuit

---

[76] Cf. Thekkedath, *History of Christianity in India*, 159.

[77] Cf. Firth, *An Introduction to Indian Church History*, 65-6.

[78] Cf. Thekkedath, *History of Christianity in India*, 162-3.

[79] Cf. Firth, *An Introduction to Indian Church History*, 66-7.

[80] Cf. Thekkedath, *History of Christianity in India*, 426.

priest reached Akbar's Court in answer to Akbar's invitation.[81] Pereira always exposed Islam as religion of error and suggested that Akbar should try to obtain some Jesuit priests from Goa, who would be able to enlighten him. To this Akbar obliged.

In response to his request Fr Rudolph Acquaviva, Fr Antony Monserrate and Fr Francis Henriques came to Akbar's court at Fatehpursikri. He gave the Jesuits full liberty to preach and make conversions. However the doctrine of Trinity and Incarnation were hard for Akbar to digest. This mission retreated after sometime, realizing Akbar was not very much interested in Christianity. A second Jesuit mission to Akbar's court was sent in 1591 at the earnest request of the emperor. The fathers were well-received.[82] Nevertheless they soon realized that Akbar had no intention of becoming a Christian. Hence the mission came to an abrupt end.

Akbar being dissatisfied by the hasty withdrawal of the second mission sent for another mission. Though the Jesuits were unwilling to go this time, for political reason, they did. Three men, Fr Jerome Xavier, Fr Immanuel Pinheiro and Bro. Benedict de Goes were sent in 1595 and this mission became a permanent undertaking.[83] Due courtesy and respect was shown unto them. He allowed them to start a school for the royal family. But, in his conversation with the fathers he avoided the subject of religion, alleging that the subject could not be properly discussed until they had learnt Persian. In 1602 the Jesuits achieved a notable success in obtaining from Akbar a written order under the royal seal expressly permitting conversion of Christianity. However Akbar till his death bed refused to accept Christianity. Yet, the mission continued till the time of Aurangazeb (1683) without much success. However, it enabled the emergence of enormous amount of Christian literature in Persian language and the influence of Christianity on Mughal paintings.

6. Robert De Nobili and His Methods

Robert de Nobili, the famous Jesuit missionary of the 17th century who started Madurai Mission in 1606 is often considered as the missionary who pioneered the notion of adaptation and inculturization of Christianity in India. It was in the context of his own encounter with the Indian cultural milieu, with its caste factor, that Fr Nobili initiated his method of adaptation and inculturization.

Robert de Nobili was born as an Italian aristocrat in September 1577 in Rome to Count Pier Francesco de Nobili, a general in the papal army, and Clarice Cioli. Cardinal Bellarmine was his uncle. He was related to at least two popes:

---

81 Cf. Thekkedath, *History of Christianity in India*, 427.

82 It has been recorded that in 1592 Pope Clement VIII wrote to the Emperor (Akbar), acknowledging the latter's good disposition and kindness towards the Jesuit priests and extending good wishes to him with love. Cf. Koodapuzha, *Christianity in India*, 232.

83 Cf. Firth, *An Introduction to Indian Church History*, 110.

Julius III, and Gregory XIII.[84] His noble birth proved to be advantageous for his later missionary enterprise, as later in Madurai he would make the declaration,

> My native city is the great city of Rome... In Rome, I was a prince, that is to say, of the caste of the rajas... there I became a sannyasi, there after I learnt the three sastras.[85]

He was educated first in Rome and then in a Duchess' house and in 1596 against the wishes of his parents the Jesuit novitiate in Naples, eventually becoming a missionary to India. It was under Portuguese Padroado that Robert de Nobili came to Madurai. Madurai was the ancient capital of the Pandyans and the center of Tamil culture and learning. It was in November 1606, that Robert de Nobili reached Madurai and ministered there till 1656.

6.1. His Methods of Indigenization

Realizing the importance of the local language, he studied Tamil. In six months he learned the language and was able to discuss religion with the learned men. He was familiar with a wide range of popular religious ideas, myths, etc., and the literature of Hinduism, i.e., such as Vaishnava and Saiva communities. Prior to Fr Nobili at Madurai, Fr Goncalo Fernandez worked there for 11 years without success. This was due to the reasons that Fr Fernandez followed a missionary method requiring the neophytes to dress, eat, and behave like the Portuguese colonials. It requires the converts to abandon the marks of their civil ranks. Following their conversion they took Portuguese names. As a result, they were strongly despised and resisted by the Hindus of high caste origin. Christian converts along with the Portuguese were considered 'paranghis' (despised foreigner) for eating beef, wine, wearing leather shoes, not bathing frequently and communicating freely with the outcastes of India. Thus, the converts were regarded as polluting, lose all titles of nobility and become infamous for the rest of their lives.[86] The method of conversion used by the Portuguese created a grave barrier for the high castes and made them shun Christianity. This is evident when Fr Nobili remarks:

> For when these heathens see that our Christian neophytes discard the caste-thread and many other time-honored practices of their own cultures and adapt the manner of foreigners, they came to think that those who apply to us for spiritual instruction, change not so much

[84] Cf. Vincent Cronin, *A Pearl to India: The Life of Roberto De Nobili* (London: Rupert Hart-Davis, 1959), 11.

[85] Cf. Dahmen, *Robert de Nobili*, 32-33, cited in Thomas Anchukandam, *Roberto De Nobili's Responsio (1610): A Vindication of Inculturation and Adaptation* (Bangalore: Kristu Jyoti Publications, 1996), 10. (Hereafter cited as Anchukandam, *Robert De Nobili's Responsio*).

[86] Cf. Thekkedath, *History of Christianity in India*, 212.

> their religious beliefs and practices as the very tenor of their civil grade; ... deprived of every civil advantage.[87]

Fr Nobili "being convinced that the deadlock was due to the identification of Christianity with paranghism, he proposed to reject that identification with paranghism and repudiate that name which applied neither to himself nor to his religion."[88] Fr Nobili firmly believed that unless the high castes were Christianized, it would be impossible to even think about Christianizing the entire people of India. In his treatise on Indian customs, Fr Nobili wrote:

> As the Brahmins alone in India represent the intelligentsia and the teaching profession, from the earliest times it became an established custom for well-nigh everyone from the inferior order, before attempting anything particularly in matters connected with the sciences and the Religious sects, to take counsel on the subject from some learned Brahmins.[89]

For this very reason, he made the high castes the primary focus of his evangelization, in order to evangelize the whole nation. He made full use of his noble background by stating that he was an Italian Kshatriya not a 'paranghi.' He described himself as a Roman Raja - Sannyasi (renunciant), which allowed him to associate with the high caste Hindus. He declared to them that he was a sannyasi, who had come to India to teach a new spiritual law. He also adapted himself to the customs of the high caste people whom he wanted to evangelize.[90] With the permission of Fr Alberto Laerzio, his provincial and Ros, the archbishop of Cranganore, he began to live the life of an Indian sannyasi and took the title of 'Guru.' The native people began to fondly address him as 'aiyer' (the master of the house). He gave up meat, fish, eggs and wine and ate only one meal a day, which consisted of rice, milk, fruit, and vegetables. In addition, none other than the high caste servants were admitted to his service – to the extent of hiring a Brahmin to cook his food. In 1607, he gave up the black cassock of the Portuguese missionaries for the common long robe of an Indian sanyasi, with a second cloth cast over the shoulder. He wore the sacred thread across his shoulder, anointed his forehead with the sandal paste and put on wooden sandals. He bathed twice a day, especially before the celebration of the Eucharist. Finally, he left the other Jesuits

---

[87] Cf. Robert de Nobili, *Indian Customs*, edited by S. Rajamanikam. (Palayamkottai: De Nobili Research Institute, 1972), 150. (Hereafter cited as Nobili, *Indian Customs*).

[88] Cf. A. Sauliere, *His Star in the East*, revised and edited by S. Rajamanickam (Madras: De Nobili Institute, 1995), 45. (Hereafter cited as Sauliere, *His Star in the East*).

[89] Cf. Nobili, *Indian Customs*, 149.

[90] See V. Cronin, "Roberto De Nobili," *New Catholic Encyclopedia* X, second edition, 478. (Hereafter cited as Cronin, *Robert De Nobili*).

and stayed in the newly-built mud-walled chapel and avoided all contact with the lower castes. The new space was presented to him by one of his Hindu admirers.[91]

His adaptation method facilitated access to him for the people of high caste origin without running the risk of losing their higher caste status and being publicly ostracized by their fellow humans. The mastery of Fr Nobili over the ornate Tamil, popular Hinduism, and his fame as a sannyasi attracted solitude, never going out of his house, and admitting visitors only with extreme reserve. For the true means of attracting these people is to excite their curiosity.[92] According to the tradition current at that time, the true original Veda had been lost. De Nobili made use of this opportunity by declaring that this Veda still exists and that it had been completed and perfected by another Veda. This was the Veda which he had come to preach - the "Sattia Veda" (True Veda). Many inclined their ears to hear him because of this revelation. Nobili's evangelistic method began to show great success wherein within the first 18 months he converted 50 people of Madurai. His first convert was a high caste Hindu Sivaite school teacher.

In 1608 Fr Nobili met and befriended Sivadarma, a Brahmin Sanskrit scholar. This friendship enabled Fr Nobili to learn Sanskrit, the classical language of Hinduism. In addition, he also acquired some knowledge of the Vedas and Vedanta. His friendship with Sivadarma moreover happened to be one of God's providence. It saved Fr Nobili from being thrown out by the Brahmins, who accused him of paranghi. At a meeting of 800 Brahmins, when his origin and status were questioned, Sivadarma defended Fr Nobili and explained that even though his skin was white Fr Nobili was a learned sannyasi and quite different from the paranghis.[93] Only because of this timely intervention Fr Nobili was allowed to remain in Madurai. It is out of this fruitful friendship that Sivadarma eventually embraced Christianity.

Fr Nobili has also been called the Apostle of the Brahmins. He lived and moved among the Brahmins, hired a Brahmin cook and scribe and kept aloof from the low castes. Yet the converts were not Brahmins alone, but Nayaks also. Out of 120 Christians the Mission had in 1611, not more than 12 were Brahmins. On the other hand, the Chettinayaks were at least 70.[94] He was the first one to make the Brahmins the target people group and find some converts among them.

Fr Nobili's research of the law of Manu and other Indian literature led him to conclude that the Punul (sacred thread) and the Kudumi (tuft of hair) were civil rather than religious - superstitious customs and therefore permissible to Brahmin

---

[91] Cf. Rajamanickam, *The First Oriental Scholar*, 213.

[92] "Letter of Fr Laerzio to the Jesuit general on 30 December 1608," cited in Thekkedath, *History of Christianity in India*, 213.

[93] Cronin, *Roberto De Nobili*, 478.

[94] Cf. Thekkedath, *History of Christianity in India*, 217.

converts.[95] He also allowed ceremonial baths and sandal paste on forehead. At the same time, he removed whatever was strictly Hindu in these practices, and Christianized them with Christian prayers and blessings. The converts were allowed to keep their caste rules and continued to live with their own families.

The Church was built in Indian style, the outcastes were separated by a balustrade and were in a lower place; and the sacraments were administered first to the high castes. For doing this he is accused of bringing caste into the Church, but it must be noted that castes distinction was there even in the time of Francis Xavier, as there were separate chapels for different caste groups. Moreover, as Rajamanickam pointed out, Christians, being a small minority could not change a universal custom such as the caste system,[96] especially in those days. It was a great achievement that Nobili had brought all of them into same Church, particularly at a time when low castes were not allowed in the Hindu temples.

His adaptation went much further than he was credited for. He Christianized the marriage and the burial ceremonies and the Pongal festival. Dadamurthi, a new convert and the landlord of the place where Fr Nobili lived, was encouraged to celebrate the Pongal Festival, planting a cross and boiling rice like others.[97] Noticing that during Brahmanical weddings a number of hymns were sung, he composed several hymns in the same manner, so that his converts could have equally joyful celebration. He retained thali (wedlock) in the Christian wedding.

His method of adaptation was much more pronounced in the language. He used Tamil terms to convey Christian ideas. He Christianized certain words and infused into them new meanings. Prasadam, for instance, signifying a gift from the temple he used for "grace," the gift from God. He used Kovil for Church and Pujei for mass. Even saints' names were made to sound Tamil. For example, he made 'Fidelis', as 'Visuvasam', Deus dedit as Sivadharma, and Peter as Malaiyapan[98] etc. He rejected the word svarga and adoption of moksa for heaven, because svarga meant a place of pleasure which satisfies every desire of man.[99] But, unfortunately all these attempts at adaptation were not received warmly or recognized.

A Parava Christian who had come from the coastal region told the high caste Christians that any of them who had been baptized by Nobili and touched by Saliva as the Roman rite required, had thereby lost their caste status and had become paranghi. This created a great commotion among the high caste Christians, and 14 of them stopped coming to the Church. While every attempt to pacify the situation failed, Fr Nobili set forth a manifesto in Tamil written on a

[95] Cf. Robert De Nobili, *Adaptation*, edited by Rajamanickam, (Palayamkottai: De Nobili Research Institute, 1971), 86-157. (Hereafter cited as Nobili, *Adaptation*).

[96] Rajamanickam, *The First Oriental Scholar*, 61.

[97] "Letter of Nobili to Provincial Laerzio Jan., 15, 1609," cited in Nobili, *Adaptation*, 85.

[98] Cf. A. Rajamanickam, "Roberto de Nobili and Adaptation," *Indian Church History Review* 1 (December 1967), 83-91.

[99] Nobili, *Adaptation*, 142-143.

palm leaf (Olai) and nailed it to a tree in front of his house. The most important lines read as follows:

> I am not a parangi... I came from Rome, where my family holds the same rank as respectable rajas hold in this country... The law which I preach is the law of the true God.... Whoever says that it is the law of the parangis, fit only for the low castes, commits a very great sin, for the true God is not the God of one race, but the God of all.[100]

Nevertheless, the damage wrought by this incident could not be fully erased. Fr Nobili had to face opposition from his colleagues and superiors too. His predecessor, Fr Fernandez, wrote memorandum after memorandum, finding fault with the method of Nobili. Matters came to a head when on 7th May 1610 Fr Fernandez dispatched to the Jesuit general a long letter, in which he rallied all the regular charges, adding that Fr Nobili had become a Hindu. The letter was received by Nicola Pimenta, an appointed visitor. The already biased Pimenta asked two theologians in Goa to examine the allegations. Pimento also ordered the provincial to conduct an enquiry among Nobili's neophyte.[101] After their examination, the theologians came up with their comments on four aspects of the Nobilian method. They argued that the thread worn by Christian Brahmins might be tolerated in view of the cross attached to it; the baths taken by de Nobili and Christian Brahmins were attacked as superstitious and the changes in the liturgical names meaningless and likely to be nothing short of dangerous errors. Finally, the separation from Goncalo Fernandez was interpreted as schismatic. Therefore, Nobili's way of functioning was considered as a serious negation of true faith and that his converts were not genuine Christians. As such, according to them, the superiors were bound under pain of mortal sin to contain the Madurai Mission. In spite of this decision, Fr Nobili continued his method of evangelization.

The Franciscan and diocesan priests working in the Pearl Fishery Coast went to the extent of saying Fr Nobili had become a Hindu. The Bishop of Cochin highly disapproved of Fr Nobili's method. His new provincial, Fr Pero Francisco, who was prejudiced against his method, gave ear to these reports and in 1612 forbade Fr Nobili to baptize.[102] Fr Pero's famous letter dated August 11, 1613 containing 34 orders has the following comment on Nobili's food: "The abstinence from meat and fish etc., must not be observed so strictly and rigorously that even in case of necessity, sickness, disgust or natural weakness, they do not touch meat..."[103] In order to defend himself against the charges and criticism

[100] Bachman. 113, cited in Neill, *History of Christianity in India*, 287.

[101] Anchukandam, *Roberto De Nobili's Responsio*, 33.

[102] Cf. Thekkedath, *History of Christianity in India*, 217.

[103] "Letter of Fr Pero to the Jesuit General Aquavira dated Nov 4, 1612," cited in Nobili, *Adaptation*, 84-85.

leveled against him, Fr Nobili set out in writing his own understanding of his mission. Hurriedly, in only a few weeks he wrote his *Responsio* (also known as Apologia) and sent it to Goa to be carried to Rome in 1610. Though it was written by Fr Nobili, it was signed by Archbishop Ros to give it an impartial hearing. In addition, Pimenta arranged for a hearing of the evidence of a number of Fr Nobili's converts. In his letter of complaint to the Jesuit general before the Goa Conference archbishop Stephen de Sa wrote,

> It is not to be permitted, most Rev Father, that Fr Robert should come to this city and live in the Professed House, without ever eating either with his brethren or what they ate, but that he should take only the food prepared for him by the Brahmins whom he had with him; nor that he should go to the new College where there were no Brahmins, and eat there only what his Brahmins had prepared and served him.[104]

Nevertheless, the Pope instructed Archbishop Sa to give a hearing to Nobili in Goa conference. In his *Adaptation* (composed in 1619), Fr Nobili defended his principle of accommodation stating that, just as Christianity legitimately adapted many of the local customs and even religious practices of the Greco-Roman world and successfully endowed these with 'Christian Significance,' it is equally legitimate to practice this adaptation when Christianity encounters Indian Civilization. He identified four propositions, which guided his adaptation of the customs of India, supporting each with examples from the adaptation that took place in the Early Church:

(1) "The evangelical preacher is to take up that manner of life which will cause his hearers to judge him worthy of being listened to."[105] This is illustrated by St. Paul who behaved as Jew among Jews and as a gentile among gentiles; when he preached in Athens he did not attack the Athenian gods but introduced his Christian God as if He were one of them, the 'unknown one.'

(2) "No practice, or custom, or habit, which itself contains no sin, has ever been disapproved or condemned by the Church, even though it was current among the gentiles as well, to whom in fact it owed its origins."[106] For example, following local custom, Christians performed frequent ablutions, veiled their wives, and exchanged rings at their weddings, even though each custom had a religious meaning for pagans.

(3) "Innumerable are the customs in honor among the blind ancient gentile nations and the emblems or insignia invented by them, which

---

[104] "ARSI, VIII-5 or Goa 336. Shembaganur Archives (SA) Photostat no. 336," cited in Nobili, *Adaptation*, 85.

[105] Nobili, *Adaptation*, 7.

[106] Nobili, *Adaptation*, 37.

no doubt fulfilled some social purpose, but were none the less mixed with various superstitious elements and other damnable ends, which customs and insignia, however, Christianity adopted for the sake of the social end they in view, (making them) honorable by simply changing their purpose."[107] An example of this is the Greek/Egyptian festival, which focused on lamp lighting in honor of the fire god which was brought into the Church as a vigil celebration of the Ascension of Christ.

(4) There were several rites and customs among the gentiles whose purpose was in no way social, but purely religious; yet the Church did not forbid them, and made scarcely any, or no change, except that she give them a new religious purpose:[108] Pagan children used to tie on their clothing little knobs to ward off demons; the early church replaced these with knobs made with the wax of altar candles, with the image of the "Lamb of God" imprinted in them.

Pointing to the parallel between Ancient Rome and South Indian society, Fr Nobili argued, if the ancient Romans were allowed to dress as they had prior to their conversion, keeping old symbols of status, etc., converts in India should likewise be allowed to maintain their signs of status, the Brahmin thread, certain names etc. This was not an accommodation to Hindu religiosity per se; elements of Indian society were to be defended and preserved precisely because they were not inherently "Hindu." Having thus made justification for his method, Fr Nobili attended the Goa conference.

The conference opened in Goa on 4th February 1619. Most of the participants to this conference were prejudiced against Fr Nobili's methods. As a result, except for the second Inquisitor Ferinand de Almeyda, the archbishop of Cranganore, Fr Ros and Jesuits declared themselves against Fr Nobili, including the archbishop of Goa. But, the Grand Inquisitor of Portugal declared himself to be in favor of Fr Nobili in 1621. Finally, Pope Gregory XV on January 31, 1623 decided the question in favor of Fr Nobili.

This decision gave new fervor and stimuli and Fr Nobili resumed his work, extending it as well to other parts of the state of Tamil Nadu. Now, in 1623 leaving the work under the care of Fr Anthony Vico, Fr Nobili went to Trichy. Like the wandering sadhus of India, he traveled from one place to another. One of his vellala converts called Yesu Adiyan succeeded in bringing about the conversion of his former guru, Muthudaiyan. Muthudaiyan was a dravida pandaram (a non-Brahmin priest) and had more than 2,000 disciples. Muthudaiyan was the first pariah convert. He managed to attract a number of his former disciples to Christianity.

---

[107] Nobili, *Adaptation*, 43.

[108] Nobili, *Adaptation*, 65.

In the meantime, Fr Nobili had started two other centers at Salem and Moramangalam. The most illustrious of his converts at Moramangalam was Tirumangala Nayak, the deposed ruler of Sendamangalam. He received baptism along with his family on Christmas Day 1625. Another distinguished convert was Nallathambi Nayak, the cousin of the ruler of the place. The work was extended to Karur by Muthudaiyam, when he was driven out of Trichy during a persecution. Fr Balthasar da Costa later provided pastoral care to this community.

Persecution erupted once again in 1640, starting at Trichy and spreading to Madurai. The refusal of a pariah Christian to give his daughter to a Hindu of the same caste triggered the persecution.[109] Fr Emmanuel Martins was arrested along with four of his neophytes. They were imprisoned, tortured and finally driven out of the town. About the same time, Fr Nobili and Fr Maya were imprisoned at Madurai.[110] The opposition in no way hindered the rapid progress of the mission work. The annual letter of 1644 reported that the Madura Mission had 4,183 Christians.[111] Lay helpers, known as catechists assisted the missionaries. These catechists played a very important role in the evangelistic work, and their service is the only explanation available how such a small number of missionaries were able to accomplish so much. By the year 1644, Trichy became the chief center of the whole mission. In 1650, Nobili was sent to Jaffna to start the Jesuit mission there. Three years later he was sent to Mylapore where he lived in a hut outside the town. He passed away in 1656 at the age 79.

6.2. His Writings

He was a prolific writer of high Tamil and later added the court language Telugu and the language of the Brahmins, Sanskrit. He is believed to have written at least 50 books in Indian languages besides a number of letters and treatises in Italian, Latin, and Portuguese. His writings reflected the methods and arguments he had used in the controversies with the non-Christians as well as the instruction to the catechumens and the neophytes. Despite his openness and pioneering achievement in learning about the Hindu religion, as an orthodox Catholic Christian of the 17th century, he carefully assessed and assimilated only in modified form, bits and pieces from the religious environment around him, and he was not tolerant.

6.3. His Thoughts on Other Religion

While he adapted the externals of Indian society, Fr Nobili had no positive comments or appreciation about Hindu religious texts, doctrines of the divine, ritual practices, etc. He apparently excluded intellectual and spiritual adaptation of

---

[109] Cf. Sauliere, *His Star in the East*, 404.

[110] Cf. S. Rajamanickam, "De Nobili in the Madurai Jail: a letter of Sebastian de Maya," *Indian Church History Review*, 18 (December 1984), 87-93.

[111] Cf. "The Annual of 1644," by Fr A. Lopez, translated by Fr L. Besse, 30-32, cited in Thekkedath, *History of Christianity in India*, 222.

Hinduism and distinguished between external and internal adaptation.[112] While his endeavor to indigenize evangelistic method is commendable, it is questionable whether he made any attempt on his part to formulate Christian theology making use of Indian philosophical categories.

He refutes the teachings of Hinduism. In his writings, which are quite often controversial and apologetic, he criticizes a variety of Hindu beliefs, particularly doctrines such as avatara and rebirth. For instance, in Punar-janma-akshepam, he argues against the doctrines of rebirth and karma. The idea of rebirth, he claims, rests upon a wrong notion of the soul. Hindus think the soul inhabits the body as a bird, lives in cage, but that is a misunderstanding. The soul is integral to the body and only together do they make one person. He attacks karma further and the Hindu notion of heaven (savarga) in Attumanirnayam (Disquisition of soul). He rejects the idea of svarga whose sensual nature is morally objectionable.[113]

In Dushna Tikkaram (Refutation of Calumnies) he presents Jesus as the divine guru (Divya Guru) who came down to earth. He sees the incarnation as God's response to the Human condition. He sees god as a physician seeking to cure humans, who find themselves ill with the disease of desire and spiritual blindness.[114] He presented Jesus as the divine guru. Thus, he portrays God as a teacher (guru) and the incarnation as a teaching process.[115] His portrayal of Jesus as the divine guru gives him the basis for criticizing the avatars popular among the people. For him if the incarnation is for the purpose of teaching humans a lesson, the teacher must be credible.[116] As such, he exclaims, what humans can learn from a god who becomes a boar or a tortoise (as did Vishnu), or from a god who takes a human form and acts scandalously and without any of the attributes one would rightly expect of a god (as did Siva)? Here is no evident salvific reason for such avatars, and hence it makes no sense to assume that a god would undertake them.[117] By describing Jesus as divine-guru and himself as a guru sent forth by the divine guru to spread the Veda, Fr Nobili enabled Hindus to situate him and his God with respect to their own culture and religion. This new god and new visitor were not invading kings, but could be counted among those mysterious teachers who sometimes appear on this earth. "Christ is the guru: 'the concealing revelation' of God among humans through the medium of human

---

[112] Cf. Francis X Clooney, "Christ as the Divine Guru in the Theology of Roberto de Nobili," in R. Costa, ed., *One Faith, Many Cultures* (New York: Orbis Book, 1980), 26. (Hereafter cited as Clooney, *Christ as the Divine Guru*).

[113] Cf. Nobili, *Adaptation*, 142.

[114] Cf. Roberto De Nobili, *Dusna Tikkaram* (Tuttukudi: De Nobili Institute, 1964), 85, cited in Clooney, *Christ as the Divine Guru*, 27.

[115] Cf. Clooney, *Christ as the Divine Guru*, 28.

[116] Clooney, *Christ as the Divine Guru*, 28-29.

[117] Clooney, *Christ as the Divine Guru*, 33.

relationships, the salvific yet demythologized and an iconic presence of the divine in the human."[118]

In conclusion, we may say that Robert de Nobili is a remarkable missionary who presented Catholic Christianity in the scholastic garb. He presented himself to the Hindus as a renouncer, dressing like an Indian Sadhu and living an austere and pure life style, even to the extent of respecting caste restrictions and avoiding the lower castes. His skill in taking Hindu customs and Christianizing them is to be applauded. His mastery of Indian languages and the contribution he made to Tamil Christianity by coining new words and phrases to replace Portuguese or Latin words is memorable. Though he could not indigenize his theology, his views on Christianity and culture are noteworthy.

7. Roman Catholic Missionaries in Madurai

7.1. John De Britto

Fr John de Britto was one of the most distinguished and successful Madurai Mission Missionaries, who endured great sufferings and eventually became a martyr. He was a Portuguese noble by birth and came to India in 1673 and joined the Madurai mission in the following year. He started his work in Kuttur in Tanjore kingdom[119] and then shifted it to Marava country (Ramnad). He worked in these places always under the threat of arrest was finally arrested and cruelly tortured.[120] After his release the provincial sent him on mission business to Portugal. During those two years he was there, though the king tried hard to retain him as tutor to his son, he came back to India and went back to Marava country again. This time he was able to baptize nearly 40,000 people. Chief among them was a man called Tadia Tevar, who was a prince of Maravas. His baptism in 1693 led to a crisis.

Tadia Tevar had five wives, and John de Britto insisted that he must keep only one and pension the others. However, one of the women who was related to the Rajah of Ramnad, appealed to her kinsman against John de Britto and it resulted in the general persecution of the Christians.[121] John de Britto was seized and afterwards he and three Christians were dragged off to Ramnad where they were imprisoned. Tadia Tevar was able to save him from immediate execution. However after sometime he was beheaded publicly in 1693.

7.2. Fr Constanzo Giuseppe Beschi

The Italian, Fr Constanzo Giuseppe Beschi, was another popular missionary who served from 1736 to 1741 in the Madurai Mission. Though in the early years of his ministry Joseph Beschi had to suffer hardship, later he won the confidence

[118] Clooney, *Christ as the Divine Guru*, 35.

[119] Cf. Thekkedath, *History of Christianity in India*, 234.

[120] Cf. Thekkedath, *History of Christianity in India*, 234-235.

[121] Cf. Firth, *An Introduction to Indian Church History*, 121.

of the mogul general Chanda Sahib who protected him. During the years when Chanda Sahib ruled Trichy (1736-1741) he is even said to have made Fr Beschi his dewan and assigned to him the revenues of certain villages, which Beschi used for the work of mission.[122] His principal station was Yella Kurichi and he covered the surroundings of Trichy.

Beschi is famous for his literary works. He produced classical Sangam epics, philosophical treatises, commentaries, dictionaries, grammars, translation works and tracts for both the Hindu Christians and non-Christians.[123] He became master of Tamil and achieved the distinction of composing a long epic poem which is regarded as a classic in Tamil. This was Thembavani (The Unfading Garland), a poem of 36 cantos in ornate high Tamil. The subject is the biblical history of Redemption, beginning with the Old Testament and fulfilled in the birth, ministry, passion and resurrection of our lord.[124] Besides his poetical works Fr Beschi also wrote in Prose. Those were the days the Tranquebar mission was in full swing. To reply to their teaching he wrote a book called 'Veda Vilakkam' (Explanation of Religion). For the guidance of Catechists he wrote Vediar Olukkam (Rule for Catechists). While the great contributions of these foreign missionaries cannot be erased from the memoirs and pages of Indian Church history, it is also important to understand that they could not have achieved thus far without the equally great assistance from the native or local teachers, guides, companions and translators who had to work under much more pressures and sacrifices.

8. The Portuguese Attempts to Latinize the Indian Christians

When the Portuguese arrived in India (1498) and then subsequently met the Syrian Christians, both parties were happy to have each other and their relations were friendly. But, as they began to live together and learn of each other, it became apparent that there were differences between them. Having come from Europe they conceived it to be their duty to bring the Syrian Christians to the Catholic form of Christianity. Thus, Latinization went on throughout the 16th century.

Efforts to Latinize the Syrian Christians began in the early years of the 16th century. By A.D. 1515 itself, around 1200 Syrian Christians embraced Roman Catholicism.[125] In 1514, a school for Syrian boys was opened at Cranganore. A few years later it was turned into a Seminary by the Franciscans, for the training of Young Syrian Christians for the priesthood. The aim of the Seminary was to Latinize the Syrian student priests. Latin and Roman Catholic rituals were taught to them. They were not taught Syriac nor were they allowed to put on Syrian

[122] Cf. also Robert Eric Frykenberg, *Christianity in India: From Beginnings to the Present* (New York: Oxford University Press, 2008), 140. (Hereafter cited as Frykenberg, *Christianity in India*).

[123] Cf. Frykenberg, *Christianity in India*, 139.

[124] Cf. Firth, *An Introduction to Indian Church History*, 122-123.

[125] Tisserant, E., *Eastern Christianity in India*, translated and edited by E.R. Hambye, S.J. (Bombay: Orient Longmans, 1957), 32. (Hereafter cited as Tisserant, *Eastern Christianity*).

dress. However, when they completed their studies, the Syrian Bishop (Mar Joseph) refused to ordain these students, on the ground they do not know Syriac and were too much westernized. Yet the efforts to Latinize continued.

After the death of the Syrian Bishop Mar Abuna Jacob, in 1549, for the six or seven years, no Bishop came from the East. Making use of the absence of the Syrian Bishop, the Franciscans in Cranganore ruthlessly carried out their efforts to Latinize the Syrians. They decided not to allow any Eastern Bishop to come to India. Nevertheless the Bishop from the Chaldean side Mar Joseph arrived after a gap of 7 years i.e., in 1556.[126] Along with him came Mar Elias and two Maltese Dominicans. In spite of the papal backing, the Portuguese, by the virtue of Padroado, resented his coming. These four were taken to custody and taught Latin, and to say mass according to Latin rite. Then they were allowed to go to Kerala to begin their work and to introduce certain Latin rites.

However, it is interesting to note that it was Mar Joseph who refused to ordain students from the Franciscan Seminary. Moreover the Jesuits in Kerala found fault with his teaching. They accused him of teaching that Virgin Mary cannot be called the Mother of God, but only mother of Christ and use of images as idolatry.[127] He was arrested and taken to Rome via Portugal. While in Portugal he could win the favor of the Queen and the Regent and he was sent back to India, without being sent to Rome, in 1565.

Meanwhile during Mar Joseph's first absence from India, the Syrians sent the request for another Bishop to Nestorian Patriarch. In reply, Mar Abraham (who was not in communion with Rome) was sent. Hence, when Mar Joseph returned there were two rival bishops. The Portuguese arrested Mar Abraham and shipped him off to Europe. But, on the voyage he escaped and went to Mesopotamia, where he transferred his allegiance to the Chaldean Patriarch and got himself re-consecrated. He went to Rome also and got himself consecrated anew as Arch Bishop of Angamali. Fortified by all these consecrations, he returned to India, with letters from the pope to the Arch-bishop of Goa and Bishop of Cochin.

When Mar Abraham arrived in Goa the Arch Bishop and the Viceroy refused to accept his documents as genuine and they asked him to remain in Dominican convent until they could be verified by fresh letters from the pope. But, Mar Abraham escaped from there and came to Kerala. As his rival (Mar Joseph) had passed away in 1569, he continued as Bishop for the next 30 years, until his death in 1597. He made sincere attempts to keep the Syrian Customs at the same time acknowledging the pope. Thus, he became a greater obstacle to the proposed Latinization.

He was invited to attend the provincial synod of Goa in 1575. He declined to attend this, suspecting it as an attempt to trap him. It is with the assurance from the Pope that he attended the second provincial Synod. After the Synod,

---

[126] Cf. Firth, *An Introduction to Indian Church History*, 75.

[127] Cf. Frykenberg, *Christianity in India*, 133.

the Jesuits became friendly and it is during this time the Jesuits established their residence (1577) and Seminary at Vaipicota. Mar Abraham attended the third Provincial synod of Goa in 1585, when a whole session was devoted to the Syrian diocese. He was obliged to sign a series of canons, some of which must have been highly unwelcomed by him. They are:

(i) Syrian Candidates for the priesthood were not to be ordained without the permission of the Bishop of Cochin and that their appointment to Churches should be in the hands of the Portuguese.
(ii) The Bishop for the Syrians should be appointed by king of Portugal and consecrated at Goa.
(iii) The Roman worship service books were to be translated into Syriac.
(iv) Mar Abraham was to be provided with an advisor, to help him to carry out the Synod's decisions, including the examination and corrections to the Syriac books in use in the Churches. The helper given was the Jesuit, Fr Francis Roz.

Though Mar Abraham signed in all these documents, from the third provincial synod, relation between Mar Abraham and Portuguese deteriorated. He showed no willingness to carry out the Synod's decisions. The Church books were not handed over for correction. When Roz examined them privately, he found the name of Nestorius still in the Liturgy. Therefore Fr Roz accused Mar Abraham of heresy. In return, Mar Abraham refused to ordain students of the Jesuit Seminary and refused to go for the Fourth Provincial Synod.

All these things having been reported to Rome, Pope ordered the Archbishop of Goa to investigate the charge against him and in the event to being found guilty, keep him in custody until further orders. Because of his illness, Mar Abraham was never brought to trial. He passed away in 1597, leaving the administration of the diocese in the hands of his arch-deacon, George.[128] At this time the newly appointed Arch-bishop of Goa to whom these papal letters were addressed was Alexis de Menezes. On the death of Mar Abraham, he decided that the time had come to bring the Syrian Christians under Roman Catholic Christianity. His plan was to appoint a Jesuit, as a Bishop of Syrian diocese. But, as arch-deacon was already appointed as Bishop he could not carry out his plan. His tireless effort to Latinize the Syrians culminated in the Synod of Diamper.

9. The Synod of Diamper

The Synod of Diamper is one of the outstanding events in the history of Christianity in India. It is the culmination of various efforts taken by the Portuguese to Latinize the Syrian Christians.

[128] Cf. Frykenberg, *Christianity in India*, 135.

9.1. The Events that Preceded the Synod of Diamper

The Portuguese were in the watch-out for an appropriate opportunity to accelerate their efforts to bring the Syrian Christians under the Roman jurisdiction. The death of Mar Abraham presented this opportunity to Alexis de Menezes, the newly-appointed Archbishop of Goa. Menezes was asked by Rome to appoint a successor to Mar Abraham and he was intending to appoint Fr Francis Roz, the Jesuit Vicar-Generál however knowing that it would not be possible instead grudgingly confirmed the archdeacon George as the administrator since George had the support of the Christians as their governor.[129] Menezes continued to plan seriously on bringing the Syrian Christians under the Roman Church and began to exert pressure on the Syrian Christians. George was alarmed of the pressure from the Goan Archbishop. Sensing imminent trouble before him the arch-deacon George called for an Assembly of Christians at Angamali. There a Solemn Oath was taken - that they would act only according to the wishes of the arch-deacon.[130]

Menezes sets out from Goa on 27 December 1598.[131] After reaching Cochin he sets out to begin his tour but met with unfavorable reception at some of the places he visited.[132] He thus began his mission of raising a group of Syrian Christians to support his plans. As the second great authority in Portuguese India, he used his power, position and prestige to influence the local prince. Beginning with the Raja of Cochin, the local rulers not only stopped opposing the schemes of Menezes, but also often put pressures on the Arch-deacon and the Syrian Christians to yield to the demands of the Arch-bishop.

In the meantime Arch-bishop also tried his best to gain the good-will of the Christians, by showing them benevolence and by giving alms liberally to the poor. Every child he met received a gold coin from Menezes. He thought that by ordaining a number of priests, he could get the whole-hearted support of those priests, their parents and relatives. Within the short space of four months, general ordinations were held in three different places. In order to impress the people more, he spent the Holy Week with the important Christian Community at Kaduthuruthy. What touched the people most was, the 'Ceremony of the Washing of the Feet' on Maundy Thursday. Menezes knelt before each of the 12 priests and washed and kissed their feet. Many of those present wept. The services of Good Friday made the people even more well-disposed towards Menezes. On the morning of Easter day, after the services, the Syrians held their customary Love Feast and Menezes was invited to come and bless the food. He did that and finished the day, going round the house in the evening visiting the sick, speaking

[129] Cf. Frykenberg, *Christianity in India*, 135. Cf. also Thekkedath, *History of Christianity in India*, 64.

[130] Cf. Thekkedath, *History of Christianity in India*, 64.

[131] Cf. Thekkedath, *History of Christianity in India*, 66.

[132] Cf. Firth, *An Introduction to Indian Church History*, 84.

kindly to them and helping them with gifts of money, regretting at the same time that their own bishops had so much neglected this part of pastoral duty. In spite of few priests' effort to divert the attention of the people, both clergy and people promised whole hearted submission to Menezes. In this way, Kaduthuruthy became the first community to be fully won-over by Menezes.[133] In this manner Mulanthuruthy and Diamper also joined the side of Menezes.

With the Arch-deacon cleverly made inactive, Menezes proceeded to make all the arrangements necessary to hold the synod which he wanted. Even the venue of the synod had been chosen carefully. The synod was to be held at Diamper, even though Angamali had a better claim to that honor. The reason for the choice was the convenience of Menezes. Diamper was already on his side, while Angamali was the strong-hold of the Arch-deacon. Besides, Diamper could be reached by water from Cochin. After making these careful arrangements he retired of the fort of Cranganore, and drafted the degrees of the synod. After drafting the decrees, he got it translated into Malayalam.

9.2. The Proceedings of the Synod of Diamper

The Synod began on the third Sunday after the Pentecost, 20th June 1599.[134] 813 Syrians (660 laymen + 133 priests + 20 deacons) and Portuguese clergy, captains and officials from the Portuguese settlement of Cochin attended the Synod. After the celebration of Mass, Menezes, who presided over the Synod, announced that he had called for the Synod because Pope Clement VIII had entrusted the administration of the Kerala Church to him. After this a Syrian Priest, Jacob of Pallurte, was appointed by general consent, interpreter for the synod proceedings, and two Jesuits were given to help him in the translation.

At the second session, it is said that Menezes professed his faith in Tridentine faith. He then asked the Syrian clergy to do likewise but some of them protested. Only after Menezes gave explanation, headed by the Arch-deacon, the Syrian Christians made their Profession according to Tridentine formula. Furthermore, Menezes mandated that all clergy not present at the synod should make their profession before Menezes on his visit to their Churches and in future the same profession should be done by all candidates for ordination.

From the third session, matters pertaining to Faith were taken up. The section on the sacraments of Baptism and Confirmation was taken. Every decree sought to Latinize the discipline and Rite of the Syrian Christians. The fourth day dealt with Eucharist, the Sacrifice of Mass, and the sacraments of Penance and Extreme Unction. On 24th June with doors closed and with no Portuguese other than officials present, the section on faith was taken up. The main content of them are:

---

[133] Cf. Tisserant, *Eastern Christianity*, 53ff.

[134] Cf. Thekkedath, *History of Christianity in India*, 69. Cf. also Firth, *An Introduction to Indian Church History*, 89.

i) Clear renunciation of Nestorianism and a statement of the Catholic Faith strongly western in tone.
ii) Renunciation of the Patriarch of the East and accepting the obedience to Pope.
iii) A careful explanation of the seven sacraments, with many details regarding their use and manner of celebration.
iv) Arrangements for administration.
v) Provisions concerning life and manners in Kerala.

The Synod came to an end on June, 26th. In those momentous seven days, the Syrian Church accepted under pressure, the Roman Catholic form of Christianity and the Pope's Jurisdiction. They have also accepted the Roman Catholic Customs. In doing that they repudiated the patriarch to whom they hitherto owed allegiance and consented to abandon many of their traditional customs.

Archbishop Menezes continued his visitation of the Syrian Churches for few more months after the Synod. To enforce the Synod decrees, he had taken with him a kind of sweet meat called 'kollukatta' to be distributed to the children and each child was delighted to find a gold coin inside.[135] The Syriac books were handed over to him for his correction or destruction. The Syriac liturgy was corrected for the use in the Church. These included the removal of the names of Nestorian Saints, the replacement of the Patriarch name by Pope's, the addition of the Roman Ceremonies of Elevation and Genuflection (bob or bow) after the consecration of the Bread and the Wine, the bringing of the Nicene Creed and the Words of Institution into the conformity with the Catholic forms, the replacement of communion by intinction (dipping communion bread into wine) by the Roman way of Communion.

9.3. An Evaluation of the Synod

From the legal-view point, as Thaliath pointed out, the Synod cannot be considered as valid piece of Church legislation for the following reasons:[136]

(1) The Synod falls within the category of Diocesan Synods. Menezes, who alone exercised legislative power in it, was neither the Bishop of the Syrian Christians nor the Pope granted him the necessary authorization to conduct such a synod. Thus, the synod of Diamper which was not convened by a proper authority was therefore not valid.

(2) The meeting of the synod and the proceedings of the synod do not seem to have been done as in synod at all. The great majority of the priests who participated in it were, those calling for a synod. Only

[135] Cf. E.M. Philip, *The Indian Church of St. Thomas* (Nagercoil: L.M. Press, 1950), 122. (Hereafter cited as Philip, *The Indian Church of St. Thomas*).

[136] Cf. Jonas Thaliath, *The Synod of Diamper* (Rome: NP., 1958), 170ff.

when Menezes saw that everything was in favor of him, he thought in that line and affixed the name of synod. Thus, the proceedings of the synod were not proper legally and thus invalid.

(3) Further, Menezes took the liberty to add more canons and regulations after the synod was over and inserted them into the Text. It was this revised text that was sent to Rome for approbation (approval or consent).

It is because of these reasons many regard the synod of Diamper as legally invalid. However, from the documentary point of view, the synod is a very important one, despite the legal invalidity of the synod. The synod of Diamper has furnished us with a document which throws much light on the situation of the Church of St. Thomas Christians during the Portuguese period. It is from it, we know about the orthodoxy of the Syrian Christians. Historically speaking, the synod is most significant as an epoch-making event in the history of the Syrian Christians. It cuts off the age-long relation the Syrian Christians had fostered with that of Eastern Church.[137] It remained in the annals of Indian Church history as the most tragic event for the Indian Christians in general and for the St. Thomas Christians in particular.

10. The Coonen Cross and Consequences

Coonen Cross Revolt was a general revolt of the St. Thomas Christians against Archbishop Garcia and the Jesuits in 1653. It turned out to be one of the most important events in the history of the Church in India. The division of the St. Thomas Christians into Syrian Catholics and Syrian Orthodox came as a result of the events closely connected with this revolt.

The root cause of the discontent which finally blew over in 1653 can easily be traced back to the synod of Diamper. The Syrian Christians disliked the severance of their ties with the East but they had to do that under pressure and Latin bishops were imposed on them. The changes brought into their worship rites and in the customs inevitably caused a tremendous amount of discontentment among them. The steps taken by the arch Bishop Garcia to introduce the Latin customs also add to their discontent. The most devastating of all was the attempt of the Jesuit Archbishop to purge the authority and the special position which the Arch-deacon had been holding for centuries in the Church of Malabar.

This attempt to demean the arch-diaconate resulted in strong resistance not only from the arch deacons but also from clergy and the laity alike, because they considered the maintenance of the arch-diaconate office essential to maintain the power, the prestige and the enviable status the Syrian Christian community had in the kingdom of Malabar. Besides, the obstinate nature of both the Arch-bishop Garcia and the Arch-deacon Thomas contributed to the revolt and which

[137] Cf. Tisserant, *Eastern Christianity*, 166.

culminated with the arrival of the Bishop from the East – Atallah (in Arabic form) or Aithalaha (in Syriac form).[138]

In response to the request for Bishop which the Archdeacon Thomas had sent in 1648, to several of the Oriental Patriarchs, a certain Mar Atallah made his appearance at Mylapore in August 1652.[139] Though Atallah was a member of a Catholic Church, the Portuguese authorities in India suspected his orthodoxy, interned him in Jesuit College at Mylapore, till he could be handed over to the officials of the Inquisition in Goa. This news reached Kerala through some seminarians who had gone to Mylapore on Pilgrimage. The Seminarians also carried with them, a letter of Atallah, addressed to the Syrian Christians and their heads. In this letter he declared himself to be "Ignatius, Patriarch of the whole of India and China," who had received all powers from the Pope.

Archdeacon Thomas spread the news that the Syrian Patriarch sent to them by the Pope in answer to the numerous petitions, had been unjustly imprisoned by the Jesuit fathers. A general meeting of Syrian Christians was held at Diamper. The meeting requested Arch Bishop Garcia's help in order to take Mar Atallah to Kerala. But, Garcia replied that even if Atallah's claim to have been sent by the Pope were true, he would not allow him to enter the diocese, since he came without the permission of the king of Portugal. This reply annoyed the Syrian Christians. In several places the people rose in rebellion, declaring the Jesuits to be schismatic and heretics, in as much as they held in prison, a holy Patriarch sent to them by the Pope.[140] When the news arrived that the ship in which Atallah was being taken from Mylapore to Goa was approaching Cochin, Arch deacon Thomas accompanied by a large number of clergy and several thousands of armed laity went to the Port to examine the bishop's credentials. On the whole, the authorities in Cochin were in favor of granting this request. Owing to the stern opposition of Archbishop Garcia it was not done and thus after two days stay in Cochin the ship left for Goa with Atallah.

The Christians after seeing off the ship lost all their aspirations of having an Oriental Bishop. In this heated excitement a rumor immediately spread that Atallah had been thrown overboard and drowned.[141] This added fuel to their anger that on 3rd January, 1653 they took a solemn oath at Mattancherry, renouncing their allegiance to Arch-bishop Garcia and the Jesuits and that, they would

---

[138] Cf. Thekkedath, *History of Christianity in India*, 91, footnote no. 2.

[139] Thekkedath, *History of Christianity in India*, 91.

[140] Cf. Joseph Thekedathu, *The Troubled Days of Francis Garcia S.J.: Archbishop of Cranganore (1641-59)* (Rome: NP., 1972), 52ff. (Hereafter cited as Thekedathu, *Troubled Days of Francis Garcia*).

[141] It is said that what actually transpired after leaving Cochin was that he was taken to Goa, tried by the Inquisition and on finding him guilty, was shipped off to Europe. Cf. Brown L.W., *The Indian Christians of St. Thomas* (C.U.P.: NP., 1956), 100, cited in Firth, *An Introduction to Indian Church History*, 101. (Hereafter cited as Brown, *The Indian Christians of St Thomas*).

recognize Archdeacon Thomas as the Governor of their Church.[142] However, there is considerable difference between the contemporary accounts and tradition preserved by the Syrian Christians, regarding the manner in which the oath at Mattancherry was taken. According to the contemporary written accounts, they took this oath inside the Church of 'Our Lady' at Mattancherry and in front of a crucifix with lighted candles and over the Bible. The Syrian Christian tradition, instead speaks of the "Coonen Cross Oath." According to this tradition a rope was tied to the open air cross that stands in front of the Church of Mattancherry, so that all could touch at least that rope when the oath was being made.[143]

Thekkedath tries to provide a solution that could be made to bring the two divergent accounts to a common agreement. According to him it is most likely that the priests and the most important lay leaders took the oath inside the Church before the crucifix and over the Bible. Since whatever space was left inside the church was occupied by all those who managed to get in there first, the larger crowd was made to be content with their places in front of the Church and around the "Coonen Cross." Hence, they might have indulged in some spectacular display of the thing described by the traditional account. And this very unusual character of the oath made in the open space must have helped to impress it in the memory of the participants and of all those who heard of it with the result that people later on spoke only of that and not of the more prosaic oath made inside the Church.[144] Later on May 22, 1653, the revolted Syrians held a counsel at Alengad to make arrangement for their future. On the alleged authority of the letter sent by Atallah they choose the Arch-deacon Thomas as their Bishop and 12 priests consecrated him. He thus assumed the title Mar Thoma I.[145] Four men committee was appointed to assist him – Kadavil Chandy, Anjilimootil Itty Thoman, Vengoor Givarghese and Palliveetil Chandy.[146] Thus the Syrian Orthodox Church saw its birth. Consequently the Syrian Christians were divided as Syrian Catholic and Syrian Orthodox.

However, after the initial adrenalin of the Coonen Cross incident subsided, some of the Syrian Christians began to harbor doubts concerning their impulsive actions in relation to the consecration of their archdeacon Thomas as archbishop. They belatedly realized that the whole consecration process was invalid. First, there was no regular authority to consecrate and hence twelve priests took upon themselves to do that on Thomas which was an invalid act; secondly, the alleged letter of Atallah's letter upon which authority they carried out the consecration turned out to be nothing but a forgery – a handiwork of Anjilimootil Itty

[142] Cf. Koodapuzha, *Christianity in India*, 97. Cf. also Thekedathu, *Troubled Days of Francis Garcia*, 59ff.

[143] Cf. Thekkedath, *History of Christianity in India*, 93.

[144] Cf. Thekkedath, *History of Christianity in India*, 93.

[145] Cf. Koodapuzha, *Christianity in India*, 98.

[146] Cf. Philip, *The Indian Church of St Thomas*, 163.

Thoman.[147] As such, even among those Syrians who remained faithful to the archdeacon Thomas, there were doubts of their position like two of the four members committee, Kadavil Chandy and Palliveetil Chandy went back to Archbishop Garcia.[148]

On the other side, Archbishop Garcia was disturbed to a very great extent with the outcome of all these that he appealed to the Portuguese Viceroy for help. The viceroy in reply advised Garcia to send some other religious orders to the Serra so that any further schisms among the Christians could be prevented. However, Garcia ignored the suggestion of the viceroy and instead sent his secretary, Fr De Magistris, to Europe with his plea before the king of Portugal and the pope.[149] At the same time, under Garcia's direction, the Goan Inquisition also sent two of its commissaries – Fr John Rangel (in 1654-55) and Fr john de Lisboa (in 1656) to the Serra to negotiate with the archdeacon Thomas. The first of the two was not successful as he was suspected of unfairly siding with the Jesuits and the Portuguese.

The second commissary Fr John de Lisboa was thus strongly advised not to contact either Archbishop Garcia or the Jesuits so that he would be spared from similar suspicion and failure. He was somewhat successful in that he persuaded the archdeacon Thomas to stop exercising his authority as a Bishop and instead write to the Inquisition to pardon him for the unfortunate event that had taken place. This was done with the implication that the commissary would appeal to Goa and its inquisitors to recommend Thomas to Rome to install him as the archbishop of the Serra. Thomas accordingly wrote to the inquisitors of Goa, admitting his mistake in following the letter of Atallah and asks for pardon. He then concluded his letter with the request for the appointment of a non-Jesuit governor or administrator for the Serra. However, Garcia while agreeing to do the rests, refused to reinstate Thomas in the position. This led Thomas to break away from his words and began to exercise his ecclesiastical powers again.[150]

Having seen the failure of the efforts of the inquisitors of Goa, Rome directly intervened and sent two groups of Carmelites – Fr Hyacinth of St Vincent and his group and Fr Joseph popularly called as Sebastiani (An Italian) and his group. When Sebastiani and his friends reached Kerala in 1657, Archdeacon Thomas went to a great extent to disturb the work of the former. However, Sebastiani with the whole-hearted support of Chandy Parampil, the vicar of Kuravilangad who was also a very prominent priest of the archdiocese, could thwart the efforts of Thomas. In addition, the political and military situation on the Malabar Coast

---

[147] Cf. Thekkedath, *History of Christianity in India*, 94.

[148] Cf. Firth, *An Introduction to Indian Church History*, 102.

[149] Cf. Thekkedath, *History of Christianity in India*, 96.

[150] Besides, it is also believed that Thomas took this step after hearing a rumor that the Inquisition in reality never forgave anyone except by fire. Cf. Thekedathu, *Troubled Days of Francis Garcia*, 89ff.

strengthened Sebastiani's cause. With their (Portuguese) lost of Ceylon to the Dutch and the imminent surrender of their hold in Malabar and Coromandel coasts, the Portuguese authorities in Cochin realized the urgency of bringing the St Thomas Christians to their fold. As a result, they were even ready to embrace the efforts of even a non-Portuguese commissary at this point of time.[151]

In 1657 the Carmelites under the leadership of Sebastiani could bring back more than 44 churches to the Roman Church.[152] Then Fr Joseph Sebastiani left for Rome and with him he took a signed statement in which the people appealed that even though they wanted to remain faithful to the Roman Church, they were not willing to be once again put under the rule of the Jesuit archbishop Garcia and hence requested the Pope to send them another Bishop. The Pope responded to this by consecrating Fr Joseph Sebastiani and sent him back to India in 1661 in Episcopal orders as a titular Bishop of Hierapolis (in Turkey in Asia Minor) and apostolic administrator in Malabar, India. By the time he reached India, Archbishop Garcia had already been dead i.e., in 1659 and thus the Carmelite Bishop made his centre at Verapoli.

Despite the persistent efforts of the Carmelites to bring back the remaining dissidents to the Roman fold and despite several conferences with Mar Thoma I, the latter along with Anjillimootil Itty Thoman did not yield. According to the accounts of Philip, Mar Thoma I and his companion were once arrested and interned at the Rajah's palace at Cochin. However, they escaped from there disguised in the clothes of two laymen who were there to visit them.[153] By 1663 when the Carmelites were compelled to leave due to political reason, 84 churches had already returned to the Roman Church and only 32 remained away. Though their number declined to a very great extent, the minority continue to remain faithful to Mar Thoma I. It was the Dutch who drove out the Portuguese in Java (1595), Malacca (1641), Ceylon (1638-58), Quilon (1661), Cranganore (1662) and Cochin (1663) and they held Cochin till 1795 when the British took it from them.[154] Thus, the administration of Bishop Joseph Sebastiani and his Carmelite colleagues came to its end. Before their departure however, he consecrated P. Chandy (Alexander de Campo to the Portuguese) as vicar apostolic.

The entrance of the Dutch into the picture helped the dissident Syrians that there was now no barrier to prevent them from renewing their connection with the Eastern Patriarchs. Earlier, under the power of the European Roman clergy and the Portuguese, they were greatly hindered but now those hindrances have been removed by the Dutch. As a result, the dissident party started to send messages across requesting for a metropolitan Bishop to be sent to them who would in turn consecrate Mar Thoma I and thus ecclesiastically regularize their

[151] Cf. Thekkedath, *History of Christianity in India*, 97.

[152] Cf. Firth, *An Introduction to Indian Church History*, 103.

[153] Cf. Philip, *The Indian Church of St Thomas*, 168-169.

[154] Cf. Firth, *An Introduction to Indian Church History*, 104-105.

stance. The Patriarch of the East who was eventually sent to them was not the one with whom the Malabar church had been in contact with before the Synod of Diamper and neither was he one from either branch of the Nestorian Church but altogether another, the Jacobite Patriarch of Antioch.[155] This Jacobite priest was none other than Mar Gregorios, Metropolitan of Jerusalem. He reached India in 1665.

There are differences of opinion regarding his consecration of Mar Thoma I. Some hold that he did indeed consecrate Thomas while others hold that it is not likely since Mar Gregorios exercised liturgical and teaching functions while Thomas functioned as archdeacon.[156] Mar Gregorios remained in India serving till his death in 1672. As a Jacobite he taught anti-Nestorian and anti-Roman teachings and attempted to reinstate oriental customs like eastern liturgical vestments, leaven bread in the Eucharist and clerical marriage. After him two more Jacobite bishops namely Mar Baseluios and Mar Ivanios came to India in 1678. Within two weeks the former died but the latter remained till 1693, carrying on the work of propagating Jacobite teaching.

Those who did not take part in the revolt of 1653 and those who revolted yet afterwards returned to the Roman fold came to be known as Palayanker or the Old Party and those who revolted and remained separate after it and who later received Jacobite bishops came to be known as Puthenkur or the New Party. Even though the majority of the Syrians who revolted in 1653 went back and joined the Roman Church, a minority continued to exist as a Jacobite Church. The division thus created at that time among the Syrian Christians continues to remain ever since.

---

[155] This Jacobite Patriarch was head of another Eastern Church and whose doctrine of the Person of Jesus Christ is opposed to that of the Nestorian Church and also to that of the Western Christianity.

[156] Brown, *The Indian Christians of St Thomas*, 112.

Chapter 4

The First Protestant Christianity in India

1. Introduction

The protestant mission began in India only in 18th century. The Tranquebar Mission and the Serampore Mission were the first two Protestant Missions in India. We shall begin with a brief analysis of the then Political, Socio-Cultural and Religious Conditions of India during the 18th and 19th Centuries and make an attempt to briefly recount the history of the Tranquebar mission followed by Serampore Mission.

2. Condition of India during the 18th and 19th Centuries

2.1. Political Condition

The earliest of India's known civilizations, the Indus Valley Civilization (about 2500 to 1700 BC), was known for its amazing artifacts and stretched throughout Northern India. Another early culture - the Vedic culture, dates from about 1500 BC and is considered one of the sources for India's predominantly Hindu culture and for the foundation of several important philosophical traditions. Outsiders who came to India during the course of its history include the Greeks under Alexander the Great, the Kushânas from central Asia, the Mongols under Genghis Khan, Muslim traders and invaders from the Middle East and Central Asia, and finally the British and other Europeans. Until the modern industrial era, India was a land popularly known for its economic as well as cultural wealth. Europeans visited the country to trade for the finest cotton textiles as well as for its special spices. Eventually, the British entered the scene and colonized the region.

In the first two centuries after Europeans arrived in India, their activities were restricted to trade and evangelism, and their presence protected by naval forces. For the entire period of the Mughal Empire, European traders were confined to trading posts along the coast. In the 16th century the Portuguese navy controlled the sea-lanes of the Indian Ocean, protecting the traders settled in Goa, Damân and Diu on the western coast. Saint Francis Xavier, a Spanish Jesuit missionary, came to Goa in 1542, converting tens of thousands of Indians along the peninsula coast and in southern India and Ceylon before leaving for Southeast Asia in 1545.

The Dutch displaced the Portuguese as masters of the seas around India in the 17th century. The Dutch East India Company was founded in 1602, two years after its main rival, the English East India Company. Both companies began by trading in spices, gradually shifting to textiles, particularly India's characteristic light, patterned cottons. By the 18th century British sea power matched that of the Dutch, and the European rivalry in India began to take on a military dimension. During the first half of the 18th century the French, who had begun to operate in India in about 1675, emerged as a serious threat to the growing power and prosperity of the English East India Company. By the mid18th century the British and French were at war with each other throughout the world. This rivalry manifested itself in India in a series of conflicts, called the Carnatic Wars, which stretched over 20 years and established the British as the primary European power in India.

2.2. Economic Condition

With the imposition of direct rule, the economy of India became even more closely linked than before with that of Britain. The opening of the Suez Canal in 1869, railroads, roads, and communications were developed to bring raw materials, especially cotton, to ports for shipment to England, and manufactured goods from England for sale in an expanding Indian market. Indian entrepreneurs were not encouraged to develop their own industries. During the 1850s, mechanized jute industries were developed in Bengal and cotton textiles in western India, mainly by British firms. Although these industries expanded rapidly from 1880 to 1914 and though an Indian iron-and-steel industry was developed in the early 20th century, India remained essentially an agrarian economy. With only small advances in public health, death rates remained high and life expectancy low.

Although local government councils had been elected prior to 1857, it was only after the Indian Councils Act of 1861 that Indians were permitted, by appointment, to participate in the Executive Council, the highest council of the land. The higher civil service had theoretically been opened to Indians in 1833, and the Queen's Proclamation of 1858 confirmed this point again. Nevertheless, candidates for the service were mandated to go to England to compete in the examination, where classical European subjects were made core content of the course. Those few who managed to overcome these initial obstacles and join the service encountered further discrimination that barred them from advancing.

2.3. Socio-Religious Condition

By 1800 Hinduism, which was the religion of at least three-fourth of the population of India, consisted, in the main, of two great groups of sects the Vishnuite[157] and the Sivaite.[158] There also existed multitudes of degraded Outcastes, held down in the dirt by Hindu law. Learning had almost ceased; ordinary education scarcely existed; spiritual religion was to be met only in the quietest places; and a coarse idolatry with cruel and immoral rites held all the great centers of population.

2.3.1. *Caste System*

According to the Hindu structure of society the rigid casteism was a must for the well being of the community. It was the norm of the society. According to Brahminism, the Brahmins were created from the head of Purusha, Kshatriyas from the shoulders, Vaishyas from the hip and Sudras from the feet.[159] Such an understanding of creation justified the hierarchical society and the die-hard system of caste. There was neither inter-dining nor inter-marriages between the high and low castes. Only the three upper castes learned the scriptures, mostly at home. The lower castes were even debarred from taking spiritual counsel from high castes. Thus, every aspect of the society was governed by caste system.

2.3.2. *Condition of Women*

Hinduism has a very low opinion of women.[160] The higher castes believed and enforced upon its women the belief that after the death of the husband, the wife's chastity and faithfulness is proved only by committing *Sati*.[161] This practice left many child widows and youthful widows who have to live the rest of their lives in sorrow. This practice was often imposed on the women by the relatives, or sometimes by the parents.[162] It is believed that on becoming *Sati* a widow purifies the families of her husband and her parents. Sometimes a widow preferred to die in the pyre of her husband in order to avoid the cruel torture of the families

[157] The Vishnuite sects were very numerous, both in the North and in the South, and they were perhaps, on the whole, more homogeneous than the worshippers of Siva.

[158] Worshippers of Siva considered that Siva is the one god, but recognized also all other gods, even Kali or Durga, Siva's wife.

[159] Zachariah, *Modern Religious and Secular Movements in India*, 2.

[160] Manu prescribed that a woman should be under the control of her father before marriage, under her husband in marriage and under the control of her son in old age.

[161] Sati is an act of widow entering the pyre of her dead husband voluntarily or involuntarily, most often involuntarily. This is never practiced among the so-called low castes.

[162] Cf. Gine, *The System of Elementary Education*, 5-6.

the rest of her life. Those who were envious of the widow's wealth insist that the widow must go to the pyre.

2.3.3. *Devadasi System and Practice of Female Infanticide*

The devadasi system was a religious custom for Hindus. The term *devadasi* means 'female servant of God.' But corrupt priests and worshippers used them to satisfy their lust, which led the devadasis to become sacred prostitutes. This practice polluted the atmosphere of the temples.

The practice of female infanticide among the Hindus was very common. Many parents considered it a liability to have girl babies, for it was the girl's father who had to pay the dowry to the boy's father. There was also a belief among the Hindus that some of the gods and goddesses required human sacrifices and such sacrifices are highly meritorious. For this purpose, children were often kidnapped and slaughtered and their blood was offered especially to the goddess Kali to appease her and receive her blessings. To some Hindus, the birth of a female child was considered to be bad omen as the girls had little regard in the society and hence in most of the situations they became the victims for any religious sacrificial rites.[163] All these factors contributed toward the pitiable condition of Indian women during the 18th and 19th centuries.

3. Background of Protestant Christianity in India

The first Protestant Christianity came to India in the early part of the 18th century. During this century the European nations that settled in India were the Dutch at Pulicat (1609), Sadras (1647) and Negapatam (1660); the British at Masulipatam (1622), Madras (1639), Cuddalore (1683) and Calcutta (1689); the French at Pondicherry (1674); the Danes at Tranquebar (1620) and Serampore (1676).[164] The French were Roman Catholics and the rests were Protestants. However, they had no intention to spread the gospel in India as their sole aim was for trade and profit.

Though the Protestant Christianity went side by side with the colonial flag it was not the colonial expansion which spread Protestant Christianity. It was the 18th century spiritual awakenings that gave Protestant Christians the biblical motive to share the gospel of Jesus Christ to others. In England the Society for Promoting Christian Knowledge (SPCK) was formed in 1698, and Society for the Propagation of the Gospel (SPG) in 1701 for the purpose of carrying the gospel to foreign land.[165] In1705 King Fredrick IV of Denmark founded the Danish Halle Mission (Tranquebar Mission), and it sent the first Protestant missionaries to India in 1706. In 1792 the British Missionary Society was founded; in 1795

[163] Cf. Gine, *The System of Elementary Education*, 4.

[164] Cf. C. B. Firth, *An Introduction to Indian Church History*, 131.

[165] Cf. Van den Berg, Johannes, *Constrained by Jesus Love* (Rotterdam: J.H. Kok and N.V. Kampen, 1956), 45.

the London Missionary Society; the Church Missionary Society in 1799; the Religious Tract Society in 1799; and the British and Foreign Bible Society in 1804. In Europe, the Netherlands Missionary Society (1796), Basel Mission (1815), and the Gossner Society (1836) were founded. In USA, the American Board of Commission for Foreign Mission (1810), the American Baptist Mission (1814), the Methodist Mission and Bible Society (1819), and the Presbyterian Foreign Mission Society (1837) were founded.[166] These Protestant missionary societies sent numerous missionaries to Asian countries, which resulted in the spread of Protestant Christianity in India also.

It was King Frederick of Denmark who first took the initiative to send Protestant missionaries to India. In 1706 Bartholomew Ziegenbalg and Henry Pluetschau were sent to India. In spite of the unwelcoming attitude, they began their work by learning Portuguese and Tamil. The first baptism took place on 12th May 1707. In the same year (1707), on 15th August the native Church named 'The Jerusalem Church' was established. In 1711 Ziegenbalg completed a translation of the New Testament into Tamil. A printing press was set up at Tranquebar in 1712.[167] Hence, a strong Christian congregation was established in South India at Tranquebar.

4. The First Protestant Mission in India

The beginning of the 18th century saw the coming of Protestant Christianity to India. The Evangelical Revival that broke out in Germany (Pietism) spread to Europe and USA. This revival created a tremendous amount of zeal for evangelism and a number of missionary societies came into being. The revival movement in the last quarter of the seventeen and the first half of the eighteenth century among the German Lutherans, is characterized by an identifiable salvation experience and inner piety that manifests itself in religious earnestness, ethical living, social activism and missionary zeal.

4.1. The Tranquebar Mission

King Frederick IV of Denmark looked for missionaries to be sent to his colonies. Since neither the Bishop nor the court preacher Franz Julius Lutkans could find suitable candidates in Denmark, Lutkans contacted his pietistic friends for recommendations of suitable candidates. When Lange was contacted, he wrote to Ziegenbalg about this proposal. Ziegenbalg, concerned about his health, did not bother to reply. Ironically, this silence from Ziegenbalg was taken to be his consent and he was recommended to be a candidate. Henry Pluetschau from Wessenbert, another fellow student of Ziegenbalg in Halle, was recommended as another candidate. They were soon ordained as Lutheran ministers by Bishop Borneman,

---

[166] Cf. Hrangkhuma, *An Introduction to Church History*, 352.

[167] Cf. V. Titus Varghese and P. P. Philip, *Glimpses of the History of the Christian Churches in India* (Madras: CLS, 1983), 53-55.

after an initial hesitation. After the ordination, Ziegenbalg was invited to preach to the king. Ziegenbalg used the occasion to expound his mission theology and program, winning the entire royal family over as supporters of the mission.[168]

They left for India on November 29th 1705 by "Princess Sophia Hedwig." They reached Tranquebar on July 9th 1706. The seven months long voyage was as Ziegenbalg described it, an 'academy of death,' replete with terrors from wind and waves, pirates and freebooters, seasickness, and a near shipwreck on the shoals off Ceylon. Ziegenbalg and Plutschau shared a cabin and had their pietistic spiritual exercises, enjoying the flying fish, studying a devotional tract under the title, 'Sophia.'[169] They had to wait on board for three days for a boat to take them to the shore, thanks to the captain of the ship who wanted to vent his anger on them, for the missionaries had prevented him from molesting a female passenger.[170] When they finally landed, they were kept in the guardhouse from ten in the morning until four in the afternoon and prevented from entering the town. Fortunately, at dusk a German-speaking Dane named Attrup took pity on them and arranged for the night with his father-in-law, Hans Paulson.

4.2. Bartholomew Ziegenbalg

Bartholomew Ziegenbalg was born on July 10th 1682 in Paulsnits, Saxony. His father was a rich grain merchant and his mother was highly influenced by Lutheran mystical piety, represented by Ardnt's True Christianity. Tragedy visited the life of young Ziegenbalg, when he lost his father and mother within a two year gap, leaving him at the tender age of ten under the care of his elder sister. His mother's last words made a permanent impression on his heart and he gave scripture a pre-eminent place in his life. At her death bed, his mother gathered all her children around herself and told them, "Dear children, I have collected a great treasure for you; a very great treasure I have collected for you." When the eldest daughter asked, "Dear mother, where is the treasure?" the reply of the dying mother was "Seek it in the bible, my dear children, there you will find it. I have watered every page with my tears."[171] This episode, no doubt, drew him closer to the bible throughout his life. During his high school days, he picked up an excellent command of Latin, Greek and Hebrew. At eighteen he had a conversion experience after nine months of spiritual struggle. He made public confession.

---

168 Scherer, *Bartholomew Ziegenbalg*, 490.

169 Scherer, *Bartholomew Ziegenbalg*, 491.

170 Beyreuther, *Bartholomaeus Ziegenbalg*, 20.

171 J. Fred Fenger, *History of the Tranquebar Mission: Worked out from the Original Papers*, translated by Francke (Madras: Leipzig Evangelical Lutheran Mission, 1906), 12. (Hereafter cited as Fenger, *History of the Tranquebar Mission*).

"While his contemporaries spent their spare time in amusements and dalliances, Ziegenbalg determined to seize the opportunity and made up for the lost time."[172]

While in Berlin, Ziegenbalg met Philip Jacob Spener. His writing aided Bartholomew to attain an ever-increasing growth in piety and theological deliberation.[173] Through Spener, he could enter the spiritually elite company of persons like Baron von Canstein, patron of the pietistic enterprise and the founder of the Canstein Bible Society.[174] He provided Ziegenbalg with a university scholarship. It is this scholarship that enabled him to enter Halle.

At Halle, Ziegenbalg was very much influenced by August Herman Francke's piety and deliberations. From Francke "he received an invincible trust in God's faithfulness, and he too wanted to participate in the spiritual springtime of God's grace."[175]

While he was there at Halle he joined a prayer group. Frankly and openly they told one another their shortcomings.[176] One of his professors, D. Breithaupt, suggested that missionary work in a distant world would be more appropriate for Ziegenbalg. He added, "When one leads one soul of such nations to God that is equivalent to one winning a hundred souls in Europe since these daily have sufficient means and opportunities."[177] Most likely, this saying helped him to consent to the missionary call that came from an unknown corner.

4.3. Their Missionary Methods

4.3.1. *Learning Language*

Realizing the value and the necessity of learning the local language for communicating the Gospel, they started learning Tamil. Besides, they also started learning Portuguese, as it was the official language then in Tranquebar. They sat along with children in their house and practiced the difficult Tamil letters on sand with their fingers.[178] To their great joy they came across an Indian by the name of Aleppa, who knew German, Danish and Portuguese, and thus it was with his help that Indian vocabulary became possible for them. Soon after Ziegenbalg worked out a Tamil-German dictionary and eventually published a grammar book. In four years his dictionary was ready with 40,000 entries.[179] Within eight months

[172] James A. Scherer, "Bartholomew Ziegenbalg," *Missiology: An International Review*, XXVI (October, 1999), 488. (Hereafter cited as Scherer, *Bartholomew Ziegenbalg*).

[173] Erich Beyreuther, *Bartholomaeus Ziegenbalg: A Biography of the first Protestant Missionary in India 1682-1719*, translated by S. G. Lange and H. W. Gensichem (Madras: CLS., 1955), 8. (Hereafter cited as Beyreuther, *Bartholomaeus Ziegenbalg*).

[174] Beyreuther, *Bartholomaeus Ziegenbalg*, 8.

[175] Scherer, *Bartholomew Ziegenbalg*, 489.

[176] Beyreuther, *Bartholomaeus Ziegenbalg*, 9.

[177] Beyreuther, *Bartholomaeus Ziegenbalg*, 11.

[178] Fenger, *History of the Tranquebar Mission: Worked out from the Original Papers*, 24.

[179] Fenger, *History of the Tranquebar Mission: Worked out from the Original Papers*, 26.

Ziegenbalg was able to read, write, and speak in Tamil and even understand the conversation of others.

4.3.2. *Schools*

They started five schools both in Tamil and Portuguese, including a school for the girls, the first of its kind in India. They also started an orphanage. The purpose behind this educational work was the training of young people who would eventually become preachers carrying the Gospel message to their fellow country people.

4.3.3. *Evangelism*

For their work of evangelism, they did not wait till they had mastered the languages. As early as November 1706, they began to catechize the Germans and Portuguese. For catechism they translated Luther's Small Catechism and some German hymns into Tamil and Portuguese. In schools and in the congregation they used with great benefits 'The Short Outline of Christian Doctrine' by Freylingshausen, a prominent Pietist professor of Halle, which was translated by July 1st 1707. They never hurried to baptize. Many months of catechism preceded baptism and continued even after baptism.

Ziegenbalg and Pluetschau pioneered the technique of leading a group of school children into the street or countryside and questioning them on their religious knowledge in the presence of adult Tamils. This catechetical approach was adapted to suit the hearers who had no knowledge of Christianity.[180] This approach proved to be effective, as most of the Tamils with whom they were working among were illiterate. They went to the people wherever they were to be found, whether in the paddy field, on the seashore, in the shadow of the tree or at the temple festivals.[181]

4.3.4. *Building New Church*

The first convert was Ziegenbalg's Tamil servant Seperumal, a Sudra. He was given the name Andreas on September 5, 1707. Following the conversion of Seperumal more Sudras became Christians. Through Ziegenbalg's trust in divine providence, he and Plustchau started and completed the construction of the church building and called it the New Jerusalem Church.

4.3.5. *Translation*

The Danish liturgy was translated into Tamil and used for worship. Within two years of his arrival, Ziegenbalg began the translation of the Bible. The translation

---

[180] D. I. Wright, "Schwartz of Thanjavur: Rajaguru?" *Indian Church History Review*, XV (December 1981), 128. (Hereafter cited as Wright, *Schwartz of Thanjavur*).

[181] Hans Werner Gensichen, "Imitating the wisdom of the Almighty," *Concordia Theological Monthly* 28 (September 1957), 836.

work was made directly from the original languages - Hebrew and Greek. The translation he began in 1708 was brought to a halt on November 19^{th}1708 when the governor Hassius imprisoned him. However, soon after his release he continued the translation and completed the New Testament and the Old Testament up to the book of Ruth. In a letter to Halle, Ziegenbalg wrote, "All the books of the New Testament are now translated; this is a treasure in India which surpasses all other Indian treasures."[182] The first part (Gospels and Acts) was printed at the mission press in 1714, and in 1715 the whole New Testament was printed. In 1723 Schultze began from where Ziegenbalg had left off and completed the entire Old Testament and the Apocrypha by 1725.[183] This printing was possible because of the printing press that had been donated by Francke.[184] It should be mentioned here that even the Tamil types came from Halle.

Francke of Halle took meticulous care to publish these letters, *Reports of the Royal Danish Missionaries in India*, *Remarkable News from India*, and *Remarkable Voyage to Proclaim the Gospel.* They gave a mass of ideological facts. As a result, enthusiasm over the mission work in India was aroused. The king of Denmark in 1711 set up a board and a budget of 2000 Taler per annum. The interest over the Tranquebar Mission spread to England through the court preacher Anton Wilhelm Boehme of the German court chapel, who was a friend of Francke. Boehme translated the letters of Ziegenbalg into English and published them in 1709.[185] Thus, impressive mission cooperation emerged between England, Germany and Denmark. Indeed it is three-corned remarkable mission cooperation. The Tranquebar missionaries worked in truly ecumenical broadmindedness without yielding their Lutheran convictions.

4.4. Relations between the Lutheran Mission and the Roman Catholic Mission

While we see a cordial relationship between the Lutherans and Anglicans, the relationship between the Tranquebar missionaries and the Roman Catholic missionaries working in and around Tranquebar was far from being cordial to each others. Ziegenbalg, filled with the spirit and theological conviction of pietism, strongly criticized the Roman Catholic methods of accommodation. He accused them of tolerating the pagan ceremonies.[186] Either through the publication of

[182] Fenger, *History of the Tranquebar Mission: Worked out from the Original Papers*, 81.

[183] Henry Victor, "Tamil Translation of the Bible by the Danish-Halle Mission during the Eighteen Century," *Indian Church History Review* XVI (June 1982), 76.

[184] Arno E. Lehmann, "August Hermann Francke and the Beginning of the Tranquebar Mission," *Lutheran World*, X (July 1963), 310. (Hereafter cited as Lehmann, *August Hermann Francke*).

[185] Beyreuther, *Bartholomaeus Ziegenbalg*, 46.

[186] Hugald Grafe, "Hindu Apologetics at the Beginning of the Protestant Mission Era in India," *Indian Church History Review* VI (June 1972), 43. (Hereafter cited as Grafe, *Hindu*

Christian literature or due to the benevolence of Tranquebar Mission a number of Roman Catholic converts, including some of their catechists, developed interest in the Lutheran faith.

4.5. The Method of Indigenization

The Tranquebar missionaries did their utmost to eradicate the rigid caste discrimination both in the divine service and in the life of the congregation. Most of their converts came from the Sudra caste, a relatively well placed caste group. As a result, the missionaries followed a conciliar policy in dealing with the issue of caste. Tranquebar missionaries were averse to the idea of any forced method and hence decided to rely on the gradual working of the Christian message in the lives of individuals to shatter the caste spirit from within rather than handle it outrightly. Thus in the New Jerusalem Church, the Sudras men sat in one nave while the Pariahs sat in the other. The report of 1727 read:

> After several long consultations, we decided that order could well exist side by side with Christian humility and unity, and permitted that pariahs [sic] and sudras [sic] sit in the church separated by one yard. But in the distribution of the sacraments, no difference was made.[187]

However, it is commendable to learn that the missionaries took every effort to elevate the standard of living of the Pariahs by finding well-paid positions for the capable and qualified Pariah children. Developing the indigenous Church was the aspiration of the mission for Ziegenbalg and his colleagues. Nevertheless, neither Ziegenbalg nor his successors were willing to abandon their resolve to establish an Indian Church.[188] Defending his proposal to build this large church in Tranquebar, he wrote,

> In the land of thousands of temples and mosques, the building of a large and beautiful house of God by the first Evangelical mission in India, much more than a mere hut which quickly falls into ruin, was of significant meaning, an encouragement to concentrated work and a testimony to a great hope.[189]

Such was the interest that Ziegenbalg showed concerning the church. Tranquebar missionaries were determined to have an indigenous church in the real sense that it was "in India and part of India."[190] The first Tamil lyric book containing 48 songs was published in 1714. The number of songs in the Tamil

---

Apologetics at the Beginning of the Protestant Mission Era in India).

[187] Beyreuther, *Bartholomaeus Ziegenbalg*, 64.

[188] Gensichen, *Tranquebar Then and Now*, 27.

[189] Beyreuther, *Bartholomaeus Ziegenbalg*, 71.

[190] Gensichen, *Tranquebar Then and Now*, 24.

lyric book rose to 160 adding the compositions of Schultze. Ziegenbalg is also credited with the introduction of the typical Indian form of preaching, sermon-in-song.[191]

Ziegenbalg also indigenized wedding ceremonies of the Tamil Christians. The young couples were adorned according to the Tamil customs. The congregation goes on procession in the street, leading the couple all the way to the Church. Ziegenbalg also adapted the Thali, a symbol of marriage, worn by Tamil women. Ziegenbalg also adapted the local burial ceremony. A funeral is conducted in utmost reverence. All the congregational members go to the house of the deceased. They sing and read from the scriptures the words of comfort.

The missionaries also adapted the local clothing to some degree. Ziegenbalg occasionally dressed himself according to the custom of Tamils, "in white turban, about the body a white apron, over the shoulders a red stripped cloth, on the feet red sandals without heels."[192] Schwartz went a step ahead of Ziegenbalg and wore Indian clothes and adapted Indian food.[193]

4.6. Christian Frederick Schwartz

The Tranquebar Mission reached its peak days in the tenure of Christian Frederick Schwartz. After the demise of Ziegenbalg, Grundler led the mission for a year. Then the leadership fell on Benjamin Schultze, and then Bosse. Schwartz was born at Sonnenberg in Prussia on 26th October 1726. Schwartz spent the first 11 years in Tranquebar, working along with John Balthasar Kohlhoff. Within a year he gained proficiency to preach in Tamil. He made repeated travels to Madras, Cuddalore, Nagapattnam, Trichy, and Tanjore, mostly for the purpose of serving communion to the Europeans and for preaching the Gospel to the locals. He elevated himself above the rest, that the history of the Tranquebar Mission could be connected to his name. He served in India for 48 years continuously from 1750 and left his mark both upon the church and on the society with which he was connected. Though a missionary by calling, he was actively involved in diverse work such as chaplain to the British East India Company, diplomat, civil servant, school master, 'friend' of Raja Tuljaji of Tanjore and guardian of an adopted son of King Tuljaji - Serofoji.[194] He says,

> One of the principal labors of a missionary ought to be to train up young natives for future catechists. Whenever I met with a promising youth, I spare neither pains nor expense to qualify him for the work.[195]

[191] Beyreuther, *Bartholomaeus Ziegenbalg*, 72.

[192] Lehmann, *It Began at Tranquebar*, 124.

[193] Fenger, *History of the Tranquebar Mission*, 164.

[194] Wright, *Schwartz of Thanjavur*, 137.

[195] "Schwartz to Rev Dr Knapp, 22 January, 1771," cited in Wright, *Schwartz of Thanjavur*, 137.

In 1762 Schwartz with missionary Klein, went to Tanjore on Captain Johann Wilhelm Berg's invitation. On his way back, he went to Trichy, which belonged to Arcot Nawab, a Mohammedan ruler. The British offered him the position as British Chaplain in 1762 to conduct public worship for the Europeans on Sundays.[196] His ecumenical spirit led him to accept that mission but only after consulting his colleagues in Tranquebar.[197] He never neglected his duties as a missionary to non-Christians that he spoke to the Hindus regularly in the Fort of Trichy (and later at Tanjore), and in the surrounding villages. He seizes every opportunity to communicate the Gospel: a funeral procession, a group of pilgrims' en route to a holy place and people working in the fields, all attracted his attention.[198]

He built an orphanage and a school in Trichy. Schwartz also committed himself to the care for the congregation. Before baptism, a thorough catechism is given to the aspirants, lasting two to three months. He never admitted more than 30 or 40 to the Lord's Supper at a time, so that they could be properly instructed.[199] His most important innovation to keep the congregation together was his introduction of morning and evening congregational prayers.

Schwartz developed a strong relationship with the local Mahammedan ruler, Hyder Ali. In order to communicate with him, Schwartz learnt Arabic and Hindustani. Owing to this friendly relationship, when he built the school, initial funds came from Hyder Ali.[200] In April 17th 1769 he visited Tanjore. After preaching to the Tamil congregation there, he went to visit Tuljaji, a Hindu king, on invitation. He shared the Gospel with the king, who was very much pleased to have Schwartz and expressed his desire for Schwartz to stay at Tanjore permanently.

In 1780, Hyder Ali overcame Tanjore and threw the economy of the country into a disarrayed state. Even within this situation, Schwartz was allowed to preach and convert. Once Hyder Ali issued his army chief the following order, "Permit the venerable Padre Schwartz to pass unmolested, and show him respect and kindness; for he is a holy man, and means no harm to my kingdom."[201] Such was the respect Schwartz had with the native rulers. After the death of Hyder Ali, his son Tippu Sultan sustained the same relationship with Schwartz. However, when

---

[196] Fenger, *History of the Tranquebar Mission: Worked out from the Original Papers*, 158.

[197] Hans Werner Gensichen, "Christian Frederick Schwartz," in Gerald H. Anderson, ed., *Biographical Dictionary of Christian Missions* (New York: Macmillan Reference, 1998), 606.

[198] "Kiernander's Cuddalore Diary, 1757, entries for 29 April, 1 May, 1 July," cited in Wright, *Schwartz of Thanjavur*, 129.

[199] Lehmann, *It Began at Tranquebar*, 62-63.

[200] Fenger, *History of the Tranquebar Mission*, 13.

[201] W. P. Walsh, *Heroes of the Mission Field* (London: Hodder and Stoughton, 1883), 242, cited in Justus, *Schwartz: A Missionary in Politics 1750-1798*, 44.

the British wanted Schwartz to negotiate with Tippu Sultan, Tippu never granted permission for it.

Schwartz's relationship with the Maratha kings of Tanjore was also remarkable. He had free access to the then king Tuljaji. King Tuljaji, at his old age and having no male child to succeed him, adopted Serofoji, a grandson of his cousins, as heir to the throne. Shortly before his death, Tuljaji installed Schwartz the guardian for his adopted son. Pointing to Serafoji, Tuljaji said, "This is not my son, but yours, into your hand I deliver him."[202] Schwartz accepted Serofoji's guardianship. In the meantime, Tuljaji also appointed his half brother Amar Singh the legal successor of Tuljaji. Following this, Amar Singh began to plot against Serofoji and the widow of Tuljaji. On hearing this, Schwartz intervened and arranged not only for the education of Serofoji but also his ascendance to the throne. In October 1798, Serofoji was proclaimed king of Tanjore. As Schwartz was determined to help them in their days of trouble, he was gratefully remembered by Serofoji in the monument he erected for Schwartz. This speaks volumes of the character of Schwartz.

During this time he also met a Maratha Brahmin lady by the name Clorinda, who asked for baptism. Schwartz refused her baptism since she was living with a European officer. However, on his second visit, finding that the officer had passed away, he proceeded to baptize Clorinda. She became instrumental in founding of the Tinnevelly Mission. On her request Sathyanathan was sent there and this led to the awakening of vibrant Christianity in that region. Tranquebar Mission, after the days of Schwartz, quickly declined. Some of the Churches founded by the mission were taken over by the Anglicans while most of the Churches that were later ministered to by the Leipzig Mission form what we call today, 'The Tamil Evangelical Lutheran Church.'

5. The Serampore Mission

The history of Serampore Mission can be traced back to the year 1799, with the arrival of Daniel Brunsdon, William Grant, Joshua Marshman and William Ward. Brunsdon and Grant died within the next two years. Meanwhile Ward visited William Carey at his residence with the protection of Danish Passport. After long deliberation between them Carey decided to join the new missionaries at Serampore, with his family consisting of four sons, and wife on the 10th of January 1800.[203] Thus, the Serampore Mission started on 10th January 1800 under the protection of the Danish flag at Serampore. It was agreed by them

---

[202] William Hickey, *The Tanjore Maratha Principality in Southern India: The Land of the Cholas: The Eden of the South* (Madras: Foster Press, 1874), 90-91, cited in Justus, *Schwartz: A Missionary in Politics 1750-1798*, 44.

[203] Cf. E. L. Wenger, "The Serampore Mission and Its Founder," in Wilma S. Stewart, ed., *The Story of Serampore and Its College* (Serampore: The Council of Serampore College, 1961), 1-2. (Hereafter cited as Wenger, *The Story of Serampore*).

to live together as one family, having all things in common. Concerning this settlement John Clark Marshman writes:

> It was determined to form a common stock, to dine at a common table and to give each family a trifling allowance for personal expenses. All the missionaries were to be considered on a footing of equality and to preach and conduct social devotions in turn. The superintendence of domestic arrangements was to be entrusted to each missionary in rotation for a month.... One evening in the week was to be devoted to adjustment of differences and the renewal of their pledge of mutual love; and it was resolved that no one should engage in any private trade, and that whatever might be earn should be credited to the common stock.[204]

The missionaries had come to India for one paramount purpose, i.e., to bring to the people of that land the knowledge of the love of God revealed in Christ. They invested every means to fulfill this purpose.

5.1. The Founders of Serampore Mission

5.1.1. *William Carey*

William Carey was born, on August 17th 1761, in the Village of Paulerspury, Northamptonshire. His father was a weaver, but later rose to be Parish clerk and village schoolmaster. At the age of six Carey worked out sum in arithmetic in his own mind; that after having learned to read, he manifested an interest in the subjects of science, history and travels and that his scientific taste became prominent at an early age. His room was filled with the insects he had collected to mark their development, and he endeavored to acquire a knowledge of drawing to assist these researches. At the age of twelve he obtained a copy of 'Dyche's Latin Vocabulary' and committed nearly the whole of it to memory, and carefully studied the brief sketch of a grammar prefixed to it.[205]

Carey's parents could not afford to send him to school, so at the age of 14 he joined Clarke Nichols, a shoemaker at Hackleton as his apprentice. He found a commentary on the New Testament, which was interspersed with word in shoemaker's shop. He learned Greek from Tom Jones, a journeyman who was educated at Kidderminster. He was brought up as a strict churchman, as the son and grandson of the Parish clerk.[206] At the same time Mr. Sutcliff, a minister in

---

[204] Marshman, *Life and Times of Carey, Marshman and Ward*, 124-125.

[205] Arthur, C. Chute, *William Carey: A Sketch of Beginning in Modern Missions* (Chicago: Goodman & Dickerson, 1891), 7. (Hereafter cited as Chute, *William Carey*).

[206] Cf. Marshman, *Life and Times of Carey, Marshman and Ward*, 3, 4. Cf. also Chute, *William Carey*, 9-10.

Olney gave him a Latin Grammar and advised him to study it diligently. He improved his acquaintance with languages in Latin, Greek, and Hebrew.

By the age of 18 Carey started preaching in the pulpits. While attending one of the Associations' meetings at Olney, at which he was obliged to fast all day, not having the means of purchasing a meal, some friends from Earl's Barton, a neighboring village, were lamenting about their spiritual destitution to Mr. Charter, the independent minister at Olney. Charter at once advised them to request Mr. Carey's services. They called on him soon after, and he accepted their request, and in that village he preached from Sabbath to Sabbath for three years and a half, and once a month in his native village of Pury.[207]

Mr. Nichols died and Mr. Carey took over his business and married his sister before he had reached the age of twenty.[208] After his marriage he rented a cottage at Hackleton. However, trade became dull, and he was constrained to sell off his stock at a great sacrifice. At this time he was attacked by fever which troubled him for eighteen months, even in this crisis he had to move from place to place to dispose off his goods to procure family bread. The Barton congregation where he serves could not raise enough funds to buy the clothes to wear in their service. At this period he was reduced to great suffering.[209]

At the age of 24 he moved to another village called Moulton where he took in-charge of a Baptist Church, from where he developed missionary zeal, and work in a school. At Moulton he preached four times a week, which increased the number of congregations as well as his cultivation of his natural gifts. In 1789 he moved to another town called Leicester. At the Easter meeting of ministers at Clipstone in 1789, Carey urged that something should be done immediately, on that very day, towards the formation of a Society to propagate the Gospel in heathen lands.[210] However, his proposal was not accepted for another eighteen months, but was asked to print the pamphlet, which was written at Moulton under the title, '*An Enquiry into the Obligation of Christians to Use Means for the Conversion of the Heathens.*' And this appeal was substantiated in May 1792, where he preached a sermon based on Isaiah 54:2-3, in which he explained and enforced two principles: '*Expect Great Things from God; Attempt Great Things for God.*'[211]

The next meeting was held at Kettering on the 2nd of October 1792. After the service, twelve ministers of the Northamptonshire Association of Baptist Churches met together and founded a society to be called 'The Particular

---

[207] Cf. Marshman, *Life and Times of Carey, Marshman and Ward*, 5, 6.

[208] His illiterate wife possessed no feelings in unison with his own yet Mr. Carey always treated her with the utmost affection, while she manifested no interest in his aspirations for a larger sphere of labor and usefulness.

[209] Cf. Marshman, *Life and Times of Carey, Marshman and Ward*, 6.

[210] Marshman, *Life and Times of Carey, Marshman and Ward*, 14.

[211] Cf. also, Marshman, *Life and Times of Carey, Marshman and Ward*, 15.

(Calvinistic) Baptist Society for propagating the Gospel among the Heathens' which later developed into the Baptist Missionary Society of the present day.[212] The ministers consulted further and the following resolutions were proposed, and unanimously agreed to:

1. Desirous of making an effort for the propagation of the gospel among the heathen, agreeably to what is recommended in brother Carey's late publication on that subject, we, whose names appear to the subsequent subscription, do solemnly agree to act in society together for that purpose
2. As in the present divided state of Christendom, it seems that each denomination, by exerting itself separately, is most likely to accomplish the great ends of a mission, it is agreed that this society be called The Particular [Calvinistic] Baptist Society for Propagating the Gospel among the Heathen.[213]
3. As such an undertaking must be attended with expense; we agree immediately to open a subscription for the above purpose, and to recommend it to others.
4. Every person, who shall subscribe ten pounds at once, or ten shillings and sixpence annually shall be considered a member of the society.
5. That the Rev John Ryland, Reynold Hogg, William Carey, John Sutcliff, and Andrew Fuller, be appointed a committee, three of whom shall be empowered to act in carrying into effect the purposes of this society.
6. That the Rev Reynold Hogg be appointed treasurer, and the Rev Andrew Fuller secretary.[214]

The Baptist Missionary Society resolved to send William Carey to Africa, but with the timely intervention of Dr John Thomas, who once acted as the company's doctor in India for some years, the Society reviewed its resolution and decided to send its first batch of missionaries to India. Hence, they began their journey to India on the 13th of June 1793, under a Danish vessel called 'Cron Princessa Maria', commanded by captain Christmas, an Englishman. They landed in Calcutta on the 11th of November 1793.[215]

5.1.2. *William Ward*

William Ward was born at Derby on the 20th of October 1769, and was the son of John Ward, carpenter and builder. His father died when he was a child, and

[212] Wenger, *The Story of Serampore*, 1.

[213] George Smith, *Life of William Carey, Shoemaker & Missionary* (London: 1909), 29, 30.

[214] Marshman, *Life and Times of Carey, Marshman and Ward*, 17.

[215] Cf. Marshman, *Life and Times of Carey, Marshman and Ward*, 60-63.

his mother who was a very devout woman, brought him up.[216] He went through tuition under Mr. Congreve, and then of Mr. Breary of Derby, and became proficient in the ordinary branches of school education. He was distinguished in childhood for clear-headedness and thoughtfulness. On leaving school he was placed as an apprentice with Mr. Drury, who was the head of a large printing establishment in the town. Ward soon rose to the grade of corrector of the press, which gave him ample opportunities of storing his mind with varied useful knowledge. He undertook at the close of his apprenticeship, of editing the 'Derby Mercury' on behalf of his master. With his elegance in writing, Derby Mercury soon raised the circulation and it became one of the most influential papers in the country. He was led to join a political society in Derby, affiliated with the parent society in London.

In August 1796, he was baptized at Hall by Mr. Pendered, and in 1797, he renounced all interest in politics and journalism, and gave his heart and soul to the nobler vocation of communicating the divine truth to his fellow-countrymen.[217] He then decided to offer himself as a missionary of BMS without delay, in the hope of being employed in printing the scriptures. The next six months were spent being acquainted with the members of the Society, conversing with Mr. Fuller, which contributed so greatly to the success of the Serampore mission.[218]

5.1.3. *Joshua Marshman*

Joshua Marshman was born at Westbury Leigh, in Wiltshire, on the 20th of April 1768. In 1764, his father, John Marshman married Mary Couzener, who was a woman of great piety and exemplary benevolence, who lived with her husband in the practice of Christian virtues for more than half a century. It was in this atmosphere of religious piety that Joshua Marshman was trained up.[219]

When he was seven years of age, he was sent to a little village school. There was no school in the neighborhood in which writing was taught, or even simple elements of arithmetic. However, in these circumstances he developed thirst for reading, and by the time he was twelve, he had read through more than a hundred volumes.[220] At the age of fifteen, Mr. Cator, a bookseller in Holborn employed Marshman in his bookshop, with the view of providing for him in his own trade. When others retired to rest, he applied to reading and more than once fell asleep with a book in his hand, and the light burning, and thus endangered the building, to the great annoyance of the inmates of the house. He came back from London to Westbury Leigh and resumed his labors at the loom, continued to engage in

[216] Cf. Marshman, *Life and Times of Carey, Marshman and Ward*, 92, 93.

[217] Cf. Marshman, *Life and Times of Carey, Marshman and Ward*, 96.

[218] Marshman, *Life and Times of Carey, Marshman and Ward*, 98.

[219] Marshman, *Life and Times of Carey, Marshman and Ward*, 100.

[220] Cf. Marshman,*Life and Times of Carey, Marshman and Ward*, 102.

reading every work of fiction or poetry, history, geography, or travels, whichever he could get hold of.[221]

In 1791 he married Hannah Shepherd, the granddaughter of the Rev John Clark. In 1794 he joined in a school as a teacher in Bristol and he also joined the Church at Broadmead, and was received into it by baptism in the course of the year. While working as teacher he read the periodical of the Account of the Baptist Missionary Society, and his mind was gradually turned toward missionary labor in the East. With the encouragement of Dr Ryland, a committee member of the Society and his friend Grant, he offered his willingness to go to India as Missionary.[222] The Society thus sent Marshman, Ward and their associates to India on 20th of May 1799.

5.2. The Mission's Establishment of the Senate of Serampore College

With the introduction of elementary schools, which amount up to forty-five in number by 1816, the desire of the native people for learning increased so much so that the Serampore missionaries began to struggle very hard to open more mission schools with sufficient efficient teachers.[223] As the desire for higher education and a thirst for English knowledge grew among the better classes of the society, it received support and encouragement from the rulers of the land, and with the blessing of Lord Hastings, the then Governor-General, even some wealthy Hindus gave their support and opened a College for the education of the young men of Calcutta in 1816. Subsequently, agencies and associations for the upliftment of the natives began to come up substantially.

5.2.1. *The Establishment of the College (1818-1837)*

Despite the fact that the missionaries had broken off from the Baptist Missionary Society in England and its support in 1816, they decided to start a College where the natives, especially of Christian parentage, can be given a higher and more complete education.[224] On the 15th of July 1818, the missionaries issued their prospectus in which the institution was meant to be *A College for the Instruction of Asiatic Christian and Other Youth in Eastern Literature and European Science.* It was Dr Marshman who wrote the document, making it very clear that the College was to be a handmaid of evangelization and the instruction would be given in Sanskrit, Arabic, European Science and English. The medium of learning was to be Vernacular, with English as a required subject. There was also the firm hope that the College was to be considered as most importantly a divinity school,

[221] Cf. Marshman, *Life and Times of Carey, Marshman and Ward*, 105.

[222] Cf. Marshman, *Life and Times of Carey, Marshman and Ward*, 107.

[223] D. A. Christadoss, "The Story of Serampore College, 1818-1929," in Wilma S. Stewart, ed., *The Story of Serampore and Its College* (Serampore: The Council of Serampore College, 1961), 20. (Hereafter cited as Christadoss, *The Story of Serampore College*).

[224] Marshman, *Life and Times of Carey, Marshman and Ward*, 168.

where promising Christian youth for evangelistic work should go through a complete course of instruction in Christian theology.[225] Nevertheless, it was made imperative that the College should be open to all without the distinction of caste or creed thereby divesting its instruction of all sectarian character.[226]

The first year they had thirty-seven students in the College, of which nineteen were Christians, many of whom were scholarship-holders, and eighteen were non-Christians. By 1822, the Trio accomplished the completion of the main building and the College House; the Rev John Mack joined the Trio. He proved to be an invaluable asset to the College. It was Mack who took charge of the secular branches of the curriculum and Ward of the Theology department. These four missionaries, Carey, Marshman, Ward and Mack, together underwent extreme tryst of financial breakdown as they tried their utmost to keep the College and the mission running. Besides their precarious financial state, two grave calamities awaited them. The first was the unexpected death of the Rev William Ward on the 5th of March that Cholera attacked him, and he died on the 7th of March. The next calamity was the huge loss caused by the devastating floods in the Hooghly River. It washed away an embankment 250 feet long and 16 feet high in front of the Mission buildings. Badly affected by these calamities, Carey and Marshman were left to await the inevitable breakdown. The British and Foreign Bible Society offered them a grant of about 6,000 pounds, enabling them to solve their present difficulties.

As the College grew gradually with maturity, it received support from various angles in India, irrespective of class or creed distinctions.[227] Dr Marshman left for England toward the end of the year (1822) for two important purposes: to bring about reconciliation between Serampore Mission and the Baptist Missionary Society, and to raise funds for the mission over here in Serampore. However, no matter how much he tried, the first purpose for reconciliation was unsuccessful with not even a glimmer of hope of restoring cordiality in the near future. Hence, for the second purpose, he had to make tedious journey throughout the country searching for people's sympathy and support for the Serampore Mission. He returned to India in May 1829 with much discouragement but soon together with his colleagues began to gear up their energies for the work.

By 1830s, they were supporting 13 out-station missions, 17 European and Eurasian laborers, 15 native preachers, the College and some widows and orphans. Discovering that there was nowhere else to look for support, they decided to turn to the public for support. Carey thus appealed to the Christian public in England pointing out:

---

225 Cf. Christadoss, *The Story of Serampore College*, 21.

226 Marshman, *Life and Times of Carey, Marshman and Ward*, 170.

227 Marshman, *Life and Times of Carey, Marshman and Ward*, 279.

> If unceasing industry or self-denial could by any means furnish us with the supplies we beg of you, we would toil and deny ourselves with cheerful alacrity and leave you un-importune. But, our hopes are small in this respect, and they are precarious in the extreme... But a few years have passed away since the Protestant world was awakened to missionary effort. Since that time the annual revenues collected for this project have grown to the then unthought-of sum of 400,000 pounds. And is it unreasonable to expect that some unnoticeable portion of this should be entrusted to him who was among the first to move in this enterprise, and to his colleagues?[228]

Carey's appeal to the generosity of his countrymen proved to be touchingly successful. Moreover, Mr. Leechman who had joined the work of the College in 1831 also appealed to the English public for the Serampore Mission. People's response to these pleas was indeed tremendous, for, Mr. Hope, the friend and caretaker of the missionaries' interests in England, was able to send thousands of pounds by the first ship itself.

The College despite repeated troubles grew with most talented teaching staff such as Dr Leechman, and Mr. John Clark Marshman, the son of Dr Marshman, who joined the staff in 1819, so also with the number of students. Dr Carey himself conducted the Divinity classes. By now, they had gathered all the means and appliances that are essential for the education of missionaries.[229] By 1833, Dr Carey and his friends began to work for the need of Statutory Laws and Regulations, for the government and administration of the College. The Statutes tackled various matters connected with the administration of the College such as nomination to the Council vacancies, its membership, voting, denominational representation, appointment to the staff, conferring of degrees, discipline, foundations, etc.

During the time that the College was making its roots deep, the College and the Mission were compelled to sustain another great loss with the demise of the founder, Dr William Carey. He passed away on Sunday, the 9th of June 1834 i.e., while he was in his 73rd year. Thus, the whole burden of the College and the Mission fell upon the feeble shoulders of the aged Dr Marshman, the second of the Serampore Trio. Dr Marshman had to wade through so many more difficulties and trials as he struggled alone for the running of the College and the Mission.

By 1835 there were above 100 students in the College of whom 10 were Eurasians, and about 50 were Indian Christians. English language replaced Sanskrit, as there was a growing demand particularly for official purposes. In addition to Divinity for the Christian students, Greek, Hebrew, Latin, Mathematics, Logic, and Natural Philosophy were some of the other subjects

---

[228] Marshman, *Life and Times of Carey, Marshman and Ward*, 425-426.

[229] Marshman, *Life and Times of Carey, Marshman and Ward*, 463.

taught. The same year (1835), Mack and Leechman went to England for reasons of the former's health where they availed themselves of the opportunity to appeal for the Mission's support. During their absence Dr Marshman's health began to decline rapidly besides which Mr. Barclay, one of the coadjutors died of illness, and so also Mr. Hope, a staunch supporter and friend of the Mission passed away in England. Hence with all these successive loss, Mack and Leechman at the advice of friends, negotiated with the Baptist Missionary Society to take charge of the Serampore Mission, thereby to relieve the missionaries of half of the burden. After prolonged negotiations the Society agreed to the proposal.

Marshman's health deteriorated increasingly and he died on the 5th of December 1837. He was spared the pain of hearing the most distressing news of the surrender of the Mission to the Society, which arrived some minutes short after he was buried. Just one day after the burial, the two deputations met in London and the Serampore Mission passed over to the Baptist Missionary Society.[230] Dr Marshman was 70 years old when he passed away. With the passing away of Dr Marshman, the first era of the history of the Serampore mission and College came to an end.

[230] Marshman, *Life and Times of Carey, Marshman and Ward*, 518.

Chapter 5

Protestant Christianity in Different Regions in India

1. Introduction

Though Protestant Christianity began in Europe as a great force in the 16th century, its presence in India began to be felt only from the beginning of the 18th century and flourished in the 19th and 20th centuries. The growth of the Protestant missionary activities during these centuries made it the most vigorous period of Protestant mission in India. On the other hand these centuries saw the emergence of the British authority in India, the development of cultural renaissance in Indian society, the beginning of Indian nationalism and final achievement of independence in the mid 20th century. The progress of the ecumenical movement in the 20th century in India found its appearance in the Protestant Church union movements. The emergence of nationalism gave rise to the idea about indigenization of Christianity and to various other national and social development activities.

2. Christian Movements

Mass movement was not an uncommon feature in the history of the Indian Church. Before the arrival of Protestant Christianity in India, a good number of mass movements occurred in association with the Roman Catholic Church. In the 16th century, Francis Xavier baptized the fishermen of the Southwestern part of India in large numbers.[231] However, the 19th century and the early part of

[231] Philip, *Protestant Christianity in India,* 270.

the 20th century was the real period of mass movements. During this period the great attention of "mass movements to Christianity in India have occurred among the depressed classes,"[232] such as tribal people in West Bengal, Central India, in the Nilgiri Hills and in the North East India, and among the depressed classes in South Travancore, Tamil Nadu, Andhra Pradesh and North-western India.

2.1. Christian Movements in Southern India

The converts of these early years were mostly from the lower caste Sambavars. In Tinnevelly, Vedamanickam and William Tobias Ringeltaube, who arrived in Travancore in 1806 with the invitation from the former, did the main work. In 1817 with the arrival of Rev Charles Mead at Mailady, the Nadar mass movements began in this area.[233] By 1819 and the succeeding years, new stations were opened in the area with the arrival of other Protestant Christianity.[234] The Southern mass movements continued to grow. In 1851 six men were ordained and by 1880 there were 89 Indian clergy and the Protestant mission in the district celebrated the centenary in 1880.[235]

One of the largest mass movements that took place was among the Telegu speaking people in Nellore District associated with the American Baptist Mission. Mr. Periah's conversion played a significant role in the mass movements in Nellore District. As he went on preaching in the villages, by 1869 there were hundreds of Christians and by 1878 thousands were being converted to Christian faith.[236]

2.2. Christian Movement in Northern India

The mass movements that took place among the Chuhra community of Punjab was associated with United Presbyterian Mission[237] in Punjab. The first converts, were baptized on October 25, 1857. Ditt's conversion among the Chuhra community made a difference in turning his community to the Christian faith. Thus, by 1900 more than half of this Chuhra community in Sialkot District had been converted to Christian faith.[238]

The mass movements in Chota Nagpur were related with different mission organizations. The Lutheran missionaries arrived at Chota Nagpur in November 1845. The first convert took place on June 9, 1850 from Oraons aboriginal tribe followed by another two members from the tribe of Mundas who were baptized.

---

[232] J. Waskom Pickett, *Christian Mass Movements in India* (New York: The Abingdon Press, 1933), 27. (Hereafter cited as Pickett, *Christian Mass Movements in India*).

[233] Cf. Pickett, *Christian Mass Movements in India,* 40, 41.

[234] By 1870 Christian adherents numbered 30,969, and by 1900 the adherents numbered 63,152.

[235] Sherring, *The History of Protestant Missions,* 34.

[236] Pickett, *Christian Mass Movements in India,* 49.

[237] This mission began its work at Sialkot in August 1855.

[238] Pickett, *Christian Mass Movements in India,* 45.

These converts took the gospel to their native places, which resulted in the mass conversion of both the tribes. The Lutheran Mission and the Anglican Mission took very active role in this Chota Nagpur mass conversion. [239]

The mass movements among the Mazhabi Sikh community in the Moradabad District[240] and Sweepers community called Mehtars in Bundaun District in Uttar Pradesh are associated with the Church Missionary Society and Methodist Episcopal Church. Mazhabi Sikhs were professionally thieves. According to Pickett, "by 1890 they were no longer regarded as professional thieves."[241] Similar mass movements took place among the Chamars of Madhya Pradesh and Bihar[242] and the Dheds of Gujarat.[243] During 1859 several members of the sweeper caste were converted to Christianity but it was only on individual basis. However, by 1871 mass conversion took place in the Bundaun District and so by the first half of the 20th century there were huge number of professing Christians among the Sweeper's community. Mass movements took place among many other castes and areas like the Doms caste of Benares, Kumaun and Garwal Hills in Uttar Pradesh, the Mangs and Mahars castes of Maharashtra and the various Panchama castes in the Kanarese of Maharashtra and in Tamil Nadu and Orissa.[244]

2.3. Christian Movements in North East India

Mass movements took place in the North East Indian regions too. Since 1841 the American Baptist Mission, Welsh Calvinistic Methodist Mission and British Baptist have built up very large churches and communities among the Garos, Khasis, Jaintia, Lushais, Nagas and other tribes of North East India. The superintendent of the census of Assam in 1921 described the progress made by Christianity as one of the most remarkable features of the decade 1911-1921:

> In a district of 7,000 square miles, sparsely settled by less than 100,000 people, there are now 27,000 Christians, where ten years ago there were only 2,000. At present time it is quite the fashion to be a Christian, and even the Chiefs are joining the movement.[245] The impact of mass movements was great among other aboriginal people,

---

[239] Pickett, *Christian Mass Movements in India*, 47.

[240] Cf. Thoburn M. James, *India and Malaysia* (New York: Methodist Book Concern, 1896), 45. The members of this group were professional thieves.

[241] Cf. Pickett, *Christian Mass Movements in India*, 51.

[242] Among the Chamars community of Madhya Pradesh, the American Lutherans and Methodist Missions carry out the mass movements.

[243] Among the Dheds community in Gujarat, the Irish Presbyterian Mission did the mission work, which resulted in the mass movements.

[244] Cf. Pickett, *Christian Mass Movements in India*, 53.

[245] Pickett, *Christian Mass Movements in India*, 52.

such as the Santals on the border of Bengal, Bihar, and Assam,[246] and the Gonds and the Bhils of Central India and the Konds and Pans of Orissa had turned to Christianity.[247]

3. Debate on Christian Movements

Despite the many success stories, the mass movements have been seriously criticized both by the non-Christian and the Christian side. It is commonly assumed that it was from the depressed classes alone who have become Christians for economic or for motives other than spiritual. It is true that in many cases Christian mass movements in India occurred in times of famine and social deprivations. It is also true that those conversions were not always purely religious. For instance the South India mass movements took place during serious famine, which occurred during 1876-1878, after which thousands of people of the depressed classes became Christians because of the help received.[248] Thus, S. Estborn pointed out that,

> Help in times of famine or epidemic, support against oppression by land lords and money-lenders, hope for better social standards, education for their children, chances of employment in Christian institutions and other such motives might have contributed to their decisions for baptism.[249]

Yet relief work itself did not create mass movements. As Pickett carefully emphasized that some of them "owe their origin to the spiritual quest of certain zealous individuals."[250] He continued to stress that it was not the missionaries or the Church that gained mass conversion but it was the conversion of individuals who refused to be separated from their fellow caste and went among them as witnesses for Christ.[251] As such we cannot rule out genuine spiritual conversion of individuals and communities who remained faithful for life.

---

246 The work of the CMS from 1860, and Santal Mission of the Northern Churches begun in 1867, the Free Church of Scotland from 1870 and other resulted in bringing many to Christian faith.

247 Cf. Firth, *An Introduction to Indian Church History,* 198-199.

248 Sherring, *History of Protestant Missions in India*, 334. In Tinnevelly the number of the baptized in the S.P.G alone increased by 12,000 in the six years following 1877.

249 Cf. S. Estborn, *The Church Among the Tamils and Telegus* (Nagpur: n.p., 1961), 32.

250 Pickett, *Christian Mass Movements in India.* 38.

251 Pickett, *Christian Mass Movements in India,* 56.

Chapter 6

Colonialism and Protestant Christianity in India

1. Introduction

Colonialism began its journey in Indian sub-continent since 1498. The Colonial powers that came to India were Portugal, France, Holland, Denmark and Britain. The colonialists did not intend to rule the land in their initial stage but with the passage of time they conquered the country and imposed their imperialism.

2. The Colonial and their Religious Policies

2.1. The Portuguese Colonialism and Christian Mission

The Portuguese term 'Padroado' refers to the right of spiritual or religious jurisdiction granted by Pope Nicholas V to the Portuguese king, Alphonse V by his famous Bull Romanus Pontifix in 1455 over all the lands discovered or to be discovered by the Portuguese in the East.[252] The rivalry between Spain and Portugal in discovering and Christianizing those lands that were discovered by them resulted in conflicts. To solve these conflicts the Pope had divided the Globe into East and West and authorized Portuguese to evangelize the East and the West to Spain. It gave to their rulers certain rights and duties. Accordingly, the kings were granted a say in the appointment of the bishops within these regions, and in the sending of missionaries. Thus, the Portuguese came to exercise ecclesiastical patronage in India and the Padroado was strongly reaffirmed.

[252] Cf. S. Vanatius Fernando, "Portuguese Patronage (Padroado) and the Evangelization of the Pearl fishery Coast," *Indian Church History Review* XVIII (December, 1984), 94.

The expansion of European colonialism at the end of 15th century has been a significant feature in the history. The 1456 Papal Bull (Padroado) gave the right to Portugal and Spain for dominion and commercial monopoly in the lands discovered and yet to be discovered. In addition, they were given the right to evangelize and establish missions and to appoint clergy and to set up Christian congregations wherever they went and discovered. Therefore, the Padroado rights ensured Portugal for exclusive dominion over the Eastern territories. Thus, this created an inseparable link between commerce trade and Christianity for Portuguese colonial policies. With this right and zeal to evangelize India the Portuguese under the leadership of Vasco da Gama landed in India on 17th May 1497. The Portuguese under the leadership of Alfonzo de Albuquerque captured Goa in 1510 and was made the capital of Portuguese political administration in Asia and in 1534 Pope Paul III created the diocese of Goa as the bishopric of Portuguese Bishop the head of India and the East. Thus, colonial expansion and mission of Roman Catholic Church grew as twin facts of the history of Christianity in India.

2.2. The Dutch Colonialism and Christian Mission

The Dutch colonialism began in India with its capture of Cochin from the hands of Portuguese in 1663.[253] As a Protestant power they never liked the Portuguese from the very beginning and their intention was to remove the Portuguese from India as much and as early as possible. Initially like other colonialists they had no interest in mission and trade was their main purpose. The Dutch could not expand their colonialism so much except in Nagapatnam Cochin and Tuticorin. They were not interested at all to evangelize the natives as it was not profitable for the Dutch East India Company. Their commitment to spread the Calvinist Church in India was not successful. Thus, they did very little evangelism in India.

2.3. The Danish Colonialism and Christian Mission

The next colonial power that came to India was the Danish. They settled at Tranquebar in the South and Serampore in West Bengal for the purpose of their trade in India. In 1620 the Danish merchants settled in Ceylon and South India and established the trading center of Tranquebar. In 1755, the Danish East India Company (DEIC) secured a parwana from the Nawab of Bengal for the erection of a factory on sixty bighas of land in Serampore.[254] They selected fifty-seven bighas of land in mawza Akna and three bighas in Serampore for river frontage. On 8th October 1755, Mr. Soetman, and his assistant, Ziegeuebar, the Danish

[253] Cf. Kuriakose, *History of Christianity in India*, 55.

[254] Pranabranjan, Ray, "Urbanization in Colonial Situation: Serampore," in Swati Datta et al., eds., *Carey Day Souvenir 2004* (Serampore: Serampore College, 2004), 7. (Hereafter cited as Ray, *Urbanization in Colonial Situation*).

officers deputed from Tranquebar, hoisted the Danish colors on the spot where they continued to fly for ninety years.[255]

The primary purpose of Danish East India Company in setting up factory in Serampore (Bengal) was tapping of cotton yarn and cotton textile for home market.[256] In 1759 the DEIC took pattani of the remainder of the Mawzas of Serampore and Akna and the new mawza of Piarapur to extend their settlement. Serampore thus thrived under the leadership of Col. Ole Bie and a number of ships under the Danish colors began to leave the port annually. In 1773, the settlement of Serampore was brought under direct administration of the Crown of Denmark and Bie became the Crown regent. Under his administration Serampore continued to flourish in trade and commerce at the dawn of 19th century. Col.Bie died on the 8thof May 1805.[257] By 1845 the Danish Colonies in India was completely transferred to the rule of the English. The Danes ruled for 90 years in Serampore. Though they were from Lutheran background still their primary purpose was for commercial purpose and they had no interest in the propagation of their faith in India. In spite of the Danish king patronizing the mission work, the missionaries were non-Denmark in origin. The connection between the mission and colonialism was very skimpy in India. In fact the early Protestant missionaries were put into so much difficulties by the Danish governor of Tranquebar. They were denied assistance in mission activities though they were there as 'Royal Missionaries.'[258] However, in Serampore, the colonial authorities acted in defense of the Serampore Trio, and extended their help to the Trio whenever they faced problems from the Britishers and even from the local people.

2.4. The British Colonialism and Christian Mission

The British colonial rule which began in India primarily as a political expedition through the East India Company to harvest the benefits of imperialism without setting up a full-fledged political power in the 17th century, ultimately emerged as the most powerful colonial power in India by the middle of the 18th century. They had no serious plan of ruling India or interest in propagating the gospel even. By the beginning of the 19th century British hegemony extended over a large part of India. As mentioned, the British East India Company's main concern was trade and profit.[259]

Since 1659, the court of Directors of British East India Company (BEIC) declared that "it was their earnests desire by all possible means to spread

[255] Marshman, *Life and Times of Carey, Marshman and Ward*, 112.

[256] Ray, *Urbanization in Colonial Situation*, 8.

[257] Chatterjee, *William Carey and Serampore*, 27.

[258] Kuriakose, *History of Christianity in India*, 59.

[259] Cf. T.V. Philip, "Christianity in India during Western Colonialism: Conflicts, Reconciliation or Adjustment," *ICHR*, XXI/1 (June, 1987), 18. (Hereafter cited as Philip, Christianity in India during Western Colonialism).

Christianity among the people of India and allowed missionaries to embark on their ships."[260] Hence, the 1698 BEIC Charter made it clear that every company has to maintain missionaries in their factories and every ship which was over 500 tones has to employ a chaplain on board. However, when the BEIC emerged as a political power in India by the end of 18th century, this was not considered and rather they declared religious neutrality as their policy and their military chaplains were prohibited to do evangelism among the natives.

With the change of company's rule which was replaced by Crown as the legal sovereign in 1858 their policy began to turn towards the interest of interfering in the affairs of the locals. The colonialists, for the stability of their commercial trade, even began to patronize the religions affairs of India. They brought a number of temples under their management. For rebuilding or repairing of temples and salaries of the temple officials, they were paid from government treasury. There were encouragements for government officials to attend Hindu festivals in order to show their interest in celebrations. All these were done to achieve their purpose and this religious neutrality hindered the mission work and even the native Christians were not given employment. Hence, the colonialists did not really favour the mission work despite their declaration.

With the revision of the BEIC charter in 1813, the government ceased to oppose the coming of missionaries to India. Though the company's policy of religious neutrality continued, they did not assist the church or mission.[261] They continued to spent money on Temple and Mosque and their festivals. Many advocated for freedom of mission in India, yet the BEIC in spite of the revised charter, their attitude towards Christian mission were negative. On the other hand, all the oppositions, some officials supported the expansion of mission in India like Governor General Lord Wellesley who became the patron for the translation project of William Carey in Bengal (1811), even before the charter was revised; Lord William Bentinck stood firmly for the rights of Indian Christians; Lord Dalhousie worked for the betterment of the Christians. Resident Colonel Munro and Colonel Maculay helped the Syrian Christians and they were instrumental in bringing the C.M.S. mission's help to the Syrian Christians. Thus, Missionaries provided religious justification to Colonialism in India. Imperialism influenced their very act of evangelism and theology of mission.

2.4.1. *The East India Company (EIC)*

The political scenario of the country during the 18th and 19th centuries in India was marked by incessant warfare. This can be seen in the words of A.B. Purkait, "after the downfall of the Mughal Empire there was no centralized political authority in

[260] Cf. Dharmaraj, *Colonialism and Christian Mission*, 41.

[261] Cf. Roger Bowen, *So I Send You: A Study Guide to Mission* (Delhi: ISPCK, 2004), 100.

the country."[262] This led the country to experience independent rulers trying to rule each other, and did not come forward to rescue each other from the invasion of any foreign ruler. This gave the opportunity to the British East India Company to exploit the situation and take advantage on internal conflicts among the native rulers and began their supremacy in the country.[263] On behalf of the British East India Company, the resourceful British Governor-General Robert Clive grabbed Bengal in 1757 from its governor Siraj-ud-doulah. Oudh fell from the hands of Wajid Ali Shah and the titular Mughal Emperor Bahadur Shah Zafar was himself packed off in 1857 after the abortive Sepoy Mutiny.

Among the Marathas also this tendency towards disintegration due to rebellious governors like the Bhosales of Nagpur - who never accepted the authority of the Peshwa, the Holkars of Indore, the Gaikwads of Baroda and the Scindias of Gwalior distancing themselves from the authority of the Peshwa at Poona, ultimately caused the downfall of the Maratha empire.

The general increase in defense expenditure, which started with Aurangzeb's Deccan campaign against Shivaji, the firebrand Maratha leader, was kept up later by the numerous battles of Indian monarchs against each other and later against the East India Company. As Indian chieftains and kings badly needed resources to finance their campaigns they levied arbitrary taxes and declared state monopolies over the trade in profitable commodities. Exclusive monopolies for the resale of superior foreign goods were declared much to the detriment of the Indian trading community and the profits were siphoned off to finance a lavish court and feudal lifestyle. In the early days of British rule, the British Viceroys and other colonial administrators collaborated with the Indian feudal nobility to usurp this country. Unlike the fierce struggle between the Muslim monarchy and the Hindu landed nobility in the initial days of Muslim occupation, the coming of the British power saw a smooth adjustment between the pre-British landed aristocracy and the colonial power. The Jagirdars and Inamdars generally became the Zamindars in the new set-up.

In Bengal, the English East India Company (EEIC) had begun fortifying Calcutta's Fort William to defend against possible attacks by the French. Nominally a part of the Mughal Empire, Bengal was at this time virtually independent under the emperor's nawab (governor). In response to reports of unauthorized activities of the British, the nawab Siraj-ud-Dawhah attacked Calcutta in 1756. After the incident, Robert Clive, the then British governor of Fort Saint David, moved north from Madras and, conniving with the commander of his enemy's army, defeated the nawab in the Battle of Plassey in 1757. The battle marked the first stage in the British conquest of India. The French attempted to regain their position in India

[262] A. B. Purkait, *Indian Renaissance and Education: From Ram Mohan to Vivekananda* (Calcutta: Firma K.L.M. Ltd, 1992), 39.

[263] Pratap Chandra Gine, *The System of Elementary Education of the Serampore Mission* (Jorhat: ETC, 2001), 11. (Hereafter cited as Gine, *The System of Elementary Education*).

but were beaten back by the British in 1761. In 1764 the British again defeated local rulers at the Battle of Buxar. This victory firmly established British control over the Bengal region. The English East India Company continued to extend its control over Indian Territory throughout the late 18th and early 19th centuries. Besides, the British also made significant gains by means of its military strength. In the late 1700s they were drawn into a three-way conflict when the nizam of Hyderâbâd asked for British assistance against his rivals: the Marathas, and Tipu Sahib, the sultan of Mysore. In 1799 the British marched on Seringapatam, Tipu's capital, and defeated his troops. Tipu was killed defending the city. The British annexed much of Mysore outright; they controlled the remainder through a new sultan they installed. After a series of battles (1775-1782, 1803-1805, 1817-1818) with the Marathas, the British also succeeded in bringing Maratha lands under their control.

In 1773 the British Parliament passed the Regulating Act, the first of a series of acts that gave British governors greater control over the English East India Company. The Act also established the post of governor-general of India and made the holder of the office directly responsible to the British government. Warren Hastings became the first governor-general of India in 1774.

The British proceeded to make major changes in the administration of their realm. The three presidencies - Bengal, Bombay, and Madras - adopted different systems of fixing responsibility for the payment of land taxes. In Bengal, the local landed gentry accepted responsibility for a fixed amount of taxes in return for ownership of large estates. By contrast, in Madras and Bombay, peasant cultivators paid annual taxes directly to the government. A civil service system was developed that admitted British officers through a merit examination, trained them in an administrative college, and paid them handsomely to reduce corruption. Meanwhile, the development of the textile industry in Britain forced a transformation of India's economy: India had to produce raw cotton for export and buy manufactured goods—including cloth—from England, while the cottage industries that produced textiles in India were wiped out.

Until about 1800 the East India Company traders adapted themselves to the country, donning Indian dress, learning Sanskrit, and sometimes taking Indian mistresses. As British rule strengthened, and as an influential evangelical Christian movement emerged in the early 19th century, India's customs were judged more harshly. Missionaries, who had been kept out by the company for fear they would upset Indians and thus disrupt commerce, were now brought in. The 18th century company officers, such as Sir William Jones, a scholar of Sanskrit who discovered the relationship of Indo-European languages, were replaced by British subjects who felt Indian thought and literature were of no value at all. In 1835 English was enforced as the language of government.

Under the leadership of Governor-General James Andrew Broun Ramsay, 10th Earl of Dalhousie, the empire continued to expand. After two wars with the Sikhs, the Sikh state of Punjab was added in 1849. Governor-General Dalhousie also annexed Satara, Jaipur, Sambalpur, Jhansi, and Nagpur on the death of their native rulers, taking advantage of a British doctrine that declared Britain's right to govern any Indian state where there was no natural heir to the throne. The absorption of Oudh was the last major piece added to the company's possessions; it was annexed in 1856. Dalhousie's tenure was also marked by various improvements and reforms: the construction of railroads, bridges, roads, and irrigation systems, the establishment of telegraph and postal services, and restrictions on slave trading and other ancient practices.

2.4.2. *Mutiny and Revolt of 1857*

The annexation of Indian Territory and the rigorous taxation on Indian land contributed to a revolt against British rule in 1857. The revolt began among Indian soldiers (sepoys) in the service of the English East India Company in Meerut, a town northeast of Delhi. The revolt erupted when some sepoys refused to use new Lee-Enfield rifles. To load the rifles, the soldiers had to bite off the ends of greased cartridges. Rumors that the cartridges were greased with the fats of cows and pigs outraged both Hindus, who regard cows as sacred, and Muslims, who regard pigs as unclean. After taking Meerut, the mutineers marched to Delhi and persuaded the nominal sovereign of India, the Mughal emperor Bahadur Shah II, to resume his rule. The revolt spread rapidly, with local rulers playing an active part in expelling or killing the British and putting their garrisons under siege, especially at Lucknow. The revolt extended through Oudh (present-day Uttar Pradesh) and northern Madhya Pradesh. The British were able to crush it, making particular use of Sikh soldiers recruited in Punjab. The mutiny ended by 1859, with both sides guilty of atrocities.[264]

In August 1858 the British Parliament abolished the English East India Company and transferred the company's responsibilities to the British crown. This launched a period of direct rule in India, ending the fiction of company rule as an agent of the Mughal emperor. In November 1858, in her proclamation to the "Princes, Chiefs, and Peoples of India," Queen Victoria pledged to preserve the rule of Indian princes in return for loyalty to the crown. More than 560 such enclaves, taking in one-fourth of India's area and one-fifth of its people, were preserved until India's Independence in 1947. In 1876, at the urging of British Prime Minister Benjamin Disraeli, Queen Victoria took the title of 'Empress of India.'

Among the reforms introduced after the adoption of direct rule was a reorganization of the administrative system. A secretary of state, aided by a council, began to control Indian affairs from London. A viceroy (a governor

---

[264] J. C. Marshman, *The Life and Times of Carey, Marshman and Ward: Embracing the History of the Serampore Mission*, vol. I (London: Longmann & Roberts, 1859), 39. (Hereafter cited as Marshman, *Life and Times of Carey, Marshman and Ward*).

who acts in the name of the British crown) implemented London's policies from Calcutta. An executive and a legislative council provided advice and assistance. Provincial governors made up the next level of authority, and below them were district officials. The army was also reorganized after the imposition of direct rule. The ratio of British to Indian soldiers was reduced, and recruitment policies were reshaped to favor Sikhs and other 'martial races' that had been loyal during the Sepoy Rebellion. As such, during the 1800 India's political,socio-cultural life and religious conditions were in a pitiable situation.[265]

The British Government vehemently opposed the entry of Christian missions. Accordingly they adopted three policies: (a) They took under their management and patronage a large number of Hindu temples. They granted large sums of money for rebuilding important shrines, for sacrifices, festivals and for feeding of Brahmans. Even cruel and immoral rites, such as hook-swinging, practiced in the worship of gods, and the burning of widows, were carried out under British supervision.[266] (b)They strongly refused to allow any missionaries to settle in their territory. Hence, William Carey got a footing in Bengal by becoming an indigo-planter, and he was not able to devote his full time for his mission, until he settled at Serampore under the Danish flag.[267] (c)They refused to employ native Christians in any capacity, and they enforced all the rigors of Hindu law against them. Thence, in the army, if any native soldier wished to become a Christian, he was forcibly prevented by the authorities, or, was expelled from the service.[268] The policy of religious neutrality was reached in 1857, when in the throes of the Mutiny the East India Company came to an end, and the home Government became directly responsible for India.

---

[265] Cf. Aleyamma Zachariah, *Modern Religious and Secular Movements in India* (Bangalore: Theological Book Trust, 1998), 1. (Hereafter cited as Zachariah, *Modern Religious and Secular Movements in India*).

[266] Cf. Julius Richter, *A History of Mission in India*, translated by Sidney Moore (London: Oliphant Anderson and Ferrier, 1908), 185.

[267] Cf. Farquhar, *Modern Religious Movements in India*, 10.

[268] Cf. Farquhar, *Modern Religious Movements in India*, 10.

Chapter 7

Christianity and Nation Building in India

1. Christianity and National Independence Movement

1.1. The Indian National Congress (INC)

The Indian National Congress, which was organized in 1885 by the educated, politically liberal middle-class, became a mass based organization, with Mahatma Gandhi at the helm. The INC, in their initial struggle neither asked for Indian independence nor was it a violent movement. Their main interest was for social and economic reforms for the betterment of the lives of Indian citizens. It also proposed more equal share for the Indian people in the administrative services.[269] As the INC began to be mass-based movement it began to turn towards national freedom struggle. With the rise of national consciousness and the struggle for political freedom have formed the background for the Church's life and mission[270] also since the later part of the 19th century.

1.2. Indian Christians and Indian National Congress

In the initial stage a number of Indian Christians actively supported the Indian National Congress. Some of the prominent Christians were R.S.N. Subramania (a prominent barrister from Madras), G.G. Nath, a barrister from Lahore, Peter Paul Pillai of Madras, Madusudan, a lawyer from Orissa, Pandita Ramabbai, a

---

[269] Cf. Arthur D. Jeyakumar, *History of Christianity in India: Selected Themes* (Madurai: TTS, 2007), 92. (Hereafter cited as Jeyakumar, *Selected Themes*).

[270] Cf. John C. B. Webster, *The Christian Community and Change in Nineteenth Century North India* (Delhi: The Macmillan Company of India Ltd, 1976), 195-198.

Christian social reformer and Kali Charan Benarji, a leader of Bengal Christian Community.[271]

As the Congress began to agitate for political freedom, the British simultaneously began to take a suspicious and even hostile attitude toward the Congress and its activities. Consequently the Western missionaries in India and the Indian Christians began to leave the Congress with apprehension. The missionaries did not encourage agitation for Indian political freedom because India's independence would mean a decline in their supremacy.[272] In 1908 Joseph J. Ghose writing on Indian Christians and the National movement commented:

> We do not know in what way it will be of any advantage to the Indian Christians if they joined the non-Christians in political agitation. If further political rights and privileges are granted to the people of this country, our poor and small community will not have the remotest chance to be profited by them. On the other hand greater powers in the hands of non-Christians may prove dangerous to the very life of our community....[273]

This alienation of Christians from the national movement continued into the 20th century. On the other hand, there were several courageous Christians who stood for national movement such as Kali Charan Banerji, Susil Rudra, S.K. Dutta, C.F. Andrews, K.T. Paul and V.S. Azariah. For example K.T. Paul wrote in 1909:

> We will do well to realize that there is a terrible danger if we persist in the policy of keeping aloof. Materially, socially, morally and politically, viewed in fact from every standpoint, our interests are intimately bound up with those of other Indian communities. Will it ever be otherwise? Long after Britain's political mission to India is finished let us hope five centuries later, for all things earthly must end or change - we shall still be Indians.[274]

1.3. The Changed Attitude of Indian Christians towards INC

It certainly took time for the Indian Christians to change their attitude toward India's National Movement "but the change had come, and in the latter phases of the struggle an increasing number of Christians began to identify with the

---

[271] Philip, *Protestant Christianity in India,* 177.

[272] Gladstone, *Protestant Christianity and People's Movements,* 334.

[273] Joseph J. Ghose, *The Young Men of India* (Calcutta: n.p., 1908), 190, cited by Philip, *Protestant Christianity in India...,* 224.

[274] Oddie, *Indian Christians and the National Congress,* 52. Cf. also K. Baago, *A History of the National Christian Council of India 1914-1964* (Nagpur: NCCI, 1965), 37-40.

national movement."[275] Thus, in the 1930s and 40s Christians were mainly on the side of the Indian National Congress in its struggle for independence.

Therefore, the rise of nationalism had strong influence upon the growth of the ecumenical vision in India.[276] Bishop V.S. Azariah asserted that India does not need denominationalism but unity of Churches and society. To quote "the young Indian Christian cannot help being influenced by this new spirit, his patriotism moves him to do what he can to advance the interest of his own country."[277] This argument of Bishop Azariah reflects the ecumenical awareness of the Indian Church. K.T. Paul likewise with his involvement in the political life of the nation was convinced that Nationalism in India demands ecumenism. He argues that true Christianity demands true nationalism.[278] Even people like Narayan Vaman Tilak expressed this view that the national consciousness gave an impetus to the Indianness of the Church as well as to ecumenical movement in India.[279] Therefore the Indian Christians were motivated to assert their identity. This assertion of self-identity of Christians in India calls for ecumenical thinking, reflection and action.

2. Christianity and Bengal Renaissance

The term *renaissance* means rebirth or the revival of learning . It is a paradigm shift in the perspective and approaches of people towards culture, politics, society and religion. Bengal renaissance and Christianity refers largely to the socio-cultural, psychological and intellectual changes that took placed in Bengal during the 19th century. Before the coming of Christianity in Bengal, the social, political and cultural condition was very poor.[280] The practice such as *sati, child marriage, devadasis, female infanticide* and so on were prevailing the society. All these social evils were practice in the name of religion. The encounter between Bengal societies towards the Christian missionaries thus began to make different in the whole of Bengal. The educated Bengali elite also began to feel the need of modernizing Hinduism as they wanted to clip off the superficial and superstitions for their own benefit. Thus, individuals like Raja Ram Mohan Roy, Sisir Kumar Ghosh, Bhudev Mukhopadhyay and some others attempted to redefine Hinduism in modern context. Bengal renaissance has brought several changes in the Bengal society.

---

[275] K. M. Panikkar, *The Foundations of New India* (London: 1963), 53.

[276] J. W. Gladstone, "Historical Development of the Indian Ecumenical Movement and its Implications for the Future," *NCCI* 114/6 (July, 1994), 451. (Hereafter cited as Gladstone, *Historical Development of the Indian Ecumenical Movement*).

[277] See, Gladstone, *Historical Development of the Indian Ecumenical Movement*, 452.

[278] Gladstone, *Historical Development of the Indian Ecumenical Movement*, 453.

[279] Gladstone, *Historical Development of the Indian Ecumenical Movement*, 453.

[280] See also, Aleyamma Zachariah, *Modern Religious and Secular Movements in India* (Bangalore: Theological Book Trust, 1998), 2.

2.1. Social Reformation

The early 19th century saw the birth of modern Bengal society. William Carey, Raja Ram Mohan Roy and Lord Wellesley played a very pivotal role in bringing several reformations in Bengal society. They were very instrumental in eradicating so many social evil practices such as child infanticide and abolition of sati. They also entered the field of journalism in 1818 and started *Samachar Darpan* and *Friends of India* to fight against social injustice and to spread social awareness concerning social evils in the society. The practice of *Sati* was prohibited by 1829 with the order of Lord William Bentinck on 4th December. They also continued to write and publish regarding the evil practices such as burning of lepers, ghat murders, suicide, slavery etc. All these kinds of social evil practices were exposed through their news journals.

2.2. Education

Education was also another significance movement that took place during this time. The missionaries such as William Carey and Mrs. Hannah Marshman began to introduce education by opening schools for boys and girls in Bengal. In 1817 Bengali intellectuals like Dwarkanath Tagore, Prasanna Kumar Tagore and others took a major step with the influence of the missionaries and their educational works to spread western education. They started Hindu College where English was medium of instruction and the teaching of science, philosophy English literature and grammar and other Western subjects were taught. In the 1820s and 1830 Young Bengal Movement also started among the Bengal young intellectuals where they began to think rationally and freely to question all authority, to love liberty, equality and freedom and to worship the truth.[281]

2.3. Modernization of Bengali Literature

Christian missionaries like Carey, Alexander Duff and others took initiative to develop the Bengali Literature into higher level. They wrote text books and produced Bengali grammar and dictionaries and made them accessible to all. Moreover, William Carey is remembered as the Father of Bengali Prose. Native writers like Michael Madhusudan Dutt and Rabindranath Tagore wrote on Bengal literature which also impacted the renaissance movement of that time. Other Bengali writers such as Raja Ram Mohan Roy, Bankim Chadra Chattaopadhyay, Sarat Chanttaopadhyay and others brought the middle class Bengali society in the limelight through their literary work. With the introduction of printing press, Bengali literature entered into a new era.

---

[281] Bipan Chandra, *History of Modern India* (Hyderabad: Orient BlackSwan, 2009), 134.

3. Christianity and Social Transformation

3.1. Protestant Christianity and Social Activities

Nineteenth century was also a period of expansion of the social activities of the Church. The social activities in the first half of the 19th century Christian missions were directed towards bringing about a moral reform in Indian society and to liberate individuals from the age-old superstitious Hindu religion. William Bentinck initiated several measures of social and moral reforms. In the second half of the19th century, though they increased in number, they were mainly confined to philanthropic activities such as establishing and maintaining schools, orphanages, hospitals, lepers' asylums and agricultural and industrial training institutions.

3.2. Education

The educational endeavors of the Protestant Mission during the 19th and 20th centuries extinguished the belief that only the higher castes were destined to learn.[282] It started with elementary schools, followed by secondary schools and colleges, teaching through the medium of English. Thus, some of the outstanding Christian colleges such as the Madras Christian College, Noble College at Masulipatnam, Bishop College of Nagpur and St. John's College at Agra were founded. These Christian Colleges and schools exerted a powerful influence on Indian education and Indian thought.

Protestant Christianity also seriously worked for the upliftment of women in India. From the beginning of its mission it felt the urgent need for girls' education. Hence, at first it was mainly the wives of the missionaries along with a handful of single women who started the schools for girls. Some organizations were also set up to establish schools and to spread awareness for the importance of women's education. For instance, in 1819 the Calcutta School Society was formed, and in 1834 the Society for Promoting Female Education was formed in London. In 1838 Captain James founded the Scottish Ladies Association for the Advancement of Female Education in India.[283] In 1852 Lady Kinnaird began a school for girls at Dowager, and as a result the Church of England's Zenana Missionary Society and Zenana Bible and Medical Mission were started.

However, during those days, practices such as child marriages, female infanticides, the burning of widows and the purdah system were so prominent that there was little thought for the emancipation of women. Reading and writing were particularly confined to indecent girls and the idea was that education was not for respectable women. Even those who attended were rough low castes girls

---

[282] Cf. also Gladstone, *Protestant Christianity and People's Movements,* 70-72.

[283] Mar Pongener, *Key Issues in the History of Christianity in India 19th through 20th Centuries* (Jorhat: Barkataki & Co. Ltd., 2000), 90.

who often had to be paid to attend, and they came so irregularly and left at such an early age that their schooling had little effect.[284]

In Calcutta, Drinkwater Bethune, President of the Government Council of Education founded the first school for high caste girls in 1849. Missionaries in 1854 began to send ladies to teach girls in the Zenanas of Hindu families. Mrs. Mullens and Miss. Toogood, were prominent in this work in Calcutta.[285] Thus, began the Zenana schools, which was imitated in other towns and became a regular feature of the educational receiving grants-in-aid from the Government. In 1859 the American Presbyterian Mission started a girls' boarding school at Dehra Dun, from which in due time came the first female matriculate of Calcutta University.[286] Prominent among the lady missionaries from America was Izabella Thoburn, who came to Lucknow in 1870 and founded a school out of which the Izabella Thoburn College developed. In 1884 two Christian girls in Bombay namely Miss. Malabai Kukde and Mrs. Shivantibai Nikambe became the first Indian girls to pass the matriculation examination of Bombay University.[287]

Pandita Ramabai (1858-1922) became a Christian in 1883 while she was in England. After finishing her studies she went to America and stayed three more years in Kindergarten training. She wrote a book entitled *The High Caste Hindu Women,* which aroused much interest that sympathizers formed a Ramabai Association to raise money for her work.[288] Back in India she started *Sarada Saden* (Home of Wisdom) in Bombay on March 1, 1889 with the co-operation of Mahadev Govind Ranade and members from Prathna Samaj. In 1890 it was moved to Kedgaon near Pune.[289] She toured the famine area in 1896, rescuing orphan girls. She sent many to mission boarding homes elsewhere, but she was still left with many. As a result she started the *Mukti Mission* at Kedgaon. Miss Abrams of America joined her. In 1898 she went to America to raise funds for the Sarada Saden and Mukti. By 1899 buildings were erected and very large Institution was organized housing over a thousand inmates and providing a wonderful variety of occupations such as field work, dairy farming, weaving, sewing, rope-making etc.[290] Pandita Ramabai's efforts had contributed so much in transforming the position of women in India.

[284] Richter, *History of Missions in India,* 329.

[285] Sudha Kaldate, "Educated Women, Equality and Role Conflict," in Leelamma Devasia, ed., *Women in India: Equality, Social Justice and Developments* (New Delhi: India Social Institute, 1990), 57.

[286] Sherring, *History of Protestant Missions in India*, 187.

[287] E. G. K. Hewate, *Christ and Western India* (Bombay: J. Kellock, Wilson College, 1950), 286.

[288] Firth, *An Introduction to Indian Church History*, 194.

[289] Jeyakumar, *Selected Themes*, 59.

[290] Pandita Ramabai, *A Testimony* (Pune: Ramabai Mukti Mission, 1917), 16.

Today girls' education has become the rule rather than exception. There are now several laws and regulations for the protection of women from discriminations and oppressions, which open the way for Indian women to become visible in both secular and religious set up. Protestant Christianity in India has thus been in the forefront in pioneering women's emancipation movement in India.

3.3. Medical Mission

Medical work also came to occupy an important part in the mission of Protestant Church. The first mission to adopt a regular policy of sending medical persons as missionaries to India was the American Board.[291] The Protestant Christians started hospitals and dispensaries both in cities and villages. Christian medical colleges and Nurses' Training Institutes were started throughout the country during the 19th and 20th centuries. Some of the important Protestant medical colleges are like Vellore Medical College and Hospital and Ludhiana Medical College. They also started several Tuberculosis Sanatoria, leprosy asylums, mental hospitals and psychiatric clinics. In 1926 the Christian Medical Association of India (CMAI) was founded. It sponsors various forms of Medical services and is the central consultative body for Protestant medical work in India.[292] Although the Protestant Christians' involvement in the society in various levels created much disruption in the society, a large number of suppressed people found the long-awaited possibility to break the chains which had bound them for centuries under the traditional culture of the Hindu ideology.

4. Christianity and the Empowerment of Women

The coming of Christianity and its contribution towards the emancipation of women is tremendous in India. India is known as a highly patriarchal society and thus denied opportunities and rights to women.

4.1. Empowerment of Women through Education

One of the major contributions of Christianity in empowering women is through education in India. Education was considered as most needed concern from the very beginning of the Protestant Christianity in India. In several areas it was the wives of the missionaries who took the initiatives for starting schools for girls. Thus, Mrs. Hannah Marshman is very much remembered for her pioneering role in girls' education in India. In 1857 Alexander Duff started a girls school. In 1859 the American Presbyterian Mission started girls' boarding school at Dehra Dun. In 1867 the Baptist Zenana Missionary Society started school for girls. Therefore, from the very beginning Protestant Christianity was very much engaged in the empowerment of women through education.

---

[291] Cf. Firth, *An Introduction to Indian Church History*, 205-207.

[292] Cf. Philip, *Protestant Christianity in India*, 176.

4.2. Empowerment of Women through Medical Work

The Zenana Mission brought the need of medical aid for women as a result of which, lady doctors came to India. In 1870 the first medical Lady Doctor was sent to India by American Episcopal Methodist Mission. She opened a women hospital at Barilly in 1870. Another lady doctor, Ida Scudder played an important role by opening small clinic for treating women and also started training courses for women in a medical school affiliated to Madras University. She also founded Vellore Hospital which is called Christian Medical College Vellore today. In addition Ida with her mother operated orphanage for homeless children and in all these Indian women were employed which was a great source of empowerment for women in the society.

4.3. Empowerment of Women in the Church

Women have been playing a very important role in the churches throughout the centuries though they are debarred from leadership roles like men. Women had been the backbone of the church. Women are mostly involved and active in women department, youth and children ministry as men take the main role in the church even today. Yet today in several churches women have begun to take the leadership roles as much as men or even doing better than men. Many women are being ordained today. This also shows the marks of the development of Christianity in the lives of the Christian women in India.

5. Caste and Christianity

During the 19th and 20th centuries the Hindu structure of society was seriously affected by the rigid caste system. The issue of caste was another serious issue that Protestant Christianity encountered.

5.1. St. Thomas Christians' Attitude toward Caste

The St. Thomas Christians of Kerala, for several centuries have been living within the caste system. They were considered as a separate caste, and only lower to the Brahmins.[293] They derive their status within the caste system from the tradition that they are converted from high caste Hindus who were evangelized by Thomas the Apostle.[294] It is viewed that they practiced untouchability,[295] and this practice in fact prevented the St. Thomas Christians from involving in evangelistic work in the early part of the centuries, because the inclusion of the lower caste would

---

[293] L. W. Brown, *The Indian Christians of St. Thomas* (Cambridge: Cambridge University Press, 1956), 168.

[294] Cf. C. J. Fuller, *Kerala Christians and Caste System* (N.p.: n.p., 1976), 529.

[295] Duncan B. Forrester, *Caste and Christianity: Attitudes and Policies on Caste of Anglo-Saxon Protestant Mission in India* (London: Curzon Press, 1980), 11-15. (Hereafter cited as Forrester, *Caste and Christianity*).

destroy their respect from the society as higher caste.[296] Therefore, throughout the centuries the St. Thomas Christians made little effort to Christianize their non-Christian neighbors.[297] In the later centuries they neither cooperate with the evangelical activities of foreign missionaries nor did they allow the new converts to join their community since they were afraid that their noble position in the society could be endangered.[298] Thus, the Syrian Christians unquestionably assimilated the caste system.

5.2. The Roman Catholic Attitude toward Caste

The attitude of the Roman Catholic Church toward caste problem was not an issue in the initial encounter. The Roman Catholic Church regarded the caste system as the cultural institution and encouraged the people to stay within their own castes. The problem of caste occurred mainly when a large number of Paravars became Christians between 1535 and 1537. This large number of Paravars converting to Christianity led to the identification of Christianity as a religion of the low caste, and they called Christianity a Paranghi religion.[299] This led to the creation of division within the members of the Roman Catholic Church on caste basis. This was evident even with the missionary Robert De Nobili, who came to India in 1606 and established the Madurai mission, adopted his method of accommodation by cutting off all kinds of contact with his colleagues working among the low-castes.[300] Nobili was challenged by the Roman Catholics which led to the famous controversy called the "Malabar Rite Controversy," which in turn brought the papal decrees of 1734 and 1744 denouncing untouchability, as alien to Christianity. However, this strategy of adaptation or accommodation was generally accepted and practiced by the Roman Catholics saying caste was a civil or cultural institution which could be used for evangelistic purposes and maintained within the Church with only minor modifications.[301] Thus, caste discrimination was fully accommodated within the Roman Catholic Church.

---

[296] Cf. Walter Fernandez, *Caste and Conversion Movements in India* (Bangalore: Indian Social Institute, 1981), 30-32.

[297] Stephen Neill, *A History of Christianity in India: The Beginnings to A.D. 1707* (Cambridge: Cambridge University Press, 1984), 403. (Hereafter cited as Neill, *Christianity in India*).

[298] Cf. Harold Coward, *Hindu-Christian dialogue: perspectives and encounters* (Madras: Motilal Banarsidass Publication, 1993), 27.

[299] Cf. A. M. Mundadan, *History of Christianity in India*, Vol. I (Bangalore: CHAI, 2001), 388. (Hereafter cited as Mundadan, *Christianity in India*).

[300] Cf. D. Rajarigam. "Tamil Churches and Caste: A Historical Sketch," *Religion and Society*, 5/8 (December, 1958), 19.

[301] Cf. Forrester, *Caste and Christianity*, 16.

5.3. The Protestant Christian Attitude toward Caste till 1850

5.3.1. *The First Protestant Mission and Caste Issue*

Caste issue was a serious problem within the Church from the very first Protestant Mission in India. When the New Jerusalem Church was founded in 1707 distinction of caste was allowed.[302] In the Church, the Sudra men sat on one side of the nave and the others on the other, and likewise the Sudra women in one of the transepts and the other women on the other; at Holy Communion all the Sudras, men and women were administered first and the others afterwards.[303] Ziegenbalg died in February 1719, and after his death, Schultze assumed the leadership in Tranquebar Mission, with the aim to stop the castes distinction in the Church, which was strongly opposed by the members. He tried to stop the distinction by order but the result was strong opposition and discontentment from the members.[304] When Schultze left Tranquebar, the new missionaries, Walter and Pressier, who arrived in 1725, restored the old practice of caste distinctions,[305] and even today this caste distinction continues to create tensions among the believers.

5.3.2. *The Baptist Missionary Attitude towards Caste*

From the very beginning the Bengal Baptist Missionaries headed by William Carey strongly opposed the practice of casteism. They considered caste distinction as incompatible with the Gospel. They wholeheartedly advocated egalitarian ideals among the believing Christians.[306] They regarded caste system an aspect of idolatry, which needed to be removed from the society. They considered departure from caste as a dynamic affirmation of conversion, and a defense against the reversion to Hinduism.[307] The Baptist Missionaries insisted on not intolerance of caste system among the Christians but to encourage the converts to enter into inter-marriage among the castes. Hence, in 1803, Mr. Prasad the first Brahmin convert married a Sudra convert in order to break the rigid caste system.[308]

5.3.3. *Anglicans' Attitude towards Caste*

Anglican Mission attitude towards caste was not so serious in the initial stage. In May 26, 1826 Bishop Reginald writes, "the old school of Missionaries tolerated all this as a merely civil question of pedigree and worldly distinction, and in

---

[302] Cf. M. K. Kuriakose, *History of Christianity in India*, 69.

[303] J. Richter, *A History of Missions in India*, 108.

[304] Firth, *An Introduction to Indian Church History*, 137.

[305] Richter, *History of Missions in India*, 110.

[306] Cf. M.A. Laird, *Missionaries and Education in Bengal, 1793-183* (Oxford: n.p., 1972), 37-43.

[307] Sushil Madhava Pathak, *American Missionaries and Hinduism* (Delhi: Munshiram Manoharlal, 1967), 158 (Hereafter cited as Pathak, *American Missionaries*).

[308] Forrester, *Caste and Christianity*, 27. Cf. also Kuriakose, *History of Christianity in India*, 76.

the hope that, as their converts became more enlightened, such distinction would die away."[309] However, with Bishop Daniel Wilson of Kolkata it became intolerable with the caste distinction within the church and thus in 1833 when he visited South India he was saddened and shocked to see the serious practice of caste within the church. Sudra and Adi Dravida Christians sat separately in the Church. This caste discrimination forced him to issue a strong letter ordering that the distinction of caste be abandoned, decidedly, immediately and finally, which immediately provoked a pandemonium.[310] Serious problem emerged among the Sudra Christians of Madras, Tanjore and Trichinopoly. This new policy led many members of the old congregations join the Leipzig Mission after 1846, as it was willing to let old caste distinctions be kept.[311] Thus, caste distinctions in the Church was never absent throughout the nineteenth and twentieth centuries.

5.3.4. *Towards the Protestant Consensus on Caste*

By 1850s majority of the Protestant Christians in India have come to realize that caste system is a serious evil that needed to be rooted out completely from the Church. The Anglican, Presbyterian, Congregationalist, and other non-Lutheran missions were in fact from the very beginning, intolerant towards the presence of caste feelings in the Church.[312] The Lutherans, before the Anglicans had taken up the mission, condoned caste. Like Vepery, the Tanjore and the Trichy churches of Tamil Nadu were full of discord, with large numbers rejoining the Hindus or the Lutheran or Roman Catholic Churches, where caste was tolerated, at that time. On many occasions Christians argued that caste is a civil institution, equal with the European class systems.[313]

The American Mission pursued stringent efforts against the observance of Caste among the Christians. They did not permit caste distinction and converts were mandated to relinquish their caste in order to join the Christian community.[314] In 1847 they insisted their employees to demonstrate their rejection of caste by taking part in the 'love-feast', by eating with Christians from various castes.[315] A resolution of the Madras Missionary Conference in 1848 put forward a significant attitude of Protestant Christians towards caste, where it states that "only those who broke caste by eating food prepared by a pariah should be entitled to baptism."[316] And Protestant consensus on caste was very clear with

---

[309] Kuriakose, *History of Christianity in India*, 109.

[310] Firth, *An Introduction to Indian Church History*, 162.

[311] Richter, *History of Missions in India*, 168.

[312] G. A. Oddie, *Social Protest in India: British Protestant Missionaries and Social Reforms 1850-1900* (New Delhi: Manohar, 1979), 51.

[313] Cf. Hugald Grafe, *History of Christianity in India*, 99.

[314] Cf. Forrester, *Caste and Christianity*, 40.

[315] Cf. John S. Chandler, *Seventy-five Years in Madurai Mission* (Madura: n.p., n.d.), 140.

[316] Richter, *History of Missions in India*, 170.

the resolutions of Madras Missionary Conference in 1850 and 1858 which was supported by the Missionary Conferences of Calcutta and Bombay Missionary Conferences.

5.4. The Protestant Christian Attitude toward Caste Post-1850

Post 1850 Christian attitude toward caste and Indian culture has become more tolerant. This change was due to the influence of the interpretation of the ideologies such as of Maxmuller and Sir Moneir Williams and the influence of the steadily increasing liberal theology in the west. The liberal minded missionaries like Farquhar and Lucas, while not denying that caste-system was incompatible with Christianity, felt the positive side of caste system.[317] In the 1860s and 1870s, thousands of people of low caste were converted to Christianity. This also required the missionaries to reassess their attitude toward caste among the Christians. Lots of Christians began to allow caste within the church again with the hope that it would positively impact more Hindus to be attracted toward the Christian gospel.

However, in the beginning of the 20th century the National Council of Churches in India and the World Council of Churches condemned the concept of untouchability, which is still practiced in India despite being abolished from India's constitution in 1950. In a joint affirmation of faith, the churches described Casteism as a sin, apostasy and rebellion against God and a crime against human beings. In spite of all the oppositions the practice of caste continues to create problems within the Indian Church today.

6. Christianity and Communalism

India is a pluralistic and multi-religious country. Diverse religions and communities are safeguarded by the Indian Constitution which provides freedom of religion. All communities are entitled to freedom of conscience and are free to profess, practice and propagate religion. However, the sad reality is even after more than seventy three years of independence one can find politicization of religion and this has cause communal tension among the different communities and this has become the biggest menace of postcolonial India. In India communalism has become a socio-political problem and becoming more and more complex today. Communalism was part and parcel of the British Policy of Divide and Rule. The British suppressed all forms of harmony of people of India and introduced divide and rule by instigating the Muslims against the Hindus and vice versa. The British in order to rule the people of India divided the people into various communities by spreading the feeling of distrust and hence sowed the seeds of communalism which ultimately led to the partition of India. The same spirit of divide and rule continued to exist in India today. Communal tension is very much prevalent throughout the subcontinent of India even today.

---

[317] Cf. Forrester, *Caste and Christianity*, 195.

6.1. Causes of Communalism

6.1.1. *Religious Factor*

One of the factors that cause communalism in India is religion. Religious fanaticism has been a big cause of communal tension. Religious movement of revivalism is gaining strength in India. Religious communities in India have been busy trying to showcase their own strengths against one another that they are creating dissension and chaos in the country. Conflicts over disputes of sites for construction of religious places of worship are becoming the trend in India. These facts reflect the role of religions in spreading communal feelings and tensions in the country.

6.1.2. *Political Factor*

In India today, political leaders, parties and organizations do not have any inhibitions whatsoever, to use the communal factor for securing their desirous positions in the political platform. They use communal lines and connections to gain votes and support. As such, in contemporary India, electoral politics is a common phenomenon. Communal cards are being extensively played for purpose of ascending to political power.

6.1.3. *Social Factor*

Owing to India's precarious and complex situation, the different communities have begun to harbour suspicion about and toward each other. The Muslims complain of the threat of Hindu, the Hindus complain of Muslims threat or the Christians complain of the threat from other religions and vice versa. All of these contribute to huge founded as well as unfounded tensions amongst the diverse communities. India's society is defined by serious issues of socio-economic imbalance wrought by unemployment, mass poverty, fundamentalism and disunity.

6.1.4. *Christian Response to Communalism*

Christians in India today are faced with the challenge of not merely spreading the message of peace far and wide but also are challenged to live out that message of peace and harmony. Christianity as a faith or as a way of life is founded upon the divine essence of love and peace and hence its adherents (Christians) are hard-pressed to follow that religious-spiritual and moral teaching of exemplifying love and peace of God in the midst of all complexities and challenges. In addition, Christians also carry the responsibility of reaching out to others (communities, faiths and traditions) with the teaching of God's love, peace and harmony amongst diverse peoples and amidst the challenges of communal spirits and activities.

Chapter 8

Indigenous Missionary Movement and the Rise of Indian Church

1. Introduction

The growth of Christian indigenous movement and the rise of Indian Church definitely bring changes to the history of Christianity in India. The first half of the 20th century presents the significant growth of indigenous movement in India. Indian Christians began to search for self identity among the existing Western mission organizations. In such a context several indigenous movements began in India.

2. Development and the Quest for Indian Identity

2.1. Protestant Missionaries towards Indigenous Movements

At the beginning of the Protestant Missionary movement the aim was not to establish an indigenous Church but to save souls from heathenism. The great reality for the Western missionaries was the Missionary Society, which sent them to India and the converts in India were considered as belonging to missions and not to an Indian Church.[318] The Indian Christians themselves did not have a consciousness of belonging to an Indian Church. Many Indian Christians were opposed to change from the early Western Christian forms, however irrelevant to India and its conditions. There was hardly any effort to develop an indigenous ministry. The Indian teachers and catechists were considered only as native agents

[318] Sunder Clark, *Let the Indian Church be Indian* (Madras: CLS, 1980), 10.

of Western missions. There was little concern for an Indian Church as such. Except in certain areas, there had been little attempt to build up self-governing institutions. After 1857 there were several Indian Christian leaders who began to show their opposition to the missionaries.[319] It was through such native Christian leaders that the Church was eventually led toward indigenization.

2.2. The Indian Christian Herald (ICH)

In 1868 some educated Indian Christians formed *The Bengal Christian Association for the Promotion of the Rights of Indian Christians.* Krishna Mohan Banerjea was elected as President. Missionaries considered this group as radicals. James Vaughan reported at the Allahabad Missionary Conference in 1872 "many or most of the educated native Christians are showing feelings of bitterness, suspicion or even dislike, towards European missionaries."[320] By 1870 Kali Charan Banerjea, J.G. Shome and few others started a newspaper "The Bengal Christian Herald" later called "The Indian Christian Herald" through which they demanded autonomy for the Church in Bengal and fought for Hindu customs to be retained in, or adapted for use in the Christian worship. These indigenous groups criticized the missionaries for denationalizing Indian Christians and making them into compound Christians, and having transferred the theological and ecclesiastical differences of the west to India, thereby dividing the Indian Christians into numerous denominations.[321]

2.3. National Missionary Society (NMS)

National Missionary Society of India (Bharat Christya Sevak Samaj) was founded in 1905 at Serampore at a meeting of Young Indian Christians from different parts of India and different denominations with the help of the American G. Sherwood Eddy. Prominent among them were V.S. Azariah and K.T. Paul. This was to be an inter-denominational society, supported by Indian money, manned by Indians, though it would not refuse offers of help from other countries, and committed as far as possible to follow indigenous methods.[322] Another important agent was the Christian Ashram Movement, which contributed much to the indigenization of the Indian Church.[323] Since the First World War a number of ashrams have

[319] Cf. Graham Houghton, *The Impoverishment of Dependency: A History of the Protestant Church in Madras 1870-1920* (Madras: CLS, 1983), 184.

[320] *Report of the General Missionary Conference held at Allahabad 1872-1873*, 260, cited by Baago, *Indigenous Christianity*, 3.

[321] Kali Charan Banerjea tried to introduce among the Christians the Nagakirtan (dancing and singing procession) taken from the Bhakti tradition in Bengal.

[322] Cf. Firth, *An Introduction to Indian Church History*, 253-255.

[323] Ashirvatham, *Christianity in the Indian Crucible,* 154. Among foreign missionaries, E. Stanley Jones has done much to popularize the ashram ideal. However, ashram is not meant to replace the Church, neither is it meant to replace the Christian ministry.

been established throughout India. Among the best known examples of Indian Christian ashrams are such as the Christu-kulu (the family of Christ) Ashram at Tirupattur in the North Arcot District of Madras State (1912)[324] and the Christa Seva Sangha (1921) and Christa Prema Seva Sangha (1934) in and near Poona.[325] Many Christians found the tradition of Indian spirituality an answer in the Ashram way of life and work.

The 19th century had been an age of foreign missions. Whatever the denomination might be, in practice the foreign missionary controlled the scene with an almost patriarchal influence; and the Christians in India would call themselves by the name of some missions such as C.M.S Christians, L.M.S. Christians and so on, rather than Indian Christians. There was little consciousness of being Indian Christians. However, in the years after the 1914-1918 missionary societies handed over some of the responsibilities to the Indian members for the development of fostering Indian Church,[326] and prepared it to take full responsibility for its own life and work. Hence, Diocesan Council was formed in 1917, consisting of the Bishop, all the clergy and lay representatives of all the parishes.[327] All the departments of the work were brought under the administration of the Bishop and Diocesan Council. It was accelerated still more when the diocese entered the Church of South India in 1947.[328] Therefore, the 20th and 21st centuries have seen considerable progress towards indigenous Christianity in India.

2.4. Friends Missionary Prayer Band (FMPB)

Friends Missionary Prayer Band was founded by Mr. P. Samuel in 1967. The main aim of this indigenous missionary movement was on church planting and Bible translation. The organization was to be self supporting, self-propagation and self-government. They decided to appoint leaders only from native, they raised their missionary support from within India through individuals, churches and institutions.

2.5. National Missionary Council of India (NMCI)

National Missionary Council of India was founded in 1914 at Nagpur. The purpose of this NMCI was to represent all the Protestant missionary organization working in Indian soil. In order to give equal wieghtage to the Indian Church with the foreign mission organization the NMCI changed to National Christian Council. The sole aim was to equally give both the Indian church and Missionary

---

[324] Ashirvatham, *Christianity in the Indian Crucible*, 155.

[325] Firth, *An Introduction to Indian Church History*, 256.

[326] Cf. Firth, *An Introduction to Indian Church History*, 259-260.

[327] Cf. P. Appasamy, *The Centenary History of the C.M.S. in Tinnevelly* (Palamcottah: n.p., 1923), 218, 231.

[328] Cf. Firth, *An Introduction to Indian Church History*, 260-261. Tinnevelly received its first Indian Bishop in 1953.

Societies to participate in the administration as well as in mission in India. To be more complete the name again was changed in 1979 to National Council of Churches in India (NCCI).

3. Indigenization of Indian Christianity

3.1. Bhakt Singh

Bakht Singh was born on 6th June, 1903 to Sikh parents Shri. Lal Jawahar Mal and Smt. Lakshmi Bai Joya. He did his early education in a Christian missionary school. He accepted Jesus Christ as his personal savior when he was studying engineering in Canada on 4th Febraury 1932. He returned to India in 1933. His parents were not very happy with his new faith yet with reluctance accepted him with a request that he will keep secret his new faith. Because of his refusal he was excommunicated from his home and family. However, that did not disturb him and he began his preaching which attracted many people to listen to him. He was considered as one of the finest evangelists of Indian Christians. He was a well known Bible teacher as well as good preacher who pioneered the Indian Church Movement and contextualization of Gospel within Indian Church. He founded Hebron Ministries through which he planted several indigenous churches and toured to several other countries for the purpose of church planting. It is believed that he planted more than 10,000 indigenous churches throughout India. He died on 17th September 2000.

3.2. Subha Rao

K. Subha Rao was born in 1912 to a very strong Hindu family of Kamma caste in Godavari District. From his early age he became an atheist and opposed all the faiths. He was more critical about the religious practice of Hindus and particularly he opposed the life and practice of *sadhus* and priests. In the midst of this in 1942 he had a vision of Christ talking to him. This event in his life changed him into a Christian. As soon as he accepted Christ he started his ministry of healing which attracted many towards the gospel. Though he accepted Christ, he refused to accept the church, its sacraments teachings and clergy.[329] He rejected Christianity as a religion and the church as having any significance. It is believed that his movement has more than 300,000 followers by 1966.[330] Though he confesses Christ and rejected church and Christianity, he remained a faithful devotee and servant of Christ within the Hindu community until his death in 1981.

---

[329] See the detail Kaj Baago, *The Movement Around Subba Rao: A Study of Hindu-Christian Movement around K. Subba Rao in Adhra Pradesh* (Bangalore: CISRS, 1968), 10.

[330] Cf. David B. Barret, ed., *World Christian Encyclopedia* (Nairobi: Oxford University Press, 1982), 89.

3.3. The Hindu Church of Lord Jesus

The first of these movements took place in Tinnevelly, in 1858, where a group of Nadar Christians broke away from the Church Missionary Society and formed *The Hindu Church of Lord, the Lord Jesus*. A similar movement started in West Bengal through the Indian Pastor Lal Behari Dey. He opposed the exclusive missionary control of the church, advocating that Indian ordained ministers should be put on equal footing with the missionaries. For this cause he brought forward a proposal for a *National Church of Bengal* comprising all the Christians.[331] However, the missionaries dismissed the movement as unacceptable.

3.4. The National Church of Madras

The National Church was formed on 12th September 1886 under the leadership of S. Parani Andi or Pulney Andy in Madras. The constitution of the National Church of India said, "it was unreasonable for Indian Christians to adhere to different Western denominations, which were products of political revolutions and dissension in Europe particularly since Christianity was Asiatic in origin."[332] Between 1894 and 1895 some Indian Christians in Tinnevelly, South Travancore and Bombay left their missions and joined the National Church. In 1900 a group of Christians in Kolar joined the National Church. By 1922 the National Church had congregations in Madras, Bangalore, Travancore, and Kolar apart from the mother congregation in Madras.[333]

Therefore, the national consciousness gave Indian Church leaders a certain amount of self-confidence and they began to voice the demand for freedom to manage their own affairs. They strongly felt that the Church in India should be truly Indian. One of the most important occasions on which this took place was the first All India Conference of Indian Christians in December 1914.[334] The gathering was an indication of the Christians' reaction to the swirling nationalist movement. Parallel with political progress went a new demand from Indian Christians for a more Indianized Church and worship. Therefore, "the growing spirit of indigenization showed itself in a gradual introduction of Indian music and Indian lyrics in worship, indigenous style in Church architecture, and indigenous methods of proclaiming Christ."[335] In 1933 in a circular letter addressed to all the LMS missionaries in India by G.E. Phillips, the LMS Foreign Secretary wrote "the naturalization of Christianity in India must definitely and

[331] Kaj Baago, *Pioneers of Indigenous Christianity* (Bangalore: CLS, 1969), 1. (Hereafter cited as Baago, *Indigenous Christianity*).

[332] Baago, *Indigenous Christianity*, 8.

[333] Cf. Baago, *Indigenous Christianity*, 11-12.

[334] Bengt Sundkler, *Church of South India: The Movement Towards Union 1900-1947* (London: Lutterworth Press, 1954), 86. (Hereafter cited as Sundkler, *Church of South India*).

[335] Philip, *Protestant Christianity in India*, 187.

consciously become the aim of the Missions, if they would conserve their work. Our work must become really indigenous or be lost."[336]

3.5. Bengal Christo Samaj

By 1887 the indigenous group left the Church and formed *the Calcutta Christo Samaj.*[337] The purpose behind it was to propagate the Christian truth and promote Christians, and to bring all Indian Christians together by eliminating the denominational spirit passed on by the Westerners.[338] The members met weekly in a private home (Banerjea's place) for common worship, led by members in turn, both men and women. No pastor was elected as such and also performed baptism by lay people.[339] K. C. Banerjea in 1892 charged the missionaries as responsible for having Christianity been considered a foreign religion in India. He further pointed out at the Bombay Missionary Conference that same year that a truly indigenous theology could develop only if the Indian Church was left alone to work it out. Christo Samaj met with much opposition from the missionaries who feared a split among the Indian Christians that could lead to the losing of the educated members of their different Churches to the Samaj. After seven years of existence the Christo Samaj was finally dissolved in 1894.[340]

[336] Cf. J. W. Gladstone, *Protestant Christianity and People's Movements in Kerala: A Study of Christian Mass Movements in Relation to Neo-Hindu, Socio-Religious Movements in Kerala 1850-1936* (Trivandrum: KUTS Publications, 1984), 335. (Hereafter cited as Gladstone, *Protestant Christianity and People's Movements*).

[337] *Indian Evangelical Review* (January, 1187), 372, cited by Baago, *Indigenous Christianity,* 7.

[338] Cf. Baago, *Indigenous Christianity*, 8.

[339] Its confession was the Apostolic Creed only. No fixed liturgy was followed. The Samaj strictly followed the principle of Christian toleration in regard to worship and discipline.

[340] Cf. Baago, *Indigenous Christianity,* 6.

Chapter 9

Indian Christianity and Ecumenical Movement

1. Introduction

Divisions in the Christian Community can be traced back to the period of the New Testament itself. Church history has often been written in the context of those divisions. But, time had come that the History of the Church should be treated from the perspective of unity or of 'oikoumene' and not of division. The noun 'ecumenism' and the adjective 'ecumenical' are derived from the Greek word 'oikoumene,' which is used in the New Testament to mean the Roman Empire (e.g. Luke 2:1) or, simply, the whole inhabited world (Matthew 24:14). Gradually, the term came to refer to the whole Church, as opposed to that which is divisive, or to the whole faith of the Church, as opposed to that which is partial.[341] Therefore, the word is now used to designate a modern Christian movement concerned with the unity and the renewal of the Church and its relationship to God's reconciling and renewing mission throughout creation.

2. Indian Ecumenical Movements and the Issue of Church Union

Protestant Christianity came to India in the form of a number of foreign missions from Europe and America. Each of the denominations maintained its position and propagated its own method of teaching and its own pattern of organizing discipline, as a result, the Christian denominations came into existence in India -

[341] Cf. Michael Kinnamon, "General Introduction," in Michael Kinnamon and Brian E. Cope, eds., *The Ecumenical Movement: An Anthology of Key Texts and Voices* (Geneva: WCC Publications, 1997), 1.

Methodist, Baptist, Anglican, Presbyterian and so on. This vast array of different denominations with divergent views on non-essentials and different practices brought many problems among the Christians in India. As such, the picture that they could present before the people of other faiths was one of division and disunity.

2.1. Co-operation in Mission

Inevitably as missionaries moved into India, they encountered problems requiring joint consultation. Though they upheld their own denominational positions they found it imperative to consult together on common problems. In 1852 missionaries working in Bombay met inter-denominationally and constituted for themselves "the Bombay Missionary Union."[342] The objective of the union was to encourage Christian fellowship and to provide a platform for exchanging ideas on how best they could extend Christian faith and work in India. In Calcutta, a similar conference came into being in about 1830. Following the local level conference in 1855, the first general conference of Bengal Protestant Missionaries[343] took place in Calcutta in order to deal with questions connected with common work, and this example followed in other parts of India.[344] On January 6-9, 1857, it took place in Benares[345] and on December 26, 1862 to 2nd January 1863, at Lahore.[346] The conference provides a criterion for assessing the relationship of missionaries to the growing churches in India.

Missionaries in South India also began coming together inter-denominationally. The first of these met at Ootacamund from April 19 to May 5, 1858 and in Bangalore from June 11 to 18, 1879,[347] that was followed by

---

[342] Cf. Hogg, *Ecumenical Foundations,* 18. The representatives were from the American Board, the London Missionary Society the Church Missionary Society, and the Scottish Missionary Society.

[343] Fifty-five members attended from six missions: The Baptist Missionary Society, the London Missionary Society, the Church Missionary Society, the Cathedral Mission, the Church of Scotland, and the Free Church of Scotland Mission.

[344] *Proceedings of a General Conference of Bengal Protestant Missionaries held at Calcutta on Sept. 4-7, in 1855.* The conference incorporated its opinion in resolutions. Respecting the progress of the Gospel on vernacular preaching, respecting female education and finally an appeal to the missionary societies of Europe and America for one hundred new missionaries within the next five years to raise the total number of Protestant missionaries in India to five hundred.

[345] Cf. J. Gregson, "Benares Missionary Conference," *Calcutta Christian Observer,* vol. 18/2 (December, 1857), 114.

[346] *Report of the Punjab Missionary Conference held at Lahore in December and January 1862-63 on the communion service, 1863,* 127. This was the largest gathering of the kind yet held in Northern India, enlisting 71 persons, many of whom were laymen and eight of whom were Indians including one Rajah.

[347] One hundred and eighteen persons, 14 of them Indians, were present from 15 societies.

Madras Conference from January 2 to 5, 1900.[348] In 1872 from December 26 to January 1, 1873, the first National General Missionary Conference was held in Allahabad.[349] The members in their coming together confirmed a felt unity and desire for increased co-operation.

The following decennial conferences were repeated in 1882 at Calcutta.[350] Twenty-seven societies were represented and in 1892 from December 29 to January 4, 1893 at Bombay. In these conferences, missionaries from all over the country came together to read papers describing the work done in their various fields, to consider points of policy and inter-mission relations, and the difficulties. It was in one of these conferences held at Madras in 1902, the principle known as comity was agreed upon by which each mission was recognized as occupying certain territories and it was agreed that other missions should abstain from entering and working in those territories.[351] However, the comity never applied to the larger towns, nor could it be fully carried out in some other places where more than one mission were already at work.

2.2. Formation of the Church of South India

The Church Union Movement in South India, which eventually resulted in the formation of Church of South India on 27th September 1947, is one of the greatest contributions of the Indian Church in the ecumenical movement. Long before the birth of Church of South India the need for mutual consultation and co-operation was keenly felt among the various Protestant or Evangelical Churches in South India.[352] Under these dismal circumstances the need for united action and closer co-operation was felt in several quarters.

In India, the Organic Union started at the beginning of the 20th century. In October 1901, a Federal Union took place between two Presbyterian Missions in South India, one connected with the American Arcot Mission of the American Dutch Reformed Church and the other with the United Free Church of Scotland Mission.[353] Similar Federal Union took place in 1904 with the Congregational Churches of the American Missions in Madura and Jaffna, and the Congregational Churches of the London Mission in South Travancore. This further opens the

---

[348] Cf. Hogg, *Ecumenical Foundations*, 21-23.

[349] K. S. Latourette, *A History of the Expansion of Christianity* Vol. VI (USA: Harper, 1945), 129. Cf., Hogg, *Ecumenical Foundations,* 23; 136 persons attended. Of these twenty-eight were native members.

[350] Cf. Hogg, *Ecumenical Foundations*, 23. Invitations were sent and 475 persons attended, of whom forty-six were natives.

[351] Cf. J. Richter, *A History of Missions in India*, 229.

[352] They included the Anglican, Baptist, Lutherans, Presbyterians, Methodists, Congregationalists and small bodies.

[353] Cf. Bengt Sundkler, *Church of South India: The Movement towards Union 1900-1947* (London: Lutterworth Press, 1954), 37, 38. (Hereafter cited as Sundkler, *Movement towards Union*).

vision for wider Union for the Presbyterians and the Congregationalists. As a result of negotiations that began from 1905, an agreed basis was found in disregarding denominational differences and realizing their "essential oneness of Christian faith."[354] Thus, the first fruitful result of an Inter-denominational Union was the South India United Church,[355] which was inaugurated on 24th July 1908.[356] This was a union of all the Congregationalists and Presbyterians in South India and the Jaffna District of Ceylon, and in 1919, after the war, the Basel Mission of Malabar District also joined the Union. The South India United Church[357] order was a mixture of Congregationalism and Presbyterianism. The North Tamil Church Council of the LMS came into the Union only after a year. J.H. Wyckoff, a leading missionary of the American Mission in Arcot says, "Some of the strongest opponents to the formation of the SIUC were Indians themselves."[358] In May 1919, an informal meeting took place at Tranquebar to consider the question of wider Church Union in India. Those present were members of the Lutheran, Methodists, Anglican and SIUC. Hence in September 1919, the General Assembly of the South India United Church appointed a committee to confer with the representatives of the Anglican and Mar Thoma Churches, and such other bodies, as they may deem wise, with a view to the possibility of Union. In February 1920 the Episcopal Synod of the Anglican province in India[359] appointed a similar committee. In 1926 the Methodist Church of South India came into the negotiations.[360]

The Joint Committee of the three Churches found agreement on the Scriptures as the supreme authority in faith, on the Nicene Creed as the authorized summary of Biblical doctrine, and on Baptism and the Holy Communion as Sacraments of the Gospel except the question of ministry. The question of the ministry was because the Anglicans do not accept non-Episcopal ministries as possessing equal authority and validity with their Episcopal ministry. On the other hand, the non-Anglicans were unwilling to do anything that might seem to

[354] Sundkler, *Movement towards Union*, 42.

[355] This was the name originally taken by the Madras-Arcot Group in 1901, from whom it passed to the South India United Church 1908.

[356] Manickam, *Formation of CSI*, 10.

[357] It was the amalgamation of the then American Arcot Mission (AAM), the United Free Church of Scotland Mission (UFCSM), the London Missionary Society (LMS) and the American Board of Commissions for Foreign Missions (ABCFM), representing the Presbyterian and Congregationalist traditions.

[358] Sundkler, *Movement towards Union*, 43.

[359] From 1930 onwards to be known as the Church of India, Burma and Ceylon.

[360] Cf. S. C. Neill, "Plans of Union and Reunion 1910-1948," in Ruth Rouse and S. C. Neill, eds., *A History of the Ecumenical Movement: 1517-1948* (Geneva: WCC, 1986), 474, 475. (Hereafter cited as Neill, *Plans of Union*).

cast doubt on the ministry that they had previously exercised.[361] In the end, the joint committee decided to allow for a period of at least thirty years, during which the Churches would be growing together and the process of unifications would come to completion. According to the constitution of the Church of South India during the thirty-year period the expectation of Church of South India was:

> The bishops of the diocese of the Church of India...accepted as bishops of that Church...all the other ministers of the uniting Churches...ordained as ministers of the word and of the Sacraments are acknowledged as such having the status of presbyters in the Church of South India...for the thirty years succeeding the inauguration of the union, the ministers any Church whose mission have founded the originally separate parts of the Church of South India shall be received as ministers of the Church...after this period of thirty years, the Church of South India will determine whether there shall continue to be any exceptions to rule that its ministry is an episcopally ordained ministry...the status of those at that time already received as ministers in the Church of South India shall not be affected by any action which the Church may take.[362]

In fact, the thirty year period was reviewed by the sixteenth Synod of the Church of South India in 1978 and it was unanimously resolved that:

> On completion of the thirty year period as stipulated in the constitution chapter II.21, the CSI solemnly proclaimed that hereafter there shall be fully unified ministry of episcopally ordained ministers in the CSI and that in as much as the United Church is the basic reality which gives unification to the ministries Episcopal and non-Episcopal, the present practice of receiving ministers from any Church with which the CSI is in full communion shall continue and that the period of such 170 reception shall be indefinite.[363]

From 1929-1947 i.e., from the publication of the first edition of scheme to the inauguration of union, it took quite a long time. However, on 28th of January 1943, the Methodist Synod decided that the Methodist Church in South India should enter into Union with the other two Churches. And in 1945 the Anglican decided to join the scheme of Church in South India with the Methodist and South India United Churches. In September 1946 the South India United Churches General Assembly accepted the terms of the Union. The Joint Committee on Church Union in South India on 3 December 1946

---

[361] Cf. Neill, *Plans of Union*, 474. Various schemes of conditional ordination and supplemental ordination were carefully considered and rejected.

[362] *The Constitution of the Church of the South India*, Chapter II, 21 (Madras: CLS, 1952), 18.

[363] *The Constitution of the Church of South India* (Madras: CLS, 1982), iv.

recommended the inauguration of Union in the month of September 1947.[364] Therefore, the most ambitious and far reaching project of Church Union in the first half of the twentieth century was the one which led to the formation of the Church of South India which was inaugurated on 27th September 1947, in the Cathedral of St. George at Madras.[365]

In 1950 the North Tamil Christian Council unanimously decided to merge with the Church of South India as part of the new diocese of Coimbatore.[366] The Bombay-Karnataka Council of the United Basel Mission Church in India joined the Church of South India in 1958. Thus today the CSI consists of 21 Dioceses covering entire South India.[367] Therefore the CSI is the outcome of a long drawn-out battle of faith and long period of negotiations. The measure of unity achieved by the CSI is a great contribution to the ecumenical movement as a whole today.

2.3. CSI Negotiation with Other Churches

CSI's role in ecumenical movement did not end with its inauguration. It had been engaged in negotiations with several Churches in India to enter into a wider union with them. With this in mind, the CSI sent a call for wider union with Lutheran and Baptist Churches. A Joint meeting of CSI-Lutheran and the Baptist Churches took place from 14-16 December 1948 in Madras. The group at the end of the meeting recommended the formation of two bodies i.e. an Inter-Church Group to carry on the conversations of union and a Theological Commission to study the theological issues involved.[368] The Joint Commission (JC) of CSI-Lutheran and the Baptist met in June 1949 at Tambaram for three days. The JC resolved to meet again in 1949 and discuss the theological issues. Hence, the meeting was held on 21-23 September 1949 at Madras. The meeting discussed and resolved the following decisions:

i. that the conversations between the three Churches groups should continue,
ii. that all the possible efforts should be made to keep the Churches informed of the progress of these discussions through printed reports

---

364 Cf. Arangaden, *Church Union in South India*, 197.

365 Cf. Neill, *Plans of Union*, 475.

366 William Moses, "The Coimbatore Diocese," in J. W. Gladstone, ed., *United to Unite History of the CSI 1947-1997* (Chennai: CSI Synod, 1997).

367 Cf. Manickam, *Formation of CSI*, 23. The CSI Diocese: 1. Coimbatore; 2. Dornakal; 3. East Kerala; 4. Jaffna; 5. Kanyakumari; 6. Karimnagar; 7. Karnataka Central; 8.Karnataka Northern; 9. Karnataka Southern; 10. Krishna Godavari; 11. Madhya Kerala; 12. Madras; 13. Madurai and Ramnad; 14. Medak; 15. Nandyal; 16. North Kerala; 17. Rayalaseema; 18. South Kerala; 19. Tiruchy-Thanjavur; 20. Thirunelveli; and 21. Vellore Diocese.

368 K. M. George, *Church of South India: Life in Union (1947-1997)* (Delhi: ISPCK, 1999), 133. (Hereafter cited as George, *Life in Union*).

of these meetings together with the statements discussed and agreed upon and not agreed upon,

iii. that the Theological Commission should continue its works.[369]

However, the Baptist withdrew their participation from the Inter-Church group after this meeting. Unfortunately there was no further progress with regard to union with the Baptist.[370] This led to the setting up of the CSI-Lutheran Joint Theological Commission in 1950. This Commission met six times in November 1950, November 1951, November 1953, March 1954, April 1956 and April 1959.[371]

During the sixth meeting of CSI-Lutheran Joint Theological Commission (JTC) in April 1959 recommended that the CSI and Lutheran Churches in India appoint an Inter-Church Commission with representatives from both the uniting Churches. The CSI Synod approved the recommendation on Inter-Church Commission and the Lutheran also accepted and approved the Inter-Church Commission in 1960.[372]

The first meeting of the Inter-Church Commission took place at Bangalore from 22-24 August 1960. The Commission decided to implement the 1955 recommendations such as Pulpit and Altar fellowship, setting up of joint organs for evangelizing unoccupied areas, joint planning for proper pastoral care. The Commission appointed a special committee to prepare a common Catechism for use both in the CSI and the Lutheran Churches. However, after several rounds of Inter-Church Commission consultations the CSI and the Lutheran Churches could not establish the proposed Church of Christ of South India.

2.4. Formation of the Church of North India

The formation of the United Church of North India (UCNI) took place in 1924. Eleven missions were represented in it, and its area stretched from Bengal and Assam to Gujarat and Punjab. Series of consultations with a view of wider Church Union began in North India in 1929.[373] In 1951 the United Church of Northern India, the Anglican Church of India, Pakistan, Burma and Ceylon, the Methodist Church in Southern Asia, the British and Australian Methodist Church and the Council of the Baptist Churches in Northern India formed a Negotiating Committee. In 1957 the Church of Brethren and the Discipleship of Christ joined the negotiations.

---

369 Paul, *CSI-Lutheran Conversations*, 3.

370 George, *Life in Union*, 134.

371 R. D. Paul, *The First Decade: An Account of the Church of South India* (Madras: CLS, 1956), 93. (Hereafter cited as Paul, *The First Decade*).

372 Cf. Paul, *The First Decade*, 14-16.

373 James Kellock, *Breakthrough for Church Union in North India and Pakistan* (Madras: CLS, 1965), 2. (Hereafter cited as Kellock, *Church Union in North India*).

The movement for wider union took actual shape in 1929 when conversations were set afoot between representatives of the UCNI, the Baptist, the Anglicans, the British and Australian Methodists and the American Methodist-Episcopal.[374] These conversations were known as the Round Table Conference. The first Round Table Conference (hereafter RTC) was held in Lucknow on 10-11 April 1929.[375] In the general discussion it was revealed that a pure Congregationalism, recognizing the absolute autonomy of each separate congregation, was not acceptable in India and was rarely found in operation.[376] However, all the elements of real value in Congregationalism were to be preserved in a united Church as had been done to some extent in the UCNI. It was agreed to recognize the place of the child in the Church and the necessity of a definite profession of faith on the part of every member.[377] There was agreement on the necessity of order in the observation of the Sacrament of the Lord's Supper.

The second RTC was held in Delhi on 18-20 November 1930, and appointed a Continuation Committee to work on the various aspects of the union. The committee discussed the different types of Church polity such as the Diocese, the Congregation and the Synod. Each diocese is under the charge of a Bishop and functions through Diocesan Council. The Congregations are the local groups of Christians organized for Christian life and worship within the fellowship of the Diocese. The Synod is the organ of the whole Church, comprising the entire Diocese, and it is the supreme supervisory and legislative body of the Church. [378] And the third RTC was held at Lucknow on 6-8 April 1937. It was also agreed that the proposed United Church's statement of doctrine should be as brief as possible; and all the representatives present were prepared to accept the following three clauses:

i) the United Church holds the faith which the Church has ever held in Jesus Christ, the Redeemer of the world, in whom men are saved by grace through faith, and in accordance with the revelation of God which He made, Himself God incarnate, it worships one God, Father, Son and Holy Spirit.
ii) it accepts the Holy Scriptures of the Old Testament and New Testament as containing all things necessary to salvation, and as the ultimate standard of that faith.

[374] Kellock, *Church Union in North India*, 3.

[375] It was represented by Australian Churches of Christ, Australian Methodist Church, Baptist Church, the Church of the Brethren Mission, Methodist Episcopal Church, Wesleyan Methodist Missionary Society, the Indian Mission Disciple of Christ, and the United Church of Northern India.

[376] Cf. D. K. Sahu, *United and Uniting: A History of the Church of North India* (Delhi: ISPCK, 2001), 34. (Hereafter cited as Sahu, *United and Uniting*).

[377] S. F. Bayne, *Ceylon, North India and Pakistan* (London: SPCK, 1960), 12.

[378] For detailed information cf. Kellock, *Church Union in North India*, 42-46.

iii) it acknowledges the witness of the Apostles' Creed and the Creed commonly called the Nicene Creed to that faith, which is continually confirmed in the spiritual experience of the Church of Christ.[379]

The Joint Council became a separate platform for negotiations, which continued from 1931-1945. Its first meeting was held at Allahabad in December 2-4, 1931. The first plan of Union in 1940 was issued after its fifth meeting in 1940 with a revised edition after the sixth meeting in March 1942.[380] During the fifth meeting of the Joint Council, at the request of the RTC the representatives of those Churches associated with the RTC were present.[381]

After seven RTC meetings, in 1951 the Negotiating Committee[382] (hereafter NC) replaced the RTC. The first plan of union as prepared by the NC in 1951 was not accepted by the uniting Churches because of the intention regarding the unification of the ministry, and because the matter of unification of the episcopate of the Anglican and Methodist Episcopal Churches was not clear.[383] Therefore, the second meeting of the sub-committee on the unification of the two episcopates took place at Lucknow on 30 – 31st January 1953. The meeting brought out an agreed statement that "the Churches before uniting agreed that the Episcopate of the United Church should be both constitutional and historic, meaning the Episcopate which is historic continuity with that of the early Church."[384] This led to the revision of the Plan of Union in 1954.[385]

The proposal set forth in the Plan of Union for unifying the Ministry of the United Church through the rite of mutual laying-on of hands with prayer was continually in the foreground of thought and discussion. The detailed proposals for a Unification of the Ministry were included in 3rd edition of the Plan as follows:

---

379 Kellock, *Church Union in North India*, 4.

380 The second, third and fourth meetings of the Joint Council were held in 1935, 1936 and 1939 respectively.

381 *Plan of Union, Joint Council, 1940* (Calcutta: New Indian Press, 1940), 115.

382 Negotiating Committee consists of Council of Baptist Churches of North India, the Church of Brethren, Church of India, Pakistan, Burma and Ceylon, the Methodist Church (Australia and British), the Disciples of Christ, Methodist Church in Southern Asia, and the United Church of North India.

383 Cf. Sahu, *United and Uniting*, 45, 46.

384 Kellock, *Church Union in North India*, 65. Cf. also Prabhudan Adhikari, "Episcopacy in the CNI," *The North India Churchman* (June, 1979), 2.

385 Cf. Kellock, *Church Union in North India,* 73. It included (a) the assertion of the words 'as the inspired word of God' in respect of OT and NT; (b) the assertion that while some men who have been deacons may later be ordained presbyters, the deaconate properly represents a distinctive calling in the Church; (c) agreement on the distinctive functions of the deacon being a specific share in the public worship, sharing responsibility in Church administration and a pastoral function under the direction of the presbyter.

1. the inauguration of the Union: the solemn formation of the Church of North India
2. the bringing together of the two episcopates - Anglican and American Methodist
3. the Representatives Act of the Unification of the Ministry
4. the Declaration and Confirmation of the appointments of existing Bishops and the Consecration of new Bishops
5. the Diocesan Services of Unification.[386]

With this third edition the real breakthrough came in this whole matter of Unification Rite. The unification was not based on the agreement of interpretations but unanimity of trust.[387] They accepted the principle of the unification of the ministry by the mutual laying-on of hands in a solemn act of humility and rededication with prayer. Therefore, the uniting Churches pledge themselves and fully trust each other that any Bishop or presbyter officiating in the rite will do so with the sincere intention of placing himself unreservedly in the hands of God, to be used as He wills, as a channel of His grace, commission and authority.[388]

In 1969 the Convention of the Churches of the Disciples of Christ accepted the Plan to join the Negotiation. In 1969 the Church of Brethren decided to join the Union. The Methodist Church (British and Australia) had voted in favor of Union in 1969. In 1966 the General Council of Church of India, Pakistan, Burma and Ceylon (CIPBC) favor the proposed united Church. In 1968 the UCNI decided to join the Union. Methodist Church in Southern Asia (MCSA) in 1970 rejected the Union Plan.[389]

Therefore, six uniting Churches[390] came together in one visible fellowship to form the Church of North India on 29th November under the presidency of Rev

---

[386] D. M. Kennedy, "The CNI History," *Indian Church History Review* 6/2 (December, 1972), 108. (Hereafter cited as Kennedy, *The CNI History*).

[387] Kennedy, *The CNI History*, 110.

[388] *Plan of Church Union in North India and Pakistan* (Madras: CLS, 1965), 52.

[389] D. M. Kennedy, "Work in Progress: The CNI History," *Indian Church History Review* 8/1 (June, 1973): 15. (Hereafter cited as Kennedy, *Work in Progress*). It was stated that the MCSA's decision to be out from the union was due to misunderstanding, i.e., during discussion of the Women's Committee's report a well known MCSA women leader Mrs Agnes Loyall, wished to make a statement on Women's work, but permission was not granted. During a discussion of Episcopal Support and Endowments, Rev H. A. Townsley of MCAS asked a short statement be recorded in the minutes. But the Negotiating Committee did not accept it to be put in the minutes but in the appendix. The other reason was that during the Nagpur Meeting there was a request from the Agra Annual Conference of the MCSA for a postponement of the inauguration but the committee rejected this request. All these reasons led the MCSA to be out of 1970 Union.

[390] The CIPBC had 340,000 members, UCNI 18,8000 members, CBCNI 110,000 members, the Church of Brethren 18000 members, the Methodist Church (British and Australia) 10,000 members, and the Disciples of Christ 7,500 members. The total of 673,500 members of CNI represented various heritages in North India.

Gurbachan Singh in 1970. The General Assembly then solemnly declared, "that these six Churches within the area of union have become one Church of North India."[391] The inauguration of the Church of North India took place in the All Saints' Cathedral compound in a great tent at Nagpur on the morning of Sunday 29th November 1970. The Most Rev Lakdasa De Mel,[392] Rev Dr Benjamin Pradhan, and Rev C.C. Pande, became the nucleus of the ordained ministry of the CNI.

2.5. CSI-CNI-MTC

With the inauguration of CNI in 1970 an attempt has begun for still wider ecumenism. The CNI in 1972 expressed their desire for wider union and witness in India. The CSI and the Mar Thoma Church welcomed this move and the result of which was the formation of a Joint Theological Commission (JTC).[393] The objectives of the Commission were:

> to explore the possibilities of close co-operation between the CSI, the CNI and the MTC and to discuss question of Faith and Order and other relevant issues so that they may eventually be led to union, keeping in mind the ultimate goal of Christ's people in India for the fulfillment of Mission of the Church. [394]

During the second meeting held at Bangalore from 3-4 June 1975 the JTC discussed the name for the proposed united Church. The third meeting of the JTC was held at Tiruvalla, Kerala on 10 September 1976 in which the JTC converted itself as Joint Council of the three Churches.[395] The first meeting of the Joint Council of the three Churches was held at Nagpur from 4-6 July 1978. The aims of the Joint Council are "to serve as the common organ of the three Churches and of the whole Churches of Jesus Christ in India and to help the Churches to fulfill the mission of evangelization of the people of India, and to witness to the righteousness of God revealed in the Gospel of Jesus Christ by striving for a just society."[396] Thus, the Joint Council is an attempt to manifest organic oneness through a common structure, which retains the autonomy of the Churches.

---

391 Kennedy, *Work in Progress*, 20.

392 Metropolitan of the CIPBC.

393 The first meeting of the CNI-CSI-MTC Joint Theological Commission met at Madras, on 16 January. Cf. George, *Life in Union*, 150.

394 *Minutes of the First Meeting of the Joint Theological Commission of the CSI-CNI-MT Churches January 16, 1975* (Madras: CLS, 1975), 13.

395 Russel J. ed., *The Joint Council of the CNI, CSI and Malankar Mar Thoma Syrian Church: A Brief History and Interpretation* (Delhi: ISPCK, 1984), 16. (Hereafter cited as Russel, *The Joint Council of CNI, CSI and MTC*).

396 *The Constitution of the Joint Council of the CNI, CSI and MTC* (Delhi: ISPCK, 1981), 6.

The second meeting of the Joint Council met at Charal Mount, Kerala on 5th May 1979. The main discussion at the meeting was the name of the proposed New Church. One of the difficulties was that the Mar Thoma Church's constitution prohibited any change of its name and therefore the Church could not unite with other Churches to become part of a Church bearing another name.[397] At the Executive Committee Meeting of the Joint Council held from 25-26 June 1982, they decided to remit different proposals for the name of the proposed New Church such as 'Uniting Church in India,' 'The Church of India,' and 'Bharat Christian Church.'[398] During the third Joint Council meeting from 22-24 January 1983 at Madras, the proposed name of the Church was discussed and resolved that it will be decided only after the CSI-CNI-MTC further clarified the adoption of common name as envisaged in the Constitution of the Joint Council.[399]

The Executive Committee meeting on 11-14 November 1999 at Charal Kunnu, Kerala unanimously recommended that the name "the Communion of the Churches in India" be adopted.[400] The new name was adopted and announced at the Executive Committee Meeting held at Calcutta on 11-14 November 2000.[401] Therefore, the Communion Churches in India by CSI-CNI-MTC has been constituted as the wider union and expression of visible unity among the different denominations of different traditions by having its own identity of traditions and remaining as autonomous Churches.

[397] *Marthoma Church Constitution* chapter 16 section 388.

[398] Cf. *Minutes of the Executive Meeting of the Joint Council of CSI-CNI-MTC, June 25-26* (Bombay: 1982), 10.

[399] *The Constitution of the Joint Council of the CNI, CSI and MTC* (Delhi: ISPCK, 1981), 3.

[400] *Reports of the Executive Committee Meeting held from 11-14 November 1999* Kerala, 6.

[401] *Reports of the Executive Committee Meeting held from 11-14 November 2000 Calcutta*, 8.

Chapter 10

History of Christianity in North East India

1. Introduction

North East India (NEI) consists of eight states namely Arunachal Pradesh, Assam, Manipur, Meghalaya, Mizoram, Nagaland, Sikkim and Tripura. It covers the total area of 2, 55,000 sq. km and hence accounts for more than 7.7% of the total geographical area of the country and has more than 3.88% of the total population of India. These people consist of more than 200 schedule tribes. The land is mostly mountainous and hilly though there are plateaus and valleys in Assam, Arunachal Pradesh, Tripura and Manipur. The people of this region are considered by many scholars and social scientists as sociable and hospitable people.[402] The ethnic composition of the race of this region is extremely complex. Majority of the inhabitants of the population are of Mongoloid race. It is difficult to ascertain how many languages are being spoken in this region and this has created diversity of culture and historical assessment to ascertain the cultural history of the various groups become more complex.[403]

However, all these states come under a political arena known as North Eastern Council (NEC), which came into being by an Act of Parliament in 1971

---

[402] Cf. Verrier Elwin, *The Tribal World of Verrier Elwin* (New Delhi: Oxford University Press, 2002), 226-228.

[403] Cf. Frederick S. Downs, *History of Christianity in India: North East India in the Nineteenth and Twentieth Centuries*, vol. V, Part 5 (Bangalore: CHAI, 1992), 1-3. (Hereafter cited as Downs, *History of Christianity*).

and started functioning from August, 1972.[404] The region has internationally been connected with the rest of the country through a narrow corridor in North Bengal and its border with China and Bhutan in the North, Myanmar to the East and Bangladesh in the West. The region has 38.4 million populations out of which 4.3 million were Christians as per 2001 Census, which is 12% (approx.) of the country's Christian population.

The socio-cultural life of the people is extremely multifaceted. The people of the region can be roughly divided into two categories on the bases of geographical location. The first group is the plains people, inhabiting the plains of Assam, Manipur and Tripura and was more or less Sanskritized[405] with the migration of the Aryans from North India.[406] The other group who inhabited the hill areas is called the Tribals. Evidently the people of the latter group were Mongoloid in their racial stock.[407] Minorities of these populations follow their traditional religions, whereas the majority of the tribals have followed Christianity.

2. The Political Scenario

Till 13th century North East India was not much known to the outside world. The people lived in their own world without much interference from the outside world as well as even among themselves as they rarely had any contact with one another outside their own village or tribe. By 1230 AD Ahoms[408] began to plunder this region and gradually controlled Assam especially the Brahmaputra Valley by the end of the 13th century. Chu Kapha was the first Ahom Raja of Assam.

In 1790 Ahom king Gaurinath Singh requested the Britishers to help him solve this political conflict within his territory that in 1792 the British sent captain Welsh to Ahom territory. At this time internal crisis further increased and the Burmese seeing the situation took advantage of it and controlled the Ahom kingdom. Skirmishes with the British on the borders of Bengal contributed to the first Anglo-Burman war of 1824-1826. The British after their victory signed the 'Treaty of Yandabo' which removed the dominance of Burma in this region. Assam came under the complete control of the British India in 1826, Cachar in 1832, Naga Hills in 1877, Lushai Hills 1892, and Eastern Frontier Tracts and some other regions in 1898. Thus, the whole region gradually came under the British administration.

---

[404] Cf. Amar Khrishna Paul, *Northeast A-Z General Knowledge* (Panbazar, Guwahati: Good Books Distributors Pub., 2003), 265. (Hereafter cited as Paul, *Northeast*).

[405] Cf. K. Thanzauva, *Theology of Community: Tribal Theology in the Making* (Aizawl: Mizo Theological Conference, 1997), 12.

[406] Cf. Frederick S. Downs, *Christianity in North East India: Historical Perspectives* (Guwahati: ISPCK, 1983), 5. (Hereafter cited as Downs, *Christianity in NEI.*).

[407] Cf. PangerImchen, *Ancient Ao Naga Religion and Culture* (New Delhi: Har-Anan Pub. 1993), 13.

[408] The Ahoms, a Shan tribe from central Asia who were of Tibeto-Burman race.

With India's independence in 1947, 15th August, Assam became a State of India, Arunachal became the 24th State of Indian Union on 20th February 1987; Manipur became full-fledged State of Indian Union on the 21st January 1972, Mizoram was instituted on 20th February, 1987 as one of the States of India; Nagaland was constituted as the 16th State of India on December 1st 1963; Tripura was organized as the State of Indian Union 1972; and Sikkim was constituted as the 22nd State of India on 16th May 1975 and was included as the 8th sister state of North-East India on 2002. Today politically North-East India has central parties as well as local people's parties. Today in Nagaland, Mizoram and Meghalaya the political life is dominated by Christians. Christianity has grown in number, after independence. It is among the Hills people that Christian movement has taken momentum.

3. Christianity and the North East India

The introduction of Christianity in the North East India was in a very denominational form of the western Christianity. This opened the field with so many names like Roman Catholic, Baptist, Presbyterian, Lutheran, Anglican, and now there is the addition of charismatic groups and independent Churches. The early Christian missions that worked in India were based in England, Wales, the United States, Australia, New Zealand, Germany and Italy. Majority of the Christians in NEI come from tribal milieu. Therefore, many historians and social scientists categorized the tribal Christians as illiterate, heathen, barbarian, and so on. It was true that they were not educated in the western sense as the invaders of these regions were, but, the tribals were also well educated in their own cultural traditions which were adequate for them at that time. Hence, in order to understand the development of History of Christianity in NEI one need to understand the importance of their world without imposing or looking at their life and witness through prejudiced eyes.

4. Different Christian Missions in NEI

4.1. Roman Catholic Mission

The earliest Christian contacts with NEI were made by the Roman Catholic missionaries in the 17th and the 18th centuries.[409] It is believed that these Roman Catholic missionaries were looking for a route to Tibet or to the interiors of China. Some are of the opinion that they were visiting Christian community associated

[409] Cf. C.B. Firth, *An Introduction to Indian Church History* (Delhi: ISPCK, 2001), 267. Cf. also F. S. Downs, "Rangamati: A Christian Community in North East India during the Seventeenth and Eighteenth Centuries," *ICHR* XII. 2 (Dec, 1978): 88; See also David Syemlieh, *A Brief History of the Catholic Church in Nagaland* (Nagaland: n.p., 1990), 35-36.

with the Moghul garrison at Rangamati in Lower Assam.[410] For unknown reasons this community had disappeared by the 19th century.

The Catholics revived their work when in 1850 Assam was attached to the Vicariate Apostolic of Lhasa. However, significant missionary work only began after 1889, when the Prefecture Apostolic of Assam, Bhutan, and Manipur was created and entrusted to a young German order, the Salvatorian Fathers. Roman Catholics became active once again in 1921, when the Pope had entrusted the work to Salesians of Don Bosco. They worked in Shillong and Garo hills in 1933. By the beginning of the Second World War, Catholics have increased from 5,000 to 50,000. Today Catholics have established their centers in all the North Eastern States. They have even reached the remotest places of the whole NEI with their social services, educational systems and church mission.

4.2. Serampore Mission

The first protestant missionary to preach the Gospel in NEI was an Indian Christian of the Baptist denomination, by the name Krishna Pal who was sent by the Serampore Mission. He preached for several months at Pandua at the foot of the Khasis Hills. He also converted seven persons and baptized them.[411] After working for eight months Krishna Pal went back to Serampore without establishing any regular work or mission centre in that area.

In 1819 the Serampore Mission translated the New Testament Bible into Assamese and the whole of the Bible in 1833.[412] In 1824 they also published Bengali script New Testament for Khasi-Jaintia people as they were not having their own alphabets during those days.[413] In 1829 at the request of Commissioner, David Scot, the Serampore Mission and Baptist Missionary Society started a center at Guwahati. James Rea[414] was sent to Guwahati for the mission. He started a school at Guwahati, in the Brahmaputra Valley with assistance from Serampore. 12 students were enrolled in the school - three Khasis and nine Garos. However, no record of such is available whether these people became Christians or not. After some years of labor, in 1836 Rev James Rea baptized six persons and a church was organized with 12 members.[415] Sadly, as F. S. Downs pointed

[410] Cf. F.S. Downs, *The Mighty Works of God* (Guwahati: CLC, 1971), ii. (Hereafter cited as Downs, *The Mighty Works*). Cf. Firth, *An Introduction to Indian Church History*, 267.

[411] Out of seven converts two were Khasis namely U. Duwan and U. Anna; one Assamese and other four identities are not known. Cf. Downs, *The Mighty Works*, 11.

[412] Cf. Downs, *The Mighty Works*, 11.

[413] Cf. O.L. Snaitang, *Christianity and Social Change in North East India* (Shillong: Vendrame Institute, 1993), 66. (Hereafter cited as Snaitang, *Christianity and Social Change*).

[414] James Rea originally came to India as East India Company officer. But after coming to India he experienced a religious experience which compelled him to join Serampore College for Theological Studies and was the first Serampore graduate to serve in the North East India.

[415] 12 members were inclusive of the six converts, the missionary, wife and some local British officers.

out "none of the Indian members of this first church in the Brahmaputra valley remained faithful."[416] By 1837, when Bronson visited Guwahati there were no local Christians left in the church. Rev Rea and Robinson left the mission with disappointment and joined the government service. Thus, in 1838 the BMS donated both the Guwahati and Cherrapunji mission fields to the American Baptist.[417]

4.3. Baptist Mission

4.3.1. *Baptist in Assam*

In 1835 British commissioner, Francis Jenkins extended invitation to the American Baptist Union[418] working in Burma to come to the NEI to undertake a mission work among the Khamti and Singpho tribes.[419] But, the American Baptist Mission sent the first missionaries to NEI not for the Khamti and Singphos but for the purpose to reach China and to evangelize the Shan tribes while they make NEI as strategic place for their China and Shan tribe's Mission. The two missionary couples who came to Sandiya on 23rd March 1836 were Mr. and Mrs. Nathan Brown and Mr. and Mrs. Oliver Cutter. On 17th July, they were joined by Mr. and Mrs. Miles Bronson and Mrs. Jacob Thomas.[420] Thus, Downs has rightly pointed out that for "five years the missionaries working in Assam were identified as workers in the Shan Mission."[421]

By 1836 the field missionaries felt that they cannot have both the Shan Mission and a Brahmaputra Valley Mission. By the end of 1837 Mr. Brown had mastered the Assamese language and in 1838 he began to translate the Gospel of Matthew. Therefore, in 1841 they turned their whole attention toward Brahmaputra Valley Mission. The first Assamese convert took place in 1841 by the name Nidhiram. In 1845 at the missionary meeting the first church in Assam was organized at Sibsagar and later at Nagoan and Guwahati respectively.[422]

The first educational institution in Assam was established at Nagoan as they opened the orphanage which served both as an orphanage and a school. The orphanage was the source for increased number of converts and those converts became very important for the Assam Christianity in the later years. The progress of the missionary work was not so fruitful that even after almost twenty five years

---

[416] Downs, *The Mighty Works*, 12.

[417] Cf. Downs, *The Mighty Works*, 12-13.

[418] Later it was changed to American Baptist Foreign Mission Society.

[419] Cf. Joseph Puthenpurakal, *Baptist Mission in Nagaland* (Shillong: Vendrame Missiological Institute, 1984), 50. (Hereafter cited as Puthenpurakal, *Baptist Mission*).

[420] In 1838 the Bronson Family, together with Mrs. Thomas moved to Jaipur at the suggestion of Mr. C. A. Bruce, a British Officer, to organize work there for the Singphos and preparing way for Shan mission evangelization.

[421] Downs, *The Mighty Works*, 14.

[422] Cf. Downs, *History of Christianity*, 70. Cf. also Downs, *The Mighty Works*, 13.

of mission work in Assam there were only 54 members in the three churches, i.e. Sibsagar, Nagoan and Guwahati.[423] Nevertheless, the mission continued their work in Assam at the same time. Today Assam Baptist Convention has six Associations,[424] 575 churches and 32503 baptized members.[425]

4.3.2. *Baptist among the Karbis*

In the late 1850s the American Baptist began their work among the Karbi tribe. It was not successful as the people were so much influenced by Hinduism. However, they continued their work not on regular basis but through the bordering areas of Assam Valleys. The Karbi Anglong Baptist Convention was formed in 1980 and now they have 13 Associations with 331 churches and 28997 baptized members.[426]

4.3.3. *Baptist in Garo Hills*

In the 1860s the American Baptists also began their work among the Garos. A School was started by a Political officer among the Garos at Goalpara in 1847. The first two converts namely Omed and Ramkhe of Watrepara village were baptized in 1863.[427] They were from this school. Ramkhe started a school at Damra and Omed established Rajasimla as the first Christian village among the Garos. On 15th April 1867, Omed was ordained as the first NEI minister and Rajasimla Christians were organized as a church. Within a year the number of believers increased to 150 and by 1875 there were 400 members of the church. The American Baptist Mission (ABM) started a center at Goalpara and in 1877 at Tura, which became the largest ABM station in Assam. In 1875 the Garo churches were organized into an association and had its first meeting in Goalpara.[428] In 1875 the Garo churches were organized into an association and had its first meeting in Goalpara.[429] By 1900, the Christian community grew to be 10,000. Today the Garos have 17 associations and 1783 churches. The total baptized members of Garo Baptist Convention as per the reports of 2017-18 is 314340.[430]

---

[423] Cf. Downs, *The Mighty Works*, 13.

[424] They are UBCA, KABS, NDBA, MABA, SBA and SDBA.

[425] *The Annual Report of the General Secretary, Assam Baptist Convention Presented at the 68nd CBCNEI AGM held at Diphu Town Baptist Church, 27th – 29th April, 2018*, 3.

[426] *The Annual Report of the General Secretary, Karbi Anglong Baptist Convention Presented at the 68nd CBCNEI AGM held at Diphu Town Baptist Church, 27th – 29th April, 2018*, 1.

[427] Cf. F.S. Downs, "Origin of Christianity in the Garo Hills of Meghalaya," *ICHR*, Vol. 1 (June, 1972), 1-3.

[428] Cf. Downs, *History of Christianity*, 79-80.

[429] Cf. Downs, *History of Christianity*, 79-80.

[430] Cf. *Report of the Regional Secretary of the Garo Baptist Convention Presented at the Annual Meeting of CBCNEI held at Diphu Town Baptist Church, Karbi Anglong from April 27-29, 2019*, 58.

4.3.4. *Baptist in the Nagas Hills*

The Baptists Missionaries Mr. Nathan Brown, one of the Missionaries in Sandiya requested the Home Board in America for a Missionary to work among the Nagas. In reply to the request in 1839 on 22nd July, Mr. and Mrs. Cyrus Barker were appointed as the missionaries to the Nagas. They reached Jaipur on 14th May 1840. Prior to their arrival Mr. Bronson made few visits to the Nagas and was allowed to stay in Namsang Village. In 1840 Mr. and Mrs. Bronson with his sister Rhoda Bronson began their work in Namsang Village. However, their work among the Nagas was cut short with the concept that it was not worth all the trouble in comparison with the possible harvest among the Assamese. Thus, in 1841 the Naga mission was abandoned.[431]

The interest of Baptist Mission among the Nagas re-started under Edward Winter Clark, his wife Mary Mead Clark and Godhula Rufus Brown, an Assamese in the early 1870s. Mr. Clark asked Mr. Godhula in 1871 to learn some of the Naga dialect in order to see the possibility of entering into the Naga Hills. By 1872 Godhula visited five times a Naga village of Deka Haimong and his wife joining the last visit. They brought nine Nagas to Sibsagar who were baptized by Clark at the Dikho River. On their return the converts built a chapel in their village. Thus, the first Church in Nagaland came into being in December 1872.[432] Soon after that Clark also visited Deka Haimong and on 22nd December 1872 he baptized another 15 Nagas.[433] In 1876 Clark also moved to stay in the Naga Hills, at first Molungyimjen (Haimong), later shifted to newly formed village of Molungyinsen where the first mission was started in North East India outside government station. Later in 1894, the Mission center was transferred to Impur, which was regarded as its Missionary colony and it's headquarter of Ao Baptist Church Association till today.

In 1878 Rev C.D. King was appointed to work in the Naga Hills and established a mission station at Kohima and founded the Kohima Baptist Church in Angami area.[434] The first Angami Naga, named Eurasian was baptized on June 21, 1885.[435] Gradually, with the contribution of W.E. Witter and family, the Mission work was expanded to a third center in Nagaland for the work among the Lotha Nagas at Wokha in 1885.[436] They opened a school for children and enrolled

---

[431] Cf. Puthenpurakal, *Baptist Mission*, 50-53.

[432] Cf. Downs, *The Mighty Works*, 65.

[433] P. T. Philip gives this date as 11th November 1872. Cf. P. T. Philip, *The Growth of Baptist Churches in Nagaland* (Guwahati: CLC, 1976), 55. (Hereafter cited as Philip, *Baptist Churches in Nagaland*). On the other hand, F.S. Downs considers 11th December 1872 as the actual date of baptism. Cf. Downs, *The Mighty Works*, 65.

[434] Cf. Puthenpurakal, *Baptist Mission*, 96-97.

[435] Cf. S.W. Rivenburg, "Historical Sketch of the Angami Naga Mission," *The Assam Mission of the ABMU* (December, 1886), 87.

[436] Cf. Puthenpurakal, *Baptist Mission*, 101-102.

14 boys. Later, through the untiring missionary labor of E.W. Clark, the first converts from the Lotha tribe, Nkhao and Shanrio, were baptized by Haggard at Impur on 2nd Oct. 1898.[437]

Historically speaking, the Nagaland Baptist Church Council was organized in 1935 at Kohima as the Naga Hills Baptist Church Advisory Board and it was renamed as the Naga Hills Baptist Church Council in 1937. But, the Nagaland Baptist Church Council as such was reorganized only in 1953 and then functioned as a true organization, though somewhat in provisional sense until 1960, under a constitution laid down to guide its working. Incidentally, at first the name was Naga Baptist Church Council and only after the inauguration of Nagaland as a separate State a consequential amendment was made, and then it was regularized as Nagaland Baptist Church Council as it is used today. The NBCC is a constituent member body of the CBCNEI, and also maintains historical relationship with American Baptist Missions. According to 2012 statistic report, NBCC consisted of 20 Associations with 1661 Churches, and 6.38 lakhs members and four Associate members.[438]

4.3.5. *Baptist in Manipur*

William Pettigrew came to India under the sponsorship of private society, the Arthington Aborigines Mission.[439] But, after coming to India he was re-baptized by R. Wright Hay, a missionary living in Dacca.[440] In 1891 he came to Cachar, Assam. He developed an interest in the Manipuris he met in Cachar but could not enter Manipur until the acting political agent gave him permission to open a school at Imphal in 1894.[441] While he was staying in Silchar in Cachar he learned Bengalese and Manipuri.[442] Within three years he not only mastered the Manipuri, but had reduced it into writing. In 1893 he had printed two books in Manipuri on the elementary Catechism of Christianity, and a comparative study of Lord Krishna with Jesus Christ.[443]

---

[437] Cf. Downs, *The Mighty Works*, 126.

[438] Interview with Vikuo Rhi, Youth Secretary of Nagaland Baptist Church Council (28/07/2019), Kohima.

[439] This mission belongs to Mr. Robert Arthington, an English gentleman. He was a great giver to missions, his contribution being always for pioneer works, with instructions that only two workers to a place; learn the language; give the gospel to the people, then move on to other fields.

[440] The Church of England practices infant baptism. After coming to India, he became convinced of the need for believer's baptism, and accordingly received it. He joined American Baptist at Sibsagar in 1895.

[441] Downs, *History of Christianity*, 84.

[442] Cf. T. Luikhan, ed., *History of the Manipur Christian* (Ukhrul: NECA, 1948), 10. (Hereafter cited as Luikhan, *Manipur Christian*).

[443] Cf. K. M. Singh, *History of Christian Missions in Manipur and other Neighboring States* (New Delhi: Mittal Publications, 1991), 56-57. (Hereafter cited as Singh, *History of Christian Missions*).

In 1892, 12th September Mr. Dalmas, Secretary of New Zealand Baptist Missionary, and the Aborigines Mission asked for a permission to start Missionary work in Manipur to the political agent Major Maxwell[444] but the latter turned down their request and suggested them to work among the Cachar Manipuris.[445]

Having failed to obtain permission W. Pettigrew again requested Mr. A. Porteous, the officiating political agent in Manipur as Maxwell had taken leave.[446] Porteous allowed the missionary without the knowledge of the higher authorities of Assam. Although objections followed, the missionary being a British nationality undoubtedly served him well, for no American would have been given permission to enter Manipur by the political agent for any other reason.[447]

Pettigrew arrived at Imphal on 6th February of 1894 to start his school.[448] Initially he gave private tuition for the children of government officials.[449] Within a short time the first Manipuri boys' school was opened at Sinjamei Imphal, naming Pettigrew Lower Primary School,[450] now upgraded to Junior High School. Major Maxwell, when he returned from leave told Pettigrew that he must discontinue his work in Imphal.[451] He however, suggested the missionary to work in the hill areas with his own risk.[452]

Further Maxwell conveyed if Pettigrew undertake the training of the hill people, he would place at the missionary's disposal for this purpose a sum annually.[453] Thus, a notice was served to Pettigrew to stop the work:

> Under instructions of the local government I have the honor to inform you (Pettigrew) that owing to the state being administered on behalf

---

[444] Singh, *History of Christian Missions*, 57

[445] *Dairy Maxwell, Political Agent and Superintendent of the state, No. 52, dated 12th September, 1892.*

[446] Singh, *History of Christian Mission*, 58. Porteous was on friendly terms with Pettigrew who succeeded in impressing the officiating political agent to grant him permission for entry into the state and start a school in the capital Imphal.

[447] Singh, *History of Christian Missions*. 58.

[448] Cf. Singh, *History of Christian Missions*, 64.

[449] Downs, *Mighty Works*, 76.

[450] Johnah M. Solo and K. Mahengthei, eds., *William Pettigrew 40 years in Manipur and Assam* (Imphal: Modern Press, 1986), 2. (Hereafter cited as Solo, *William Pettigrew*).

[451] The reason for Major Maxwell to take this action was that the vaishnavite Hindus Meitais accused Pettigrew's teaching and preaching in the valley of being a deliberate attempt to impose them the government's religion (Christianity). Major Maxwell sensing the situation concluded that to give license to Pettigrew to preach among the Hindu Manipuris would mean to wage war against the State's native religion. Thus he was allowed to carry on for only six months. Cf. also Lal Dena, *Christian Mission and Colonialism* (Shillong: Vendrame Institute, 1988), 134. (Hereafter cited as Dena, *Christian Mission and Colonialism*).

[452] Solo, *William Pettigrew*, 2-3. During those days hill areas were under the direct administration of British government of India.

[453] Cf. Singh, *History of Christian Missions*, 63.

of the minor Raja no missionary of any denomination intending to work in the state territory can be admitted into Manipur without the previous sanction of the chief commissioner of Assam.[454]

Pettigrew is silent as to what he did, where he went next after giving up his work in Imphal before landing in Ukhrul.[455] In January 1896, he decided to begin his work at Ukhrul.[456] By this time the Arthington Mission was no longer in a position to support his work in Manipur. Pettigrew contacted the American rather than the British Mission.[457] In December 1895 he was ordained and in January 1896 his appointment as American Baptist minister was confirmed.[458]

The first thing Pettigrew did was starting a school. In this Maxwell assisted him by forcing the Tangkhul chiefs to send their boys to the school. Despite the support of Maxwell, the political agent, the early years at Ukhrul were difficult ones. The progress was very slow and setbacks were frequent. In 1901 after five years of work, twelve of the boys attending the school confessed Christ and were baptized. In 1902, the first Baptist Church in Manipur was organized at Ukhrul, and until 1916 the only one.[459] By 1917 Pettigrew had three hundred thirty five church members and five churches.[460] The growing increase in local churches and the widening of the frontier of the missionary necessitated the formation of what was known as the Manipur Christian Association in November 1916, and its first convention was held at Ukhrul in 1917.[461] In 1928 MCA was changed to

---

[454] *Notification No. 806, dated 11th December 1894 addressed to Pettigrew by Political Agent of Manipur.*

[455] At least there are two traditions about Pettigrew's work during the sixteen months gap before starting the Ukhrul mission, among the Christians of Manipur. The southern tradition, according to this, he went to the Kuki village of Sevon and asked the chief Kamkholum Singson for permission to work in that place. When the permission was denied he went to the Tangkhul area and started his work. The northern tradition has it that Pettigrew went to Mao Songson village and tried to buy land but the sixteen Khulakpas refused to give permission, informing the missionary that they wanted nothing to do with religion and asked him to leave the place immediately. Then he went to the Tangkhul area. K. Hepuni, ed., *Manipur North Naga Baptist Association Church History* (Punanamai: MNNBA Golden Jubilee Publication, 1976), 3. Cf. also R. R. Lolly, *The Baptist Church in Manipur* (Imphal: Modern Printer, 1985), 22-23. (Hereafter cited as Lolly, *Baptist Church in Manipur*).

[456] Luikham, *Manipur Christian*, 13.

[457] The reason for him to contact American Mission was due to his view on baptism and possibly because it was working among the Nagas in Nagaland.

[458] Downs, *Mighty Works*, 78. The Assam Mission records indicate that the missionary union took over the Manipur field from the Arthington Mission on 1st February 1896.

[459] Cf. Downs, *Mighty Works*, 80.

[460] Cf. Milton Sangma, *American Baptist Mission in North East India* (Dibrugarh: NEIHA, 1981), 191. (Hereafter cited Sangma, *American BM*).

[461] Cf. Dena, *Christian Mission and Colonialism*, 38.

Manipur Baptist Convention. Today MBC has 29 Associations, 1471 Churches and 220190 baptized members.[462]

4.4. Welsh (Presbyterian) Mission

The Welsh Presbyterians (Welsh Calvinist Methodists) began their work in Cherrapunji in the year 1841.[463] Cherrapunji at that time was an isolated and thinly populated village inspite of being the British district headquarters. The first missionaries were Rev and Mrs. Thomas Jones I.[464] The first missionaries were strongly opposed by the local people – the Khasis. Inspite of all the oppositions the missionaries continued their works and as a result people began to show interest in the religion of the missionaries. Gradually people began to confess Christian faith and sought membership in the church. However, strict rules were employed by the missionaries such as:

1. They should completely disclaim all traditional religious practices and rituals,
2. They should faithfully observe Sunday (Sabbath), i.e., by attending Church and not doing any work,
3. They should have knowledge of the fundamental principles of Christianity,
4. They should live in a manner befitting the Gospel.[465]

The Mission center was shifted to Nogsawlia hill near Cherrapunji in 1843 as the village chief gave this place to the missionaries. It was from here that the missionaries could begin their serious mission and the first conversion took place on 8th March, 1846.[466] Inspite of severe opposition, the Welsh Mission gradually expanded their works even toward other hill areas. However, Christian community among the Khasis and Jaintias had a slow growth till 1880s though educational system was established in many places by 1866. By 1870 the school graduates also began taking up teaching positions. By 1891 there were 2147 communicants in the Khasi churches and by 1929 it increased to 15,885. Thus, by the end of the 19th century and early parts of the 20th century the Welsh Presbyterian Mission

[462] Cf. *Report of the General Secretary of Manipur Baptist Convention for the year 2018 Presented at the Annual Meeting of CBCNEI held at Diphu Town Baptist Church, Karbi Anglong from April 27-29, 2019*, 62.

[463] Cf. John H. Morris, *The History of the Welsh Calvinistic Methodists Foreign Mission: To the End of the Year 1904* (New Delhi: Indus Publishing Company 1996), 178. (Hereafter cited as Morris, *Welsh Calvinistic Methodists Foreign Mission*).

[464] Cf. Snaitang, *Christianity and Social Change*, 70.

[465] Snaitang, *Christianity and Social Change*, 71.

[466] Cf. Morris, *Welsh Calvinistic Methodists Foreign Mission*, 179.

had strongly established both church structure and educational systems among the Khasis and Jaintias.[467]

Presbyterian mission work among the Mizos began in the year 1897 with the arrival of D.E. Jones, a missionary accompanied by a Khasi who resigned from his job as school inspector in order to be a missionary to the Mizos. In 1899 the two Mizos by the names Khuma and Khara were converted and baptized as the first Christians in Mizoram. By 1929 the Mizo Christian community grew to more than 27,720. However, the rapid growth of Christianity in Mizoram is attributed to the revival movement which started in 1906 and intensified in 1913 and further intensified in 1919 and 1929.[468]

Today the Presbyterian Church of India (PCI) is one of the mainline Protestant Churches in India with over one million believers, mostly in North East India. PCI is an apex body comprising of eight Synods such as Mizoram Presbyterian Church Synod; Cachar Hill Tribes Synod; Manipur Presbyterian Church Synod; Biateram Presbyterian Church Synod; RiBhoi Presbyterian Church Synod; Khasi Jaintia Presbyterian Synod Sepngi (KJP Synod Sepngi); KJP Synod Mihngi; and Zou Presbyterian Church Synod. The PCI has its headquarters in Shillong. The PCI subscribes to the Westminster Confession of Faith and maintains relationship with denominations such as the Presbyterian Church in the United States of America, the Presbyterian Church of Korea, and the Uniting Church in Australia, the Christian Conference of Asia (CCA), and the Council for World Mission (CWM) through PCI. It is also supported by the Welsh parent Church. Locally, it has ties with the Council of Baptist Churches in North East India (CBCNEI) and the Church of North India (CNI).

Association and Affiliation of the PCI:

- National Council of Churches in India (NCCI): a member.
- World Council of Churches (WCC) - a member.
- World Alliance of Reformed Churches - a member.
- Maraland Presbyterian Church is an affiliated church under Mizoram Presbyterian Church.

4.5. The Anglican Church

The Anglicans did not have missionaries as such in the early parts in the NEI.[469] They did have few regular chaplains to look after the spiritual affairs of the European government official members of their denomination. The earliest Anglican Mission in North East India was in the person of a clergyman, Rev

[467] Downs, *History of Christianity*, 88-90, 95.

[468] Cf. Morris, *Welsh Calvinistic Methodists Foreign Mission*, 180.

[469] Cf. Mathew, Muttumana, *Christianity in Assam and Inter-Faith Dialogue: A Study on the Modern Religious Movements in North East India* (Indore: n.p., 1984), 124. (Hereafter cited as Muttumana, *Christianity in Assam*).

A. Grastin, Chaplain of Sylhet who visited the scattered Europeans, who were beginning to come to Assam valley in 1841.[470] The Anglican chaplains who were serving in the region were appointed by the Society for the Propagation of the Gospel (SPG), who were strongly influenced by Anglo-Catholicism.[471] In 1842, Calcutta Bishop, Wilson, appointed Rev Robert Bland as Chaplain of Assam. In 1844 he reached Assam, where he took charge at Guwahati.[472] He brought with him a young man by the name Roach from Dacca to serve as a clerk as at that time Assam was within the Diocese of Calcutta.[473] To revive the Mission he toured Assam extensively including Sibsagar, Dibrugarh, Jaipur and Goalpara. It was in his time that a new Anglican Church was built at Guwahati, called 'Christ Church.'[474]

Apart from the work of chaplains on the tea gardens, a British officer Capt. J.T. Gordon, an Anglican took over a small Anglican mission in around 1848 at Tezpur. Two German missionaries, C.H. Hesselmeyer and G. Dauble were assigned to this field to work among the Kacharis, with the promise of financial help from British officials.[475] To assist Hesselmeyer, a young deacon Sydney Endle, a missionary appointed by SPG arrived at Tezpur in 1864.[476] In 1865 he was entrusted to work and minister among the tea planters and also among the Kachari tribesmen. Later in 1869, Endle was appointed Chaplain of Darrang district with the charge of Kachari Mission.[477] By 1864 there were few converts of Kacharis but the mission was not successful as expected. However, by the end of the 19th century there were more than five hundred (500) Anglican members in Assam.[478] From the beginning, the Anglican Church in Assam was under the jurisdiction of Calcutta diocese but because of detachment Assam was raised to a Suffragan diocese in 1914. Finally, the Assam Diocese was created in 1915 and Rev Herbert Pankenham Walsh,[479] was consecrated as the first Anglican Bishop in

---

470 Cf. Talibuddin, *Anglican Church*, 33.

471 This led to a conflict with the American Baptist Missionaries. Each would try to take away members from churches of the other. This problem seems to have been most intense during the middle of the century and was largely due to the attitudes of the local chaplains rather than the Church of England itself.

472 Cf. Talibuddin, *Anglican Church*, 33.

473 Cf. Talibuddin, *Anglican Church*, 33.

474 Cf. Talibuddin, *Anglican Church*, 17.

475 Cf. Downs, *Christianity in NEI*, 112.

476 They were employed by Gordon for the purpose of evangelizing the people of Bhutan. But when they failed they turned to the Kacharis.

477 Cf. Muttumana, *Christianity in Assam*, 128.

478 Cf. Downs, *Christianity in NEI*, 89.

479 Cf. M.E. Gibbs, *The Anglican Church in India 1600-1970* (Delhi: ISPCK, 1972), 352.

NEI.[480] In 1946 Nirod Biswas was consecrated the first Indian Bishop of Anglican Church in the region.[481] And in 1970 the Assam Diocese of Anglican Church merged with other diocese of Anglican Indian Church with the Church of North India which inaugurated on 29th November 1970, and thus Anglican Church ceased to exist in India as a separate body. Consequently, the Diocese of Assam became one of the Dioceses of the Church of North India.[482]

4.6. Lutheran Church

The Gossner Lutheran Mission began its evangelical activities in Chotanagpur much earlier than 1845.[483] When the missionaries came to Chotanagpur, there was a crisis between them and the local people. Thereupon thousands left Chotanagpur to work in other parts of India. Many migrated to Assam to work in tea gardens for their livelihood. Among those who immigrated were Lutheran Christians.[484] Thus, the Lutheran Mission began in Assam through these tribal emigrants. They started a small Lutheran mission in Assam particularly in the tea garden. Slowly a Church was built and a native pastor was ordained in 1900. With the request of the local people on July 10, 1919 the Gossner Evangelical Lutheran Church at Chotanagpur and Assam was established.[485] The main station of the Lutheran Church in Assam was in Tezpur, where the church members were mainly tea-garden workers and emigrants but was an active church.

The second batch of the Lutheran Mission to work in NEI was the Northern Evangelical Lutheran Church. In reality, they were Santhals, who came to Assam as tribal emigrants from Bihar in search of jobs. They embraced Lutheranism through the work of L.O. Skrefsrud and H.P. Boerresen, who worked under the Gossner Mission. As such Lutheranism flourished in various parts of Assam and also in the neighboring areas, particularly in the areas of Boros and Garos. The first three Santhal converts were Siram, Jogot and Rahgu, who took baptism in 1869.[486] Now there are 46,303 Lutheran members with 344 communities and around 60 pastors who are working in various Lutheran mission stations in NEI. In Assam alone now they have 14 parishes and two mission fields and 7500

[480] Cf. Talibuddin, *Anglican Church*, 129. During those days there was a very small clerical (clergy) staff in Assam, consisting of three Europeans - one Government Chaplain, one Additional Clergy Society Chaplain and one Chaplain Missionary and four Indians, three priests and one Deacon.

[481] Cf. Talibuddin, *Anglican Church*, 157.

[482] Cf. Talibuddin, *Anglican Church*, 209-211.

[483] Cf. Robert Reid, *Years of Change in Bengal and Assam* (London: 1966), 135.

[484] C. Becker, *History of the Catholic Missions in North East India: 1890-1915* (Shillong: Kerma KLM Pvt. Ltd., 1980), 49. (Hereafter cited as Becker, *Catholic Mission*).

[485] Cf. Becker, *Catholic Mission*, 79.

[486] Cf. Becker, *Catholic Mission*, 138.

families in Assam. Lutheran churches have spread to almost all the parts of NEI today.

5. Other Denominations

Today Christian denominationalism is a reality and its influence cannot be measured in the history of Christianity. NEI is not different from any other regions concerning the spread of denominations. Now we have many denominations apart from those discussed above. Some of them are, General Conference Baptist Mission; Australian Baptist Mission; Baptist Mid-Mission; Salvation Army; Church of God; Jehovah Witness Church; Unitarian Church; Assemblies of God; United Pentecostal Church; Seventh Day Adventists; the Pentecostal;[487] Mara Evangelical Church; Christian Revival Church; The Salvation Army;[488] The Revival Church of God; The Independent Church of India; The Evangelical Free Church of India[489] and so on. Due to these many denominations the Christian community in NEI faces tension among themselves. Some of these churches are known for their tendency to seek converts from among existing Christian groups rather than from among non-Christians.

6. Impact of Christianity on the North East Indian Society

The absence of a single language created the spirit of disunity among the North East Indian tribes and communities. It was hard for any outsider to come into contact with the region. However, with the coming of British Administration the Gospel also entered into the region. The encounter between the Gospel and the People of North East India has brought tremendous changes especially among the hills people - both positive and negative - where it was not sanskritized. The following are some of the major impact of Christianity upon the people of NEI:

6.1. Positive Transformations

6.1.1. *Religious Life of the People*

Although, the traditional religion of the tribals is basically characterized by belief in the existence of the High God or the Supreme Being, it is also constituted of observances of different kinds of gennas and taboos in order to appease the spirits so that they attain good life in this world. The function of the rites and

[487] Downs, *Christianity in NEI*, 151.

[488] Salvation Army found its foothold first in Silchar and Mizoram in between 1945-1950. At present the Headquarters is situated at Lamka in Manipur. Cf. also L. Jeyaseelan, *Impact of the Missionary Movement in Manipur* (New Delhi: Scholar Publishing House, 1996), 103-121. (Hereafter cited as Jeyaseelan, *Missionary Movement in Manipur*).

[489] Their head quarters is established at Shillong. They have twelve districts in NEI. They are: (1) Sailkot, (2) Imphal, (3) Thanlon, (4) Senvon, (5) Vangai, (6) Cachar District, (7) North Cachar Hills, (8) Kholian - Mizoram, (9) Sakordai- Mizoram, (10) Lunglei- Mizoram, (11) Darchoi - Tripura and (12) Kanlachera - Tripura.

taboos observance was to temporarily liberate people from the harmful activities of malevolent spirits. But, the acceptance of the gospel of Christ liberated them from all such fears, sacrifices to the spirits, practice of divination and omen. Thus, today almost all the ancestor religious rituals and practices have disappeared among many tribes of NEI. They found the scope for peace and eternal life in the new faith. Many became Christians initially because they were convinced that the new religion was more effective than the old religions in securing this objective. Many look upon the Sunday (no work day), in much the same way they observed the old taboo days when it was inauspicious to leave the village or carry on normal work; other substitute the Bible for the traditional charms carried to ward off evil spirits when traveling. Thus, Christianity liberated the people from a world view in which they were socially and psychologically enslaved by fear of spirits. Belief in the spirits continues, but it is no longer, the dominant element. Christ's power is seen to be greater than that of the spirits.

6.1.2. *Building of Tribal Identity*

The hill areas of North East India were uniformly administered until 1937 as backward tract exclusively under the chief commissioner of Assam. From 1st April 1937 there was a bifurcation of the administrative pattern. The Mizo Hills, Naga Hills, North Cachar Hills and N.E. Frontier Tracts were called Excluded Areas and were guarded by the 'Inner Line' which prevented the entry of outsiders without permit. The North Eastern Hill States as a result developed a special kind of identity, which remained crucial for subsequent political development. The hilly areas of NEI were not completely integrated with the politico-ecosystem of colonial period and the Inner Line system still in operation further isolated the tribal regions of North East from the rest of the country.[490]

Christianity has emerged as a strong factor of modernisation, and has given the tribes a sense of identity. The phenomenal rise of Christianity in all North Eastern states excluding Arunachal Pradesh became a symbol of tribal identity. With this the extension of British raj in the region with the formation of different administrative units helped in developing a sense of identity and alliances among different tribes.[491] In developing a sense of larger tribal identity, demand for representation of tribal population in Provincial Legislative Assembly started in the 1930s. A growing sense of ethnic identity among different communities in the North East and the fear of losing identity – all these factors combined together contributed to the growth of ethno-political movements in NEI. Indeed the tribal movement in the NEI is an aspiration and a manifestation of fight for identity. The rising tribal aspirations are expressed through movement on cultural identity crisis - the basis of this crisis is economic resources. Thus "identity crisis is an

[490] Cf. B. Datta Ray, *Tribal Identity and Tension in North East India* (New Delhi: Omsons Publications, 1989), 5. (Hereafter cited as Ray, *Tribal Identity*).

[491] Ray, *Tribal Identity*, 6-7.

urban phenomenon rooted among the rising petty bourgeoisie and middle class with definite class solidarity all over North East India."[492] Hence, Christianity provided an ideology that helped the tribal people maintain their identity in the face of serious erosion of their traditional religious, social and political institutions.

6.1.3. *New Social Order for the North Easterners*

Christianity brought great transformation in the socio-cultural life of the North East Indian society. In the ancient days they had no separate places for cattle, pigs, and fowls; all lived together in the same house or under the same roof. But, today the condition is entirely different in the region. Today in the village they have arrangement for separate stables, poultry and pens and houses are equipped with modern fillings, bathrooms, lavatories - the style or mode of living has changed to a great extent.[493] Festivals and feasts were marked with drinking rice beer, singing and dancing, but today all the festivals are replaced by Christian colors especially in the hills society. The olden educational systems, which were done in the dormitories among the hill tribes of this region, are replaced by western educational system, which was brought by Christianity.

Christianity brought the tribal wars and headhunting to their end through the Christian emphasis on love for neighbor and enemy alike, and promoted new social order. The headhunting energy and enthusiasm had been diverted towards the furtherance of the Gospel in the unreached areas by the young.[494] Villages of the same tribe that had previously been at war with each other were brought together in Presbyteries and Associations. Thus evangelism and Church structures fostered a sense of tribal and regional identity which was absent earlier. As such, the impact of Christianity on the socio-cultural life of the society transformed and directed their lives towards modern civilization.

6.1.4. *Birth of Literature for the People*

Education and Christianity came to be closely identified in North East India. Education has been one of the most powerful agencies for bringing transformation in the life of the people of NEI. The schools were not only the primary agents of evangelism but also of the new order. The education imparted by the Christians lifted the people from ignorance, illiteracy, raw lifestyles and superstitions. Education prepared them for new occupations. It gave them greater mobility and it encouraged a great deal of interaction with people not only of their own tribes.[495] Thus, education brought by Christianity

---

492 Ray, *Tribal Identity*, 9.

493 Cf. F. S. Downs, *Essay on Christianity in North East India* (New Delhi: Indus Publishing, 1994), 203. (Hereafter cited as Downs, *Essay*).

494 Cf. Sir James Johnstone, *My Experience in Manipur and the Naga Hills* (London: 1896), 29.

495 Cf. M. Horam, *North East India a Profile* (New Delhi: Cosmo Publications, 1990), 174-180.

transformed the minds and improved their way of living in and outside the community.

Moreover, the impact of Christian influence through its literacy and literature program is remarkable. In Assam, Christians were acknowledged for bringing the Assamese language renaissance by stopping the government's effort to introduce Bengali as official language. In the hill areas the impact was seen as a great one because the missions gave the various tribes their first literature. Since Christianity without the Bible was unthinkable to the Protestants, the missionaries when they entered into a new field reduced the language to writing. No hill tribe at that time had a written language. The Christian literature contributed to the developing sense of tribal identity. In providing written language, Christianity prepared the tribals to adjust to the new social, economic and political situation, in which they found themselves.

6.2. Negative Impacts

6.2.1. *Western Culture to the Erosion of Native Culture*

There is no doubt that Christianity brought great changes in the socio-cultural life of the people of this region. Foremost among those changes (and there are many indeed) would include the better living conditions of the people – hygienic or sanitized way of life, which the people of the past were not accustomed to especially in relation to the animal husbandry within close perimeter of the homes.[496] While Christianity has contributed so much toward the conscientization and development of the people, we cannot also at the same time romanticize the whole issue. Anyone with a constructively-critical mind (be it foreign or native), would be able to realize that it also has its fair share of negative impact upon the people.

Western Christianity regarded its own culture as the only valid expression of Christian culture. They considered everything non-Christian as the product of depraved human being under the control of Satan.[497] With such concept Christianity came to the people of NEI. Without indepth knowledge of the people and their culture, they condemned them as un-Christian. As a result, almost all the cultural elements of the natives (without distinguishing between good and bad or between life-affirming ones and the destructive ones), were made to be discarded and thus left to erode with the passage of time.

In the midst of diversity of the people the western style of Christianity was introduced and thus, created more difficulty for the people to come together in terms of their religious respect for each other. Therefore, Christianity contributed to the erosion of the native cultures by replacing it with the western culture,

[496] Cf. Downs, *Essay*, 203.

[497] Cf. J. T. Seamands, *Tell It Well: Communicating Gospel Across Cultures* (Missouri: Beacon Hill Press of Kansas City, 1981), 42.

which imbalances the true nature of the gospel and slows down the progress of the gospel.

6.2.2. *Christian Message of Personal Salvation Detrimental to the Communitarian Values of Old*

Christianity preached Personal salvation or salvation of personal soul while that is also very much a part of the Gospel's message, gave way to self-centered or individualistic concept and way of life for the natives. The old community-centered understanding and pattern of life gradually began to lose its hold in the minds and actions of the people. Besides, Christianity's emphasis on the 'other-worldly' aspect of salvation also gave rise to the people's insensitivity towards social concerns and justice of the people. The spread of Christianity among the people of NEI was accompanied by unhealthy individualism that is insensitive to social concerns and justice of the people as a community. Thus, Udayan Misra writes:

> Christianity and Western education brought in new values based on individualism which posed a direct challenge to the collective life-pattern of the people.[498]

So, their mind of socialism was replaced by individualism and started working for their own benefits. The good culture of community sharing of meals, meat, vegetables and their things had almost vanished. Therefore the introduction of individualism by western Christianity has affected the very life of the people and their culture. Selfishness, greed, dishonesty and corruption are rampant among the NEI society today. Christianity had failed to impart fully the Christian values among the communities in North East India. Such failure was exposed especially during the ethnic clashes between Nagas and Kukis, Garos and Rabhas, Assamese and hill tribals, Bodos and Muslims etc. All of these had revealed the extent to which Christian values have played the role negatively. Therefore, Christianity has not always been able to preserve Christian values such as love, honesty, simplicity, justice, democratic procedures, dignity of human life and so on.[499] Indeed nowhere else in India has the encounter between society and Christianity so deeply transformed and affected the people as in the society of North East India, in many areas of their lives, such as religious life, philosophy of life, marriage, family, education, economic life, political structures, status of women, and socio-cultural life.[500]

---

[498] Cf. Udayan Misra, "Naga Nationalism and the Role of the Middle Class," in B. Dutta Ray, ed., *The Emergence and Role of Middle Class in North East India* (New Delhi: Uppal, 1983), 154.

[499] S. Karotemprel, "The Impact of Christianity on the Tribes of North East India," in J. Puthenpurakal, ed., *Impact of Christianity on North East India* (Shillong: Vendrame Institute Publication, 1996), 43. (Hereafter cited as Karotemprel, *Impact of Christianity*).

[500] Cf. Karotemprel, *Impact of Christianity*, 48.

Western values based on the western worldview came to be identified as Christian values that people find it difficult to differentiate between the two. The Christianity that the tribals were exposed to, was a very divided one; divided on historical, denominational, doctrinal, catechetical and ethical basis.[501] It is a fact that historical rivalries that were prevalent in western countries were transferred to the tribal society. Due to such crisis the life and mission of the Church have slowed progress and development. Therefore, Christianity failed to eradicate division and rivalries in their presentation of the gospel wherever they went.

6.2.3. *Human-Centered View of Reality replaces Creation-Centered Worldview of the Tribal Religion*

A good number of historians, both native and foreign, often delight in recounting how the tribals in their traditional faiths lived in great fear of the powers of nature and of innumerable superstitions attached to it. While they are not wrong in holding the view that the tribals' religious life includes sacrifices to the spirits, practice of divination and omen, they fail to adequately recognize the underlying concept of people being one with the world of nature or of creation. Thus, today almost all the ancestral religious rituals and practices have disappeared among the NEI tribes as this new faith in Christ impelled them to 'a complete turning away from the old and a complete immersion in the new.'[502] Christianity came with the message of condemning the old tribal religion as satanic. Hence, it is no wonder, that some of the village authorities in the traditional world considered that the evangelists come to their villages/land to abolish the traditions of the ancestors.

6.3. Western Education Triumphs over Native Form of Learning

While Western education introduced by Christianity served as a powerful force in transforming the life of tribals, we also need to critically reflect upon the western form of education and the mentality that accompanied it. It took it for granted that western form of education is the only one or the only true and universal form of education that the uncivilized world such as that of the tribals need. It thus belittled and condemned the traditional pattern of education. In the past, the tribals maintained community-structured pattern of education especially through the Morung/dormitory system – through which young men and women receive holistic education needed for their lifetime. Thus, the western form of education does not truly connect with the life situations, aspirations, experiences and needs of the people.

---

[501] Karotemprel, *Impact of Christianity*, 43.

[502] A. D. Nock, *Conversion* (London: Oxford University Press, 1961), 114.

6.4. Western Christianity Reinforces the Subjugation of Women in Tribal Society

The tribal society from early times is patriarchal and the family inheritance follows the male line, hence no female has any right to claim property. All the tribes have a concept of difference between men and women in their social status. Among the Nagas if a girl is born the name is given on the fifth day, if it is a boy on the sixth day to show that man is superior to woman.[503] Traditional culture and its customs have several restrictions (taboos) related to women. As such, any men are held above women in almost every aspect of life in the community.

Education was one of the serious social concerns of the early missionaries among the tribals. It served as an opening toward the upliftment of the tribal community for better standard of life. When education was introduced among the tribals through the agency of western Christianity, the initial privilege was taken by the boys. However, in the course of time, Christian missionaries and evangelists encouraged the people to send both the boys and girls for learning and education. In that sense, education along with other social transformations brought by Christianity helped the community to a very great extent.

Having said that, when it comes to issue of the status of women in the tribal society Christianity also plays an important role in it. While Christianity preached the message of salvation, forgiveness and equality of all – men, women and children before God – it also endorsed the concept of the superiority of men over women. Christianity, being western in everything, missionaries coming from their own western socio-cultural set up where male domination is so potent, when they came to the world of the tribals they could not really remain true to the teaching of the Scriptures but were influenced and driven by their own male-centered worldview. The Bible as a whole was read and interpreted from the lens of men and thus they re-enforced male-domination with its support. As such even today, women in the tribal community (in both Church and society), they are not treated equally with men. Tribal communities still have a long way to go to reach a state where their women can truly be called liberated and accepted on equal terms with men. The Church in particular is still much steep in its male-oriented view of life; its total structure is defined by male-domination.

For those writers (the natives in particular) who write that tribal women are treated equally or that there is no discrimination on its women are nothing short of (intentional or not), ignoring the reality and living in a make-believe world. Unless, everyone wake up and honestly deal with the reality, the whole of the society will have a difficult time in progressing toward any real advancement mainly because it is not at all possible for any sane human community to do so when the half section of the society is subjugated.

---

[503] Lolly, *Baptist Church in Manipur*, 77.

Chapter 11

Issues of Pentecostalism in India

1. Introduction

The development of Pentecostalism in the modern and post-modern era has been phenomenal and it has seriously affected almost all the traditional churches in the world. The origin of this movement has been ascribed to Azusa Street Revival[504] by many as it is generally believed to have been responsible in giving birth to the Global Pentecostalism.[505] This revival that began in April 9, 1906 continued for few years which ignited the wildfire of Pentecostalism and that it

---

[504] The Azusa Street Revival began in April 9, 1906 when a group of black domestic servants and washerwomen who have assembled for a prayer meeting at 214 North Bonnie Brae Avenue in Los Angeles experienced "Pentecost" along with their leader William Joseph Seymour, a black holiness preacher who had been preaching about a new Pentecost. The Azusa Street Revival did play a decisive role not only toward the emergence of the Pentecostal movement but also played a key role in making it a worldwide movement. However, many suggest that the origin of modern Pentecostalism sprang out at the very beginning of the 20th century as an offshoot of Holiness Movement in the latter half of the 19th century that stems down from Wesleys' teachings on Christian perfection in the 18th century. See also, Melvin E. Dieter, "Wesleyn-Holiness Aspects of Pentecostal Origins: As Mediated through the Nineteenth-Century Holiness Revival," *Aspects of Pentecostal Charismatic Origins*, ed. by Vinson Synan (New Jersey: Logos International, 1975), 50-60.

[505] Cf. W. F. Carothers, *The Baptism with the Holy Ghost and the Speaking in Tongues* (Illinois: Carothers, 1907), 21-22. There are some Pentecostal historians who opined that Pentecostalism had its beginning in the Topeka Revival in 1901 under the leadership of Charles Parham. Cf. Steve Durasoff, *Bright Wind of the Spirit: Pentecostalism Today* (New Jersey: Logos International, 1972), 15-17.

spread throughout the globe within a decade and today grew out to be one of the largest and fastest growing denominations in the world.[506] While acknowledging that traditional or conventional understanding of the origin and development of Pentecostalism at the global scale, coming to the history of Indian Pentecostalism, we shall briefly study the subject from a postcolonial perspective.

2. What is Pentecostalism?

Pentecostalism is a movement; it is a trend within Christianity of a growing group that shares characteristic beliefs and goals that inspired them to be more pious in nature in their faith. The phenomenon of Pentecostalism is 'speaking in tongues' or ***Glossolalia.*** This tongues speaking is an ecstatic experience, one in which the cognitive grids and perceptual barriers that normally prevent people from opening themselves to deeper insights and exultant feelings, are temporarily suspended.[507] In the early days of Pentecostalism, speaking in tongues is believed to be a miracle as they spoke in the previously unknown and unlearned language, though now it is generally held to be prayer of the heart that goes beyond mere words, or that it is a spiritual language known only to God.[508] The emphases of Pentecostalism include the infilling of the Holy Spirit, speaking unknown tongues, followed by vision, faith healing, dream and dancing in the spirit, slaying in the spirit, weeping for joy, healing and testimonies, and joyous bodily movements etc. In this movements the new religious space, provided by the Pentecostalism, that is music which is more contemporary and appealing; the sermons have taken a new style of presentation and they were more narrative in form instead of long intellectual discourse; and the testimony hour provided to the individuals and giving them opportunity to tell and retell his or her story, allows the person to experience more intimate relationship with their God. They consider that the prayers for healing are more fervent and the so-called miracles are prevalent and that allow them to open their hearts to God.[509] Such concepts and movements have enabled many people to draw closer towards Pentecostalism today.

The emphasis on speaking in tongues is another characteristic of Pentecostalism. The services are done with ecstatic religious expressions. Every service had songs, testimonies spoken or read, prayers in sobs or tears, joyous shouts, prayer for the sick and speaking in tongues, altar call for salvation and sanctification. When someone gets the anointing, they would stand and preach in loud voices. Slaying in the spirit or falling under the power of the Holy Spirit is common. There are periods of extended silence and singing in tongues. Sharing of

---

[506] Harvey Cox, *Fire from Heaven: The Rise of Pentecostal Spiritually and the Reshaping of Religion in the Twenty-first Century* (Massachusetts: Addison-Wesley Publishing Company, 1995), 82. (Hereafter cited as Cox, *The Rise of Pentecostal Spirituality*).

[507] Cf. Cox, *The Rise of Pentecostal Spirituality*, 86.

[508] Cf. Cox, *The Rise of Pentecostal Spirituality*, 87.

[509] Cf. Cox, *The Rise of Pentecostal Spirituality*, 107.

testimonies about visions or dreams or unusual circumstances that brought them to the revival meetings is also very common.

3. The Origin of Pentecostal Movements in India

The origin of Pentecostalism in India is not without controversy especially in relation to the diverse views concerning it. Of the different views there are mainly three that stand out and which call for our attention here.

3.1. Eurocentric View

This is one of the most traditional views in understanding the origin of Indian Pentecostalism. It strongly holds that Indian Pentecostalism is the direct result of North American Pentecostalism.[510] This view proclaims that Pentecostal movement entered and began to spread in India through its missionaries with the Azusa Street experience namely Alfred and Lillian Garr, who came to Calcutta in the early part of the 1907 as independent pioneers, next, George E. Berg, another American missionary of German origin came to South India in 1908.[511] In 1913, another American missionary Robert F. Cook came to India with his family – wife and two daughters.[512] Beside these missionaries, there were several others whose coming had been credited as the foundation for the Indian Pentecostalism which gave way to serious historical debate from a postcolonial perspective from the native/Indian scholars and historians.

One of the main reasons for claiming that Indian Pentecostalism is the outcome of western Pentecostalism could be due to the western missionaries' own propagation or self-claims. Their mission reports were filled with news of their spirit-filled ministries among the natives whereby the native Indians for the first time experienced the outpouring of the Spirit of God. Hence, many westerners as well as uncritical Indians believed and claimed that Calcutta revival under the Garrs was the birthplace of Indian Pentecostalism. However, as mentioned, we now have several critical historians and writers who argue against such sweeping claims, like Paulson Pulikottil, who went on to prove that the history of Indian Pentecostalism began much earlier than the Eurocentric one in Kerala, South India.[513] We shall be looking at the Pentecostal beginnings that took place in Kerala a little while later hence it should suffice for us to say here that the Eurocentric

---

[510] Cf. Frank Bartleman, *Azusa Street* (New Jersey: Bridge Publishing, 1980), 19.

[511] Cf. A. C. George, "Pentecostal Beginnings in India," *DD* (2002), 41-43; A. C. George, "Pentecostal Beginnings in Travancore, South India," *AJPS*, 5/1 (2002), 24-26. (Hereafter cited as George, *Pentecostal Beginnings in Travancore*).

[512] While some date the Cooks' coming at 1913, others date it at 1912. Cf. George, *Pentecostal Beginnings in Travancore*. Cf. also Mammen Philip, *Robert F. Cook* (Vennikulam: Deepam Book Club, 1992), 30; Paulson Pulikottil, "Emergence of Indian Pentecostalism," *DD* (2002), 51.

[513] Cf. Paulson Pulikottil, "As East and West Met in God's Own Country: Encounter of Western Pentecostalism with Native Pentecostalism in Kerala, "*AJPS* 5/1 (2002).

view seriously comes under the critical scrutiny of postcolonial historiography of Pentecostalism in India and is now invalid as far as it being the womb of Indian Pentecostalism.

3.2. Native View based on Mukti Mission Revival

The second view can be named as the 'Native View,' which builds upon the history of revival at Pandita Ramabai Saraswati's Mukti Mission in Kedgaon, near Poona between 1905 and 1907. This view holds that Indian Pentecostalism had its beginning from within and not through the influence that came from outside. That being said, there are nevertheless some such as those classical Pentecostals in India who were not willing to accept the Mukti revival as part of the Pentecostal movement in the past or until recent times. Their argument was that Mukti revival could not contribute much to the Pentecostal movement in India. It is observed that Mukti Mission and its revival were pushed out from the Pentecostal movement in India mainly with the purpose of clubbing it within the main Evangelical Awakening in the beginning of the 20th century.[514] However, recently Mukti Revival came to the forefront of Indian Pentecostalism as they celebrated the Centenary of the Pentecostal Movement in India from 6-11 December 2005 wherein Mukti revival is recognized as the genesis of Pentecostalism in India. Till then, Mukti Revival was not given its due credit in the origin of Pentecostalism in India even though there is proof that it preceded the Azusa Street Revival. Thus today, with the presence of strong historical evidence, the western claim of being the cause for Indian Pentecostalism does not have any validity.

3.3. 'Pentecostal-Like Movements' View

The third view is that Pentecostalism in India began even much earlier than and after the Mukti revival through the 'Pentecostal-Like Movements.' The NIDPCM strongly affirms that these Pentecostal-like movements in India preceded North American and European Pentecostalism by not less than 40 years. For instance, the awakening of Tirunelvelli, Tamil Nadu in South India in 1860 and the Khasi Hills revival in the Northeastern region of India in 1905. It is crucial for us to take note of the tag 'Pentecostal-Like Movements' given by NIDPCM to these Indian or native revivals or why the western historians begrudge the full title of Pentecostalism to these revivals in India. Some of the westerners would argue that these Indian revivals were not revivals in the true sense of the term as they do not measure up to the western idea and definition of revival. For them (westerners), glassolalia (speaking in tongues) serve as the basic characteristic or component of Pentecostal revivalism and therefore since this aspect was seen lacking in these

[514] Cf. Michael Bergunder, "Constructing Indian Pentecostalism: On Issues or Methodology and Representation," *Asian and Pentecostal: The Charismatic Face of Christianity in Asia*, Allan Anderson and Edmond Tang, eds, (Oxford: Regnum, 2005), 187. (Hereafter cited as Bergunder, *Indian Pentecostalism*).

early Indian Pentecostalism, they categorized it as insignificant to be counted as true Pentecostalism.

It is said that the Garrs came to India with the conviction that they have this gift of tongues. Alfred Garr believed that he had been gifted with Bengali language when he was spirit-baptized through the impact of Azusa revival in Los Angeles, California, while his wife Lillian Garr with the Tibetan and Mandarin languages.[515] However, their claims later proved trouble for them when for instance Alfred Garr could not preach in Bengali that they had to abandon the use of tongues as a missionary tool though they retained them as the indispensable sign of Spirit-baptism. In this issue they came into conflict with some earlier missionaries like Minnie F. Abrams, who worked with Mukti Mission. Abrams argued against the concept that tongues is absolutely indispensable for Spirit-baptism.[516] As such, Classical Pentecostalism's stance on the necessity of tongues came under serious debate. Nevertheless, researches eventually brought out that early Pentecostals realized their error in this issue and thus led to the reformation of their theology on tongues.[517] Hence, it was due to the absence of tongue theology in indigenous Indian revivals, the western Pentecostal advocates refused to recognize Indian Pentecostalism as a full-fledged one and named it only as 'Pentecostal-Like Movements' – a blatant reflection of imperialistic western missionary attitude.

4. The Indigenous Revival Movements in India

The rise and development of the Pentecostal Movement in India is one of the major issues that captured the attention of a number of researchers of Indian Church History especially the Pentecostal historians today. India plays an important role in the worldwide revival that took place in the first decade of 20th century. There were records of number of indigenous revivals with Pentecostal characteristics in several parts of the country before western Pentecostalism had reached India.

4.1. In South India

The first indigenous revival occurred in Tirunelvelli in the Madras Province, Tamil Nadu in 1860-61 under the leadership of John Christian Aroolappan. Aroolappan was a native Anglican catechist who was trained under the pietistic missionaries and yet his indigenous revival ministry developed without any significant help

[515] Cf. Gary B. McGee, "'Latter Rain' Falling in the East: Early Twentieth-Century Pentecostalism in India and the Debate over Speaking in Tongues," *Church History: Studies in Christianity and Culture*, 68/3 (Sept 1999), 658-65.

[516] Cf. Stanley M. Burgess, "Pentecostalism in India: An Overview," *AJPS*, 4/1 (2001), 96. (Hereafter cited as Burgess, *Pentecostalism in India*).

[517] Cf. Allan H. Anderson, "Signs and Blunders: Pentecostal Mission Issues at 'Home and Abroad' in the Twentieth Century," *JAM*, no. 2 (2000), 193-210. Cf. also Gary B. McGee, "The Calcutta Revival of 1907 and the Reformulation of Charles Parharm's Bible Evidence Doctrine," *AJPS*, 5/1 (2002), 123-43.

from the missionaries.[518] His revival outreach impacted many men and women that they came to Christianity in large number. Believers began to have charismatic gifts and characteristics such as prophecy, glassolalia, interpretation of tongues, prayer for the healing of the sick, Spirit-filled convulsions and restoration of apostolic and prophetic offices. With all these present, the power of revival touched and influenced many lives.

Former Brahmin by the name Justus Joseph, a convert of Aroolappan, was also very instrumental in the spread of indigenous revival. He founded the Revival Church in 1875 with indigenous elements though he negated caste among his congregation. This Revival Church progressively entered into the twentieth century though it received heavy criticisms and discredition from the conventional missionary groups for some of its questionable practices such as its controversial prophecies.[519] Nevertheless, it serves as historically-significant part of the strong indigenous revival movements that swept India in the latter part of the 19th century before the arrival of western Pentecostalism to India.

The second indigenous revival movement in India occurred in Travancore between 1874 and 1875. In fact it is said that there were three indigenous revivals in Kerala before the coming of western Pentecostal missionaries, in the year 1873, 1895 and 1908. In these revivals, people experienced the outpouring of the Spirit through the Spirit-baptism and the subsequent gifts of the Spirit. Here again John Christian Aroolappan was instrumental in bringing revival into Travancore area. He visited Travancore as early as 1853 and 1859, conducting revival meetings that gradually attracted great number of people.[520] The amazing impact of these meetings came to be felt during the early 1860s to the 1870s especially in Mavelikkara and Tiruvalla. Once again Justus Joseph (the Brahmin convert of Aroolappan), also appears in Kerala as a powerful revivalist along with his brothers in spreading this great awakening in the Churches in Kaneeti, Thevalakkara, Njakkannal, Krishnapuram, Puthuppally, Mankuzhi, Kattanam and Cheppad.[521] However, it is said that Justus Joseph was later on excommunicated and his license cancelled because of his unbiblical teachings and practices, which resulted in the revival movement dying down.

It was through the great work of Lakshmana Rao, a great revivalist from Marthomite Church that revival flame was rekindled. It was during this time that

---

518 Burgess, *Pentecostalism in India*, 87.

519 Cf. Burgess, *Pentecostalism in India*, 87.

520 Cf. C. M. Agur, *Church History of Travancore* (New Delhi: Asian Education Service, 1990), 918, 919, cited in Ipe Kochupallikunnel, *Pentecostal Churches in Kerala and Indigenous Leadership* (Delhi: ISPCK, 2011), 8. (Hereafter cited as Agur, *Church History of Travancore*; and, Kochupallikunnel, *Pentecostal Churches in Kerala*).

521 Agur, *Church History of Travancore*, 1013, cited in Kochupallikunnel, *Pentecostal Churches in Kerala*, 9. Cf. also K. K. *Kuruvilla, Keralathile Almiya Unarve* (Malayalam) [Spiritual Revival in Kerala] (Tiruvalla: Malayalam Christian Literature Committee, 1942), 34, as cited in Kochupallikunnel, *Pentecostal Churches in Kerala*, 9.

the second wave of revival began in Kerala and once again from Tamil Nadu. Two prominent personalities were V.D. David, also known as Tamil David and L.M. Wordsworth from Ceylon around 1894-95. It was through their preaching in revival meetings that thousands of people were converted within a short span of time. It was through their encouragement that the popular Maramon Convention was started in 1895 and David is said to have preached to a gathering of about 25,000 people in that convention whereby large number of people were attracted unlike any other time under the missionaries.[522] The third wave of revival in Kerala occurred in the beginning of the 20th century. This was considered to be the greatest evangelical awakening that had a nation-wide impact. After being informed about the revival in Wales through the missionaries, a great number of hearers in Trivandrum, Cochin, Kottayam and Kunnamkulam fervently prayed for the same kind of outpouring of the Spirit upon India and the world in general. Thus, when in 1905 the great revival broke out, there were a huge number of natives participating and experiencing the movement and indwelling of the Spirit upon them. It was through the impact of this third wave of revival in Kerala that K.E. Abraham, the founder of Indian Pentecostal Church of God, experienced the baptism of the Spirit in 1914 and began his ministry.

4.2. In North India

In the North, the Sailkot, Punjab revival in 1904 is worth noting. John Hyde, an American missionary is said to be instrumental in this revival movement. Sailkot convention that was held every year had records of great revival phenomenon wherein a great number of people receive Spirit-baptisms and several other Spirit-filled gifts.[523] Another place where an equally great revival occurred was in Dholka, Gujarat. It took place at an orphanage for boys in 1905.

4.3. In Central Part of India

In central India, Mukti revival is considered the most exceptional of all indigenous revivals in India. It occurred in 1905 at Pandita Ramabai Saraswati's Mukti Mission – a mission that cared for the orphans and widows – in Kedgaon, Maharashtra. It was here that cast out and homeless women (mainly child widows) and children experienced the amazing outpourings of the Holy Spirit. It all took place under the powerful leadership of Ramabai herself in 1905. More than five hundred women met daily for prayer and they continued to experience the rich revivalism – baptism of the Holy Spirit or Fire, slaying in the Spirit, and by 1906 there were records of the gift of Tongues etc.[524] it is said that not only the inmates but

[522] Cf. Edwin Orr, *Evangelical Awakenings in India in the Early Twentieth Century* (New Delhi: Masihi Sahitya Sanstha, 1970), 96.

[523] Cf. Basil Miller, *Praying Hyde: The Story of John Hyde: A Man of Prayer* (Belfast, Northern Ireland: Ambassador, 2000), 75.

[524] Cf. Burgess, *Pentecostalism in India*, 88.

also those missionaries serving at Mukti experienced the Spirit-baptism such as Minnie Abrams who was from Methodist Episcopal Church and Albert Norton from Methodist but later on became independent. Thus, Mukti Mission under Ramabai became a great force in the history of Indian Pentecostalism in modern times.

4.4. In North East India

Another great indigenous revival that broke out in India was that of the tribal communities in the Khasi Hills in North East India in the year 1905 under the Welsh Presbyterian mission. According to O.L. Snaitang, a well-known Church historian from Meghalaya, North East India, although there had been long awaited hope of spiritual awakening among the native Christians, the Khasi revival has a link with the Welsh revival in 1904.[525] It was during the presbytery meeting at Pariong in the west Khasi Hills in 1905 that people had their first experience of revival. Subsequently from there it spread to Mizoram and Korea the following year. Another place where revival wave touched upon, near the North Eastern region, is Calcutta in the year 1907. It occurred with the coming of the Garrs as mentioned earlier. It is said that of all the revivals in India, this is the only one that can be directly connected to the Azusa Street revival since the Garrs were the products of it.

5. A Postcolonial Reading of Pentecostal Movements in India

Our study thus far on the issue of the origin of Pentecostal movements in India and the Indigenous revival movements that occurred in different parts of the country, is not to outrightly erase or demean the great contribution of western Pentecostal missionaries in India. In fact, it is historically clear that they did immensely contribute toward the establishment of Pentecostalism as an organized Church or institutionalized movement in India.[526] The main purpose of this chapter on Indian Pentecostalism is to show that there should be created sufficient space to understand that the revival work of the Spirit was already very much at work in India even much before the coming of the western Pentecostal missionaries. The western missionaries came and built upon the indigenous roots of revival that was already there.

A post-colonial approach to historiography in general does not swoon under any grand narratives and instead work with great attachment to locality and historical particularity. In this way, it achieves a place for those who are not

---

[525] Cf. O. L. Snaitang, "The Indigenous Pentecostal Movement," *Dharma Deepika*, 6/2 (2002), 6. Cf. also F. S. Downs, *History of Christianity in North East India* (Guwahati: CLS, 1992), 95-96.

[526] Cf. George, *Pentecostal Beginnings in Travancore*, 221. Here, George particularly commented on the work of the Azusa missionaries in India and in South India in Particular.

given their rightful place in history.[527] Thus, applying a postcolonial approach to the reading of the Pentecostal movements in India enables us to look beyond the presentation of the traditional western Pentecostalism that refuses to give any significant place to non-western cultures. Besides, it also helps us to look at the Pentecostal history in India from the perspective of the natives all the while making people to understand that the work of the Holy Spirit is not confined or restricted to any particular place or time but that it is universal as God and His love are. No nation or culture can have a complete monopoly over the person and work of the Holy Spirit for the Spirit works and manifests Himself/Itself wherever and whenever God wills.

[527] Cf. Ranajit Guha, "On Some Aspects of the Historiography of Colonial India," in Ranajit Guha and G. C. Spivak, eds., *Selected Subaltern Studies* (New York: Oxford University Press, 1988), 37-44.

Chapter 12

Post Independent Indian and Christian Movements

1. The Rise of Religious Fundamentalism and Christian Issue of Conversion in India

1.1. Conversion Issues during British Raj

In the beginning when the British was in power and when Protestant Christian missionaries arrived in India, the main force of prohibition came not from the Hindus but mainly from the British East India Company. The Hindus were in fact grateful and supportive of the missionaries' dedication and commitment in their reform works among the illiterate and poor Indians. However with the passage of time there appeared considerable growth of conversions among the Indian mass particularly among the Adivasis and other lower sections of the Indian society that alarmed the Hindu higher castes. They witnessed the improved status of the low caste and their greater power, for which they turned hostile toward Christian missionaries and their religion. Since then, Anti-Conversion Acts and activities began to emerge in different corners of India where Christian missionary activities began to expand.

1.2. Freedom of Religion Bill

The consecutive emergence of Freedom of Religion Bill in India that prevents Christian conversions for the whole of India through the so-called use of "force, inducement or fraud," was in fact a bill to destroy religious freedom. The Hindu fanatics mainly through the established body of Rashtriya Swayamsevak Sangh

(RSS), Vishwa Hindu Parishad (VHP), and the Jan Sangh (JS), were and are still very active in enforcing cruel anti-Christian attitudes and actions all over the country. Moreover, due to their hold on the political parties, the Government of India is also helpless in intervening and taking peace-making measures in the events of several sufferings and persecutions rendered upon the Christian minority in the country.

1.3. Anti Conversion Bills

Today Freedom of Religion has become an issue of great concern for the citizens of India. Four Legislatures: Orissa Legislature in 1968, Madhya Pradesh Legislature in 1968, Arunachal Pradesh Legislature in 1978 and Tamil Nadu Legislature in 2002 passed a bill against the Freedom of Religion.[528] The crux of the issue is that the Constitutional guarantees given to the citizens of India to 'profess, practice and propagate the religion' of one's own choice has been paralyzed indirectly by these Acts. Article 25 of the Indian Constitution reads, "subject to public order, morality and health and to the other provisions of this Part, all persons are equally entitled to freedom of conscience and the right to freely profess, practice and propagate religion."[529] However, this Constitutional Right had been violated to a very great extent in India over time again and again.

1.4. Accusation of Proselytism

The Hindu fundamentalists in India accuse Christians of proselytizing the people of India through their money power. They consider anti-conversion law as imperative for the preservation of Indian culture and heritage.[530] However, they fail to acknowledge the Constitution of India that guarantees Freedom of Religion to every citizen irrespective of caste, faith, race sex etc, which constitutes one factor of human rights. Therefore, these atrocities against the Christians or for that matter against any faith and against any individual on the basis of one's belief and faith, is an outright violation of human rights.

1.5. Conversion and India Today

Conversion in India continues to be an issue of debate in today's scenario with so much blame and accusation thrown toward Christianity. However, there are several incidents where people are being converted from one religion to another religion and therefore cannot claim that conversion is the work of Christians alone. Thus, conversion is not only to Christianity from other religions as different groups are

---

[528] Cf. Mathai Zachariah, "Introduction," in Mathai Zachariah, ed., *Freedom of Religion in India* (Nagpur: NCCI, 1979), 5. (Hereafter cited as Zachariah, *Freedom of Religion*).

[529] M. V. Pylee, *India's Constitution* (Bombay: Asia Publishing House, 1962), 6.

[530] Cf. Sebastian C. H. Kim, *In Search of Identity: Debates on Religious Conversion in India* (Delhi: Oxford University Press, 2002), 190.

changing their faiths according to the trend of modernization and according to peoples' right to personal choice.

2. Minority Rights

2.1. Who are the Minorities?

The Constitution of India uses the word 'minority' or its plural form in some Articles – 29 to 30 and 350A to 350B – but does not define it anywhere. Article 29 has the word "minorities" in its marginal heading but speaks of "any sections of citizens.... having a distinct language, script or culture."[531] This may be a whole community generally seen as a minority or a group within a majority community. The Indian Constitution Article 30 speaks specifically of two categories of minorities – religious and linguistic. The remaining two Articles – 350A and 350B relate to linguistic minorities only. Therefore, the expression "minority" means a group comprising less than half of the population and differing from others, especially the predominant section, in race, religion, traditions and culture, language, etc. The Oxford Dictionary defines 'Minority' as a smaller number or part; a number or part representing less than half of the whole; a relatively small group of people, differing from others in race, religion, language or political persuasion.

India is a land of diversities housing large varieties of people with different cultures, languages, religions, castes, races, tribes, costumes, food habits way of living, standards of living, party affiliations, and so on. Within this diversity, when it comes to religion, Hinduism is the majority religion in India with its 79.80 % population. India also has minority religions like Islam, Christianity, Jainism, Buddhism, Parsi, Sikhism etc. The National Commission for Minorities Act, 1992 of Indian Constitution says that "Minority for the purpose of the Act, means a community notified as such by the Central Government"- Section 2(7). Acting under this provision on 23-10- 1993, the Central Government notified the Muslim, Christian, Sikh, Buddhist and Parsi (Zoroastrian) communities to be regarded as "minorities" for the purpose of this Act.[532] Moreover, a special Sub-Committee on the Protection of Minority Rights appointed by the United Nations Human Rights Commission in 1946 defined the 'minority' as those "non-dominant groups in a population which possess a wish to preserve stable ethnic, religious and linguistic traditions or characteristics markedly different from those of the rest of population."[533]

---

[531] *Report of the National Commission for Religious and Linguistic Minorities* (Delhi: Ministry of Minority Affairs, 2007), 3. (Hereafter cited as *Religious and Linguistic Minorities*).

[532] *Religious and Linguistic Minorities*, 5-6.

[533] *Religious and Linguistic Minorities*, 13.

2.2. Minority Rights

Minority rights are part of the general human rights framework and must be protected through national legislation, appropriate government policies, and the support of the civil society. Internationally, Minority rights protection was for the first time formally included within the international legal framework following World War I, through the League of Nations' Minority Treaties. After World War II, minority rights received significantly less attention, with the notable exceptions of the United Nations Convention on the Prevention and Punishment of the Crime of Genocide (the Genocide Convention), and the International Covenant on Civil and Political Rights (ICCPR), which includes minority rights protection under Article 27. From the early 1990s onwards, several international and regional human rights instruments that included minority rights provisions were adopted. Some of the most relevant ones are:[534]

- The United Nations Declaration on the Rights of Person Belonging to National or Ethnic, Religious and Linguistic Minorities in 1992. The two Council of Europe treaties, the Framework Convention for the Protection of National Minorities (1995) and the European Charter for Regional or Minority Languages (1992).
- The Organization for Security and Co-operation in Europe's, Copenhagen Document (Art. 31-35) 1990.
- The Office of the United Nations of the High Commissioner of Human Rights the UN Independent Expert on Minority Issues and the UN Forum on Minority Issues.

Therefore, at the national level, a significant number of countries, including India, have adopted constitution and legislation that address the protection of minority communities and established institutions with minority protection included in their mandates. Minority rights are based on the recognition that minorities are in a vulnerable situation in comparison to other groups in society, namely the majority population, and aim to protect members of a minority group from discrimination, assimilation, prosecution, hostility or violence, as a consequence of their status. However, minority rights do not constitute privilege, but act to ensure equal respect for members of different communities. These rights serve to accommodate vulnerable groups and to brings all members of society to a minimum level of equality in the exercise of their human and fundamental rights. Yet Article 19 of the Indian Constitution expresses that, "All citizens shall have the right.

- To freedom of speech and expression;
- To assemble peaceably and without arms;

[534] G. Pentassuglia, Minorities *in International Law: An Introductory Study* (Strasbourg: Council of Europe Publications, 2002), 27.

- To form associations or unions;
- To move freely throughout the territory of India;
- To reside and settle in any part of the territory of India and;
- To practice any profession or to carry on any occupation, trade or business.[535]

Minority rights are individual and collective rights through which different groups of people of communities belonging to national minority groups are entitled to enjoy their own culture, to use their own language, to profess and practice their own religion, to have the right to freedom of expression and assembly, to have equal opportunities to education and employment, and to enjoy full participation in public life.[536]

2.3. Minority Rights and Its Provision

Our founding fathers enshrined in the Constitution ideals that sought to ensure for all citizens of India the equal opportunity to develop, by securing for them social, economic and political justice; liberty of thought, expression, belief, faith and worship; and equality of status and opportunity.[537] In order to achieve unity and integrity of the country and to allay any fears of the minority communities, the Indian Constitution Articles 29 and Article 30 were provided as protection against cultural hegemony of the dominant groups. Article 29(1) of the Constitution provides that any section of the citizens, residing in the territory of India or any part thereof, having a distinct language, script or culture of its own shall have the right to conserve the same." Article 29(2) lays down that "no citizen shall be denied admission into any educational institution maintained by the State or receiving aid out of State funds on grounds only of religion, race, caste, language or any of them."[538] Article 30(1) enjoins that "all minorities, whether based on religion or language, shall have the right to establish and administer educational institutions of their choice,"[539] while Article 30(2) lays down that "the State shall not, in granting aid to educational institutions, discriminate against any educational institution on the ground that it is under the management of a minority, whether based on religion or language."[540] Furthermore, Article 350-A establishes that "it shall be the endeavor of every State and of every local authority within the State

[535] Cf. B. Shiva Rao, *The Framing of India's Constitution, A Study* (Uttar Pradesh: Universal Law Publishing, 1967), 70.

[536] Cf. V. N. Shukla, *Constitution of India* (Lucknow: Eastern Book Company, 2001), 27.

[537] *The Preamble to the Constitution of India*, 2.

[538] *The Preamble to the Constitution of India*, 3.

[539] Cf. P. M. Bakshi, *The Constitution of India* (Delhi: Universal Law Publishing Company, 2005), 66. (Hereafter cited as Baksi, *The Constitution of India*).

[540] Cf. Baksi, *The Constitution of India*, 70.

to provide adequate facilities for instruction in the mother-tongue at the primary stage of education, to children belonging to linguistic minority groups."[541]
Article 30(1) guarantees to all minorities based on religion or language the right to establish and administer educational institution of their own choice.[542] The minority is not required to seek prior permission for the establishment of an educational institution.[543]

- The right to administer may be said to consist of the following rights:
- To choose its managing or governing body;
- To choose its teachers; and headmaster/principal.
- Not to be compelled to refuse admission to students;
- To use its properties and assets for the benefit of the institution;
- To select its own medium of instruction;[544] hence, a legislation which would penalize by disaffiliation from the university any institution which uses a language as the medium of instruction other than the one prescribed by it, offends against article 30(1).[545]

The Indian Constitution Articles from 25 to 28, dealing with right to freedom of religion. The constitution of India personifies the positive aspect of the term secularism, ie, "all religions in our country (irrespective of their strength) have the same status and support from the state."[546] This also means that no religion will be treated as national or state religion and no special privileges will be given to a particular religion. Every religion will have equal stature and respect in front of Indian state. In this regard Neera Chandhoke rightly observed: "It is not surprising that secularism in the Indian polity as a response to our conditions and mode of thought came to be conceptualized as Sarva Dharma Sambhava or equality of all religions."[547]

Article 25: Freedom of conscience and free profession, practice and propagation of religion.

(1) Subject to public order, morality and health and to other provisions of this part, all persons are equally entitled to freedom of conscience and the right freely to profess, practice and propagate religion.

---

[541] Baksi, *The Constitution of India*, 73.

[542] Kumar, Professor Narendera, "constitutional Law of India" (Delhi, Published by Pioneer Publications, Edition, 1997) p. 270.

[543] Socio Literati Advancement Society Bangalore v. State of Karnataka, AIR 1979 Karn. 217.

[544] Basu Durga Das " Shorter Constitution of India" (New Delhi, Published by Wadhwa and Company, edition 13th) p. 350.

[545] D.A.V College v. State of Punjab, AIR 1971 SC1737.

[546] Neera Chandhoke, *Beyond Secularism: The Rights of Religious Minorities* (New Delhi: Oxford University Press, 1999), 42. (Hereafter cited as, Chandhoke, *Beyond Secularism*).

[547] Chandhoke, *Beyond Secularism*, 43.

(2) Nothing in this Article shall affect the operation of any existing law or prevent the state from making any law-
    (a) Regulating or restricting any economic, financial political or other secular activity which may be associated with religion practice.
    (b) Providing for social welfare and reform or throwing open of Hindu religious institutions of a public character to all classes and sections of Hindus. Explanation 1- The wearing and carrying of kirpans shall be deemed to be included in the profession of the Sikh religions.

Explanation II –In sub clause (b) of clause (2) the reference to Hindus shall be construed as including a reference to persons professing the Sikh, Jain, or Buddhist religion, and the reference to Hindu religious institutions shall be construed accordingly.[548]

Article 26: Freedom to manage religious affairs.

Subject to public order, morality and health, every religious denomination or any section thereof shall have the right a) to establish and maintain institutions for religious and charitable purposes;

(b) To manage its own affairs in matters of religion.
(c) To own and acquire movable and immovable property; and
(d) To administer such property in accordance with law.[549]

Article 28: Freedom as to attendance at religious instruction or religious worship in certain educational institutions.

(1) No religious instruction shall be provided in any educational instructions wholly maintained out of State fund.
(2) Nothing in clause (1) shall apply to an educational instructions which is administered by the State but has been established under any endowment or trust which required that religious instruction shall be imparted in such instructions.
(3) No person attending any educational instructions recognized by the State or receiving aid out of State funds shall be required to take part in any religious.[550]

[548] James, Massey, *Minorities in a democracy: the Indian experience* (New Delhi: Manohar Publishers & Distributors, 1999), 77. See also M. Desai, *Minority Educational Institutions and Law* (Mumbai: Akshar Prakashan, 1996), 41.

[549] Basu Durga Das, *Commentary on the Constitution of India* (Nagpur: Lexis Nexis Butterworths Wadhwa, 2008), 132.

[550] M.P. Bakshi *The Constitutional Law of India* (Delhi Universal Law Publishing Company, 2001), 58.

Therefore, the Indian Constitution is a treasure where minorities can find various articles and provisions that safeguard their rights and privileges. The Constitution of India is an archetypal instance of accommodating and adjusting various claims of people belonging to multifaceted cultures and identities. In Indian Constitution, there are many ways through which the minorities safeguard their rights. Therefore it is crystal clear that, Indian Constitution has significant role and is important source of guaranteeing the rights and privileges of the minorities in India.

3. Reservation (Dalit Christians)

"*Many people have the idea that everything in India is booming business, but there are millions of Christian brothers and sisters who are literally in the shit.*" Dick Kleinhesselink

Dalit Christians are officially non-existent in India. The issue is that one cannot be a Christian and a Dalit at the same time. Dalits especially the Dalit Christians are often treated as worse than animals. Day in and day out, they have to suffer humiliation and atrocities of all kinds. The caste system is so much intertwined with the Indian culture that it is virtually impossible to escape from it. The oppression and discrimination won't stop when converting to another religion, although many converts still hope so. Fact is that caste follows you wherever you go, even into the Church, purely because the caste system is fixed in the minds of the Indian people. Christian Dalits are not recognized by the government.[551] Christian Dalits are not recognized by the government. Therefore, being a Dalit when you are a Christian is a logic used by the government to exclude Christian Dalits from the Reservation System. The most prevailing view is that Dalits constitute around seventy percent of the Christians, which is, although a minority, a 24-million-strong community in India.[552] In the north of India there are very few caste Christians; roughly seventy percent of the Church members are Dalit. Christian Dalit is not only discriminated against because he is a Dalit, but also because he is a Christian. Christian Dalits live in a caste-based society and their conversion has not been able to change that fact.[553] So, being a Christian or becoming a Christian doesn't change the status of a Dalit, let alone that it will change his life in terms of his well-being: for an Indian he is still a Dalit.

3.1. The Discrimination of Christian Dalits

According to James Massey the Christian Dalits suffers threefold discrimination: "one at the hands of members of the Indian society in general; two, from

[551] John C.B. Webster, *Religion and Dalit Liberation: an Examination of Perspectives* (Delhi: Manohar, 1999), 90. (Hereafter cited as Webster, *Religion and Dalit Liberation*).

[552] Priyanka P. Narain, *A high price for religious conversion?* (The Wall Street Journal, livemint.com, 12-03-2009).

[553] Webster, *Religion and Dalit Liberation*, 89.

the government of India...; and three from Christians of upper caste/class background."[554] The Christian Dalits are treated even worse than Hindu, Sikh or Buddhist Dalits. In the first place, in the eyes of the Indians, Christian Dalits made the 'mistake' of embracing the Christian faith, in addition to their 'crime' of being born in an untouchable caste. The consequence of this is that Christian Dalits are in fact twice discriminated: as Dalits and as Christians.[555] Moreover, the main issue here is that Christian Dalits are excluded from the Reservation System of our nation. This system is fixed by Indian law and is a form of affirmative action whereby a percentage of seats in the public sector are reserved for the Scheduled Castes, namely, the Dalits.[556] The sad thing is that, only for the Hindu, Sikh or Buddhist Dalits – Muslims and Christians are denied those benefits, as a result of a presidential order in 1950. They don't get the Scheduled Caste status, whereas under Article 17 of the Constitution it is clearly stated that no one is allowed to motivate untouchability.[557] By denying the Muslim and Christian Dalits those benefits, the state is violating its own laws that are meant to safeguard the equality of all people, irrespective of caste and creed distinctions.[558] In this way the state does not only discriminate on the basis of religion and thus a denial of religious liberty, but they also punish those Dalits who have had the courage to exercise their religious liberty and convert to Christianity or Islam.[559] Not surprisingly many Christian Dalits conceal and deny that they are Christian, in order to get the benefits of reservation.[560]

The caste structure of Indian society is even practiced in the church today. It started with the early missionaries: they were not able to put an end to the caste

---

[554] James Massey, *Dalits in India: Religion as a Source of Bondage or Liberation with a Special Reference to Christians* (New Delhi: Manohar Publishers & Distributors, 1995), 97.

[555] Godwin Shiri, *The Plight of Christian Dalits: a South Indian Case Study* (Bangalore: Asian Trading Corporation, 1997), 114. (Hereafter cited as Shiri, *The Plight of Christian Dalits*).

[556] Sukhadeo Thorat explains the system as follows: "The government's approach towards the SCs primarily draws from provisions in the Constitution, which legally abolished the practice of untouchability and the discrimination arising out of untouchability (article 17). The Constitution guarantees equality before the law (Article 14); provides for the promotion of the educational and economic interests of SCs and for their protection from social injustice and all forms of exploitation (Article 46); provides for special measures trough reservation in government service; and also reserves seats in democratic political institutions (Articles 330 and 335, 73rd Amendment Act, 1992). Finally, the Constitution provides for the establishment of a permanent body to investigate and monitor the social and economic progress of SCs on an annual basis." The SC workforce in the private sector, which employs more than 90 per cent of the SC workers, remains unprotected from possible exclusion and discrimination."

[557] Abid Shah, ed., *Indian People's Tribunal on Untouchability: Untouchability on Trial* (New Delhi: Human Rights Law Network (HRLN), 2008), 132.

[558] Shiri, *The Plight of Christian Dalits*, 239.

[559] Webster, *Religion and Dalit Liberation*, 90.

[560] M.R. Arulraja, *Jesus the Dalit* (Secunderabad: Jeevan Institute of Printing, 1996), 31.

system in the Churches; instead they maintained the status quo.[561] Moreover, there are still many people who don't want to change the situation, mainly because they still believe in their hearts that Dalits should be downtrodden, and they just want to keep the power in their own hands.[562] Sadly, Christian Dalit Women are the worst victims in this all. The Dalit women in India are one of the most oppressed groups. Often they are referred to as 'double Dalits'. They are treated as less than animals because they are Dalits and on top of that, women.

3.2. The Plea to include Dalit Christians in the Scheduled Caste Category

The emergence of some elite groups among the Dalits of India is primarily due to positive discrimination programs that have reserved a percentage of government jobs for Dalits since Independence. This is obvious in the case of the administrative and intellectual elite, but to some extent it is also true of the political elites. Inspite of several changes the condition of Christian Dalits continues to remain the same. Quotas, which reserve fifteen percent of central government jobs for Dalits, remained unfulfilled for decades in the upper classes of the administration, allegedly due to an insufficient number of qualified candidates. However, today, quotas are cornered by those Dalits whose father and/or mother have already benefited from positive discrimination policies. These Dalits often come from one special jati, or subcaste, in a given region. Therefore, such a situation tends to defeat an important part of the whole purpose of quotas, since it prevents other Dalit jatis from gaining substantial access to the reservations.

For this the Supreme Court has, once again, sought the Centre's response on a plea by Dalit Christians seeking parity in quota with their counterparts among the Hindu, Sikh and Buddhist communities. Former Chief Justice Ranganath Misra's report is crucial evidence before the court, and the religious minorities have set much hope by it. The Misra panel report, which was tabled in Parliament December 18, 2009, has defined religious and linguistic minorities as backward classes and recommended 15 percent reservation for all minorities in jobs, education and welfare schemes. The Commission, inter alia, made recommendations to give 15 percent reservation to minorities under Backward Class quota in education, government employment and social welfare schemes. Out of this 15 percent reservation, 10 percent reservation has been recommended to the Muslim Community and remaining 5 percent to other minority communities. The Commission has further recommended to include convert Dalit Christian and Dalit Muslims in the list of Scheduled Castes. Inspite of all the commission the Ranganath Mishra Commission, the Human Rights Commission, the National

---

[561] David Haslam, *Caste Out!: The Liberation Struggle of the Dalits in India* (London: CTBI Inter-Church House, 1999), 23.

[562] Satish Deshpande, *Dalits in the Muslim and Christian Communities: a Status Report on Current Social Scientific Knowledge* (Department of Sociology, University of Delhi, 2008), XI.

Minority Commission have all given a favorable recommendation to include dalit Christians into schedule caste. But, both the UPA and NDA government have not implemented it till today.

4. Ashram Movements

Christian Ashrams are of recent origin in India. The term ashram is derived from the root word *sram*, to exert or to express oneself. There has been lot of misunderstandings and misinterpretations of Christian ashram movement in India. A number of Christian beliefs and experiences contributed to the development and growth of Christian ashram movement in India. As the Christian came to contact with other faiths they also realized the need of inter-religious dialogue and cooperation. To share the faiths experience with each others in the form of dialogue became part of Christian ashram movement in India.

4.1. *Roman Catholic Ashrams*

Robert de Nobile was the first person who introduced Christian ashram in India. He adopted fully the Indian life style of sannyasin in order to reach out to the high caste Hindus of India. The next was followed by Brahmabandhab Upadhyaya who introduces two types of sannayasins, first those who lead a life of contemplation in the monastery and second those who are itinerant ones who will preach the Gospel everywhere. He opened Catholic ashram in 1899 at Jabalpur. The more permanent Catholic ashram, Saccidananda Ashram in Shantivanam in Kulitalai, Tiruchirapalli was started by Abbe Monchanin and Fr Henri Le Saux both French missionaries. Both changed their names as Swami Parama Arubi Ananda and Abhishiktananda. Both felt that contemplation and its structured form monasticism were the best means of entering into dialogue with Hinduism and of manifesting the spiritual nature of the Catholic Church. They had clearly laid down the basic principles, which govern a Christian Ashram. In 1968, Abhishiktananda handed over Saccidanda Ashram to Bede Griffiths. Under his guidance, Saccidananda Ashram became one of the leading Catholic Ashrams in India. Fr D.S. Amalorpavadass (1932-1990) opened Anjali Ashram on August 15, 1979. Anjali Ashram is to promote Indian Spirituallity, contemplation, inter-religious dialogue, social service, liberation of the poor, ecumenism and multi-religious community. Vandana Mataji started on her own Jeevan Dhara Ashram in Garkwal Hills, U.P.

4.2. *Protestant Ashrams*

The first Protestants Ashram Christukula Ashram started in 1921 at Tirupattur in Tamil Nadu by S. Jesudasan and Ferrester Paton. The main aim of the ashram was to have deeper spirituality. The daily programme consisted of prayer, meditation, work, study, recreation and village visit. Fr Jack Winslow founded Christa *Prema Seva Āshram* (CPSA) in 1927 at Shivajinagar, Pune. This ashram taught on three orders, First Order of celibate men, and Second order of celibate women and Third Order of married people. This ashram was closed down in 1962. But, it was revived in 1972 and today it continues to function as an ecumenical ashram under the name of *Christa Prema Seva Ashram* led by a Roman Catholic sister as *Acharya*. K.K. Chandy started another ashram called *Christavashram* and followed by E. Stanley Jones's ashram *Sat Tal Ashram* started in 1930 which continues to be one of the best place for Christian meditation today. Today there are more than 50 Christian ashrams in India.

5. Theological Institutions

Theological education as a dynamic process does not take place in a vacuum rather it occurs in the context of the Church and Society. Theological education is part of the churches' ministry and hence the period that students spent in the seminaries becomes the period of ministerial formation for them. Therefore, this calls for a closer interaction between the theological institutions and the churches. Yet this can be developed only on the basis of mutual responsibility, respect and accountability between the church and theological education. Keeping this in mind few theological colleges and seminaries in India were chosen out of many for our brief reflection.

5.1. United Theological College (UTC)

United Theological College was established in 1910. The college is situated in Bangalore, Karnataka state of India. The college was first name "The United Theological College of South India and Ceylon" as "a Christian College where students may obtain a sound theological education". It was established through the coming together of the London Missionary Society, the Wesleyan Methodist Missionary Society, The United Free Church of Scotland, the Arcot Mission of the Reformed Church in America and the Trustees of the Jaffna College Funds and the S.P.C.K. in Scotland also gave their support.[563]

As this was an ecumenical institution, ecumenical churches, missionary societies and other organizations from various regions of India and from abroad joined the College to support for furthering of ecumenism through theological education. Church and Missionary Society and the Society for Propagation of the Gospel also joined the college to support further. In 1959 the Danish Missionary Society became a supporting body of the college. In 1960 the Basel Evangelical Mission and the Kolhapur Church Council joined to support the college as part of the supporting body. In the year 1961 the Church of South India and in 1963 Mar Thoma Church joined the supporting body of the college. In 1967 the Council of Young Men Christian Association in India joined and in 1969 the Church of India, Pakistan, Burma and Ceylon as the supporting body. Also the

---

[563] "The United Theological College," *http://www.utc.edu.in/* (Assessed on 16/8/2019), at 4:00 pm, 1. (Hereafter The *United Theological College*).

Board of Global Ministries of the United Methodist Church became one of the contributing bodies in 1969.[564]

Following the merger of the Gurukul Lutheran Theological College and Research Institute with the United Theological College for B.D., M. Th. and other degree programmers in June 1971, several Lutheran Church and Missions (Andhra Evangelical Lutheran Church, South Andhra Lutheran Church, Church of Sweden Mission, the Lutheran Church of America, the American Lutheran Church-both presently merged in the Evangelical Church of America, India Evangelical Lutheran Church and the Leipzig Evangelical Lutheran Mission) became supporting bodies of the College. The Malankar Jacobite Syrian Church became a contributing body in 1979.[565]

The first home of the College was a building on Mission Road, Bangalore city, formerly used for the seminary, which had been founded and maintained by the London Missionary Society from 1841 under the name 'Bangalore Theological Seminary'. The permanent site of the College at 17 (new number 63) Miller's road, Bangalore, was acquired in 1912, and the building was first occupied in 1914. In 1919, a year after Serampore College was granted permission by the Act of the Government of Bengal to grant degrees in Theology, the College was affiliated to the Serampore College for the B. D. Degree.

In 1949, the Y.M.C.A Training School was re-opened, and in September 1950, eight new rooms were added to the Hostel by the Council of Y.M.C.A's to provide accommodation for their students. In 1976, the Senate of Serampore College granted autonomy to the College for the B.D., B.R.E., and D. R. K. Courses. Under the autonomy the College has the freedom to set its own curriculum, evaluate the candidates and recommend them to the Senate for the award of the degree or diploma. Dr L. P. Larsen, was the first Principal of the College and at present Rev Dr Chilkuri Vasantha Rao is the Principal of the College. The college is offering several courses particularly Bachelor of Divinity (BD), Master of Theology (M.Th), Doctor of Theology (D.Th). The college also offers diploma courses like Diploma in Proficiency Counseling (DPC), and Diploma in Women Studies (DWS).

Master of Theology Degree of the Senate of Serampore College is offered in the department of:[566]

1. Old Testament M.Th.
2. New Testament M.Th.
3. Christian Theology M.Th.
4. Christian Ethics M.Th.
5. History of Christianity M.Th.

---

[564] *The United Theological College*, 1.

[565] *The United Theological College*, 4.

[566] *The United Theological College*, 5.

6. Christian Ministry (Counselling) M.Th.
7. Christian Ministry (Christian Education) M.Th.
8. Religion (Hinduism) M.Th.
9. Missiology M.Th.
10. Women's Studies M.Th.

Doctor of Theology Degree of the Senate of Serampore College is offered in the department of :

1. Old Testament D.Th.
2. New Testament D.Th.
3. Christian Theology D.Th.
4. Christian Ethics D.Th.
5. History of Christianity D.Th.
6. Christian Ministry (Counselling) D.Th.
7. Missiology D.Th.
8. Women's Studies.

5.2. Andhra Christian Theological College (ACTC)

Andhra Christian Theological College (ACTC) was founded in 1964. It is situated in Telegana state of India. It is affiliated to the Senate of Serampore College (University) The College was founded with the coming together of the Andhra Evangelical Lutheran Church, the Church of South India, the Convention of Baptist Churches of Northern Circars, the Methodist Church in India and the South Andhra Lutheran Church. Good Samaritan Evangelical Lutheran Church also joined the college in 1992.

Dr. William D. Coleman was the first Principal of the college. Under the able leadership of Rev Dr A. John Prabhakar, the college is offering courses like:[567]

1. Bachelor of Divinity (BD) Serampore
2. Master of Divinity (M.Div) ATA
3. Master of Theology (M.Th)

Distance education

1. Bachelor of Christian Studies (B.C.S.)
2. Master of Christian Studies (M.C.S.)
3. Diploma in Christian Studies (Dip. C.S.)

5.3. Union Biblical Seminary (UBS)

In 1951 the Evangelical Fellowship of India (EFI), was founded, and with the establishment of EFI soon decided that there ought to be made available a

[567] "Andhra Christian Theological College," *https://en.wikipedia.org/wiki/Hyderabad* (Assessed on 24/08/2019), at 2:00 pm, 1.

ministerial training of a good standard to those called to serve in the church. It was the effort of evangelical churches that began to express the need of having a place for training the young leaders of the church. Hence, in 1953 the Union Biblical Seminary was constituted as a joint effort of eleven mission and church groups at Yavatmal. Rev Dr Frank Kline was chosen as the first Principal, and the Bible School of which he was already Principal was merged into the new institution. In 1975, the Union Biblical Seminary Association decided to relocate the Seminary to the city of Pune. So the Seminary was relocated in 1983 to the new campus at Bibvewadi, a southeastern part of the city and about 8 kilometres from the Pune Railway Station. The campus is on a beautiful hillock, overlooking the city.[568]

The Union Biblical Seminary is unique as it represents evangelical Christians from almost all the major Indian ethnic, linguistic and cultural groups as well as from other countries. The vision of UBS from its founding is the fulfilling of the Great Commission in the contemporary socio-economic, cultural and religious context of India. This involves training committed men and women to become more effective ministers and mission leaders who will facilitate the Indian Church in fulfilling its calling. Today, there are more than thirty churches, Christian Institutions, missions and Christian organizations represented in the Union Biblical Seminary Association, the body that governs the Seminary. UBS is affiliated to the Seante of Serampore College (University). At present Rev Dr Pravin Paul is the Principal of the College. Under his able leadership the UBS offers several courses today:[569]

1. Bachelor of Divinity (BD) Serampore
2. Master of Divinity (M.Div) Asia Theological Association
3. Master of Theology (M.Th) ATA
4. Master of Thcology (M.Th) Serampore
5. Doctor of Theology (D.Th) Serampore

UBS is offering Master of Theology (M.Th) Serampore Degree in the discipline of:

1. Old Testament,
2. New Testament,
3. Christian Theology,
4. Christian Ministry (Christian Education & Counseling)
5. Missions.

[568] "Union Biblical Seminary," *https://www.ubs.ac.in/* (Assessed on 21/8/2019), at 9:00 pm, 1.

[569] Union Biblical Seminary," *https://www.ubs.ac.in/* (Assessed on 23/8/2019), at 8:00 pm, 2-4.

UBS is offering Doctor of Theology (D.Th) Serampore Degree in the discipline of:

1. Old Testament
2. New Testament
3. Christian Theology

UBS also offered other courses such as:

1. Post-Graduate Diploma in Pastoral Counseling (UBS Christian Ministry Division) Duration: One year.
2. Comprehensive Children Ministry Training Program (6 months)

Distance Education offered by UBS:
Courses offered in English

1. CMS - Certificate in Ministerial Studies (1 Year)
2. M.Div - Master Of Divinity (4 Years)

Courses offered in Marathi

1. CMS - Certificate in Ministerial Studies (1 Year)
2. B.Th - Bachelor of Theology
3. M.Div - Master of Divinity (4 Years)

Course offered in Hindi

1. CMS - Certificate in Ministerial Studies (1 Year)
2. B.Th - Bachelor of Theology
3. M.Div - Master Of Divinity (4 Year)

5.4. Senate of Serampore College (University)

Serampore College was established on July 15, 1818 at Serampore by William Carey, Joshua Marshman and William Ward. The missionaries released prospectus in which the institution was meant to be *A College for instruction of Asiatic Christian and other youth, in Eastern Literature and European Science,*[570] at Serampore West Bengal. It was Dr Marshman who wrote the lengthy document making it very clear that the College was to be handmaid of evangelization and that the instruction would be given in Sanskrit, Arabic, European Science and English.[571] There was also firm hope that the College was to be considered as most importantly a divinity school, where a promising youth for evangelistic

[570] Cf. *Senate of Serampore College Regulations for Internal and External Candidate: Relating to the Bachelor of Divinity Degree*. December, 1962, 6-10.

[571] Woba James, *Revisiting Ecumenical Theological Education in India: With a Special Reference to the Senate of Serampore College* (Delhi: Christian World Imprints, 2016), 57. (Hereafter cited as James *Revisiting Ecumenical Theological Education in India*).

work should go through complete course of instruction in Christian theology.[572] The College was open to all persons of any caste or creed, and the founders insured that no denominational test would apply to faculty members.[573] Since Serampore was a Danish Colony, Frederick the Sixth, king of Denmark, issued Serampore College its Royal Charter of Incorporation on February 23, 1827, in Copenhagen, Denmark (Charter, 1, Charter, 2, Charter, 3). The charter came in response to Joshua Marshman's visit with King Frederick in August 1826; the charter gave Serampore College the privilege of awarding degrees in Arts and Theology. William Carey, Joshua Marshman, and John Clark Marshman (Joshua's son) were designated as members of the first Council.[574]

On February 22, 1845, the ownership of Serampore College was transferred to the British Government after Denmark sold all of its Indian assets to Great Britain. The management and operation of the College continued without interruption under the direction of a Master and Council. In 1856, the Baptist Missionary Society in England took over the management of the College, and in 1857, the College became affiliated with the University of Calcutta. In 1883, the College closed as an Arts College and began functioning as a Christian Training Institution and a theological institute for the Baptist Churches in Bengal. Affiliating again with the University of Calcutta in 1911, Serampore College, in 1913, rose to the standard of the Bachelor of Arts degree. The College faculty was interdenominational.[575]

In December 4, 1915, the first group of Bachelor of Divinity students graduated: Rev I. W. Johory, Rev N. G. Kuriakos, a priest in the Orthodox Syrian Church; and Mr. D. M. Devasahayam, London Missionary Society, South India. From 1916 through 1927, sixty-nine additional students earned the Bachelor of Divinity degree through Serampore. During the Centenary Year of the College in 1918, the Bengal Legislative Council passed the Serampore College Act 1918, for the purpose of enlarging the College Council and forming a new interdenominational Senate that would confer theological degrees for all Christian denominations in India.[576] Today under the leadership of Dr. Vansanglura more than 50 colleges and seminaries affiliated themselves with the Senate of Serampore College (University) in India.

---

[572] Cf. James *Revisiting Ecumenical Theological Education in India*, 57.

[573] J.C. Marshman, *History of Serampore Mission or Life and Times of Carey Marshman and Ward*, Vol. II (Calcutta: 1859), 168. (Hereafter cited Marshman, *History of Serampore Mission*).

[574] Cf. Marshman, *History of Serampore Mission*). 192.

[575] Joshua Marshman, *The Life and Times of Carey, Marshman, and Ward: Embracing the History of the Serampore Mission*, Vol. 2 (London: Spottiswood and Co. Printers, 1859), 107.

[576] See detail, James *Revisiting Ecumenical Theological Education in India*, 66-68.

5.5. Eastern Theological College

Eastern Theological College (ETC) was founded in the year 1905 by Rev S. A. D. Boggs and was assisted by Rev Henry Goldsmith. It started as a Bible Training Centre with 18 students. The pioneering work grew into groups of schools like Jorhat Christian School, a Middle English School, a Normal School and an Industrial School and later High School by 1914. The pioneering leaders soon felt the need of upgrading the training into more intensive training for further evangelization of the region. Therefore, the program for College level of theological education was proposed to the missionary conference and in 1950 the Council of Baptist Churches in North East India (CBCNEI) accepted the proposed program. Therefore, in the fall of 1950 a historic step was taken when the Jorhat Bible College was established with Rev J. W. Cook as its first Principal. Meanwhile in 1955 the High School was closed down due to severe financial and administrative difficulties. In 1953 the College was renamed as Assam Baptist Theological Seminary but again in 1957 the College changed the name into Eastern Theological College as it is known till today.[577]

In 1966 the College received the first native principal in the person of Rev Dr J. H. Thumra. Today under the able leadership of Rev Prof. Dr Narola Imchen the College is offering several courses for furthering theological education and ministerial formation. The following courses are being offered in the college today:

1. Bachelor of Divinity (BD) Serampore
2. Master of Theology (M.Th) Serampore
3. Doctor of Theology (D.Th) Serampore

The College also fosters the Senate's program of Theological Education by Extension on the following course:

1. Bachelor of Christian Studies (B.C.S.)
2. Diploma in Christian Studies (Dip. C.S.)

The college also offered courses under CBCNEI

1. Master of Arts (MA) in Holistic Child Development
2. Master of Arts (MA) in Peace Studies

ETC is offering Master of Theology (M.Th) Degree in the discipline of:

1. New Testament,
2. Christian Theology,
3. Christian Ministry (Christian Education & Counseling)
4. History of Christianity.

[577] *The Eastern Theological College Prospectus* (Jorhat: ETC, 2016), 2.

ETC is offering Doctor of Theology (D.Th) Serampore Degree in the discipline of:

1. New Testament
2. Christian Theology
3. History of Christianity

Eastern Theological College as the premier theological training and ministerial formation college of CBCNEI, continues to play a significant role in promoting and training men and women for theological education in the region and beyond.

Conclusion

The subject of the History of Christianity in India is an interesting as well as challenging one. What little has been attempted to cover in this book, I hope that this could set the readers to develop critical questions in their minds so as to push them to venture into the fields for further research for the benefit of many and especially for the future generation of Church historians. We shall try to summarize the issues dealt with in this book by way of conclusion. The first chapter on the subject of the **Origin of Christianity in India**, we conclude that we still endorse or stand in line with St Thomas tradition – that the Apostle Thomas should continue to be credited with the origin of Christianity in India. We hold this view on the basis that thus far there is/are no other view(s) strong enough to challenge and defeat this tradition.

The second chapter holds that there were ties between the **Indian Christianity and Its Relation with the Christians of thc East** as early as 3rd and 4th centuries. Besides, there were also a number of native converts living as Christian community in India in the early centuries who were later joined by the immigrants through which the Christian community in India was strengthened and this also led to the over-dependence of the Church in India upon the Eastern Church.

The third chapter analyzed the strenuous and sometimes even underhanded attempts of the **Roman Catholic Christianity in India** and the resultant disturbing events of the Synod of Diamper and the Coonen Cross revolt of 1653 and the eventual strained relationship between the Catholic Church and the Syrian Christianity.

The fourth and fifth chapters dealt with the **Protestant missions in India** (18th and 19th centuries) and the Protestant Christianity in India in the 19th and 21st centuries respectively. The former specifically analyzed the first two Protestant missions – Tranquebar and Serampore Missions, and their mission strategies and methods while the latter dealt with the spread of Potestant Christianity to different regions in India in the 19th and 20th centuries. In all of these, we have noted how

Christianity in India had to struggle to wade through the tides of varied factors all affecting (both positively and negatively), the emergence of native or Indian Christianity.

The sixth chapter analyzes the **colonial religious policies in India** in relation to Christian mission. This chapter discussed the relation between colonialism and different religious policies in India.

The seventh chapter on **Christianity and Nation Building in India,** the writer has emphasized the role of Indian Christians in Indian National Independence Movement, the influences of Christianity in Bengal Renaissance. It also brought out the contributions of Protestant Christianity in Social Activities such as medical, education and Empowerment of Women. It also analyzed how Christians tackle the problem of Caste systems and the rise of Communalism in India.

The eight chapter on **Indigenous Missionary Movements and the Rise of Indian Church** reveals the development of Indian Christian indigenous movement and its growth such as the Indian Christian Herald, National Missionary Society, Friends Missionary Prayer Band, Indian Mission Society and National Missionary Council of India. Also this chapter also brings out aspects of indigenization of Indian Christianity.

The ninth chapter on **Indian Christianity and Ecumenical Movement** dealt some of the serious issues that come under the Indian ecumenical movement like the issue of Church Union with the objective of transforming the Indian Church from its western-orientedness to being truly Indian and from being divided to being united as one. It eventually led to the formation of the Church of South India on 27th September 1947 and the Church of North India in November 1970.

The tenth chapter on the **History of Christianity in North East India** traced the origin of Christianity in the region through the twin agencies of British power and the Christian Missions. We conclude that while Christianity tremendously brought social and religious transformation, it also is seriously responsible for the erosion of the tribals'/natives' cultural values and their connected identity as people of the land and soil.

The eleven chapter on **Issues of Pentecostalism in India** shows us that Pentecostalism is a movement that swept (and is still sweeping) India with its amazing influence, making it the fastest growing Church in India since its inception. We especially deal with the issue of its origin from an Indian post-colonial perspective, claiming our own origin against the conventional claim of the western Pentecostalism.

The last and final (twelfth) chapter on **Post Independent Indian and Christian Movements** reveals the rise of religious fundamentalism, where the issue of conversion, freedom of religion bill, anti conversion were dealt. The last chapter also dealt several other topics such as, Minority Rights, Reservation for Dalit Christian, Christian Ashram Movements and Theological Institutions in India.

Bibliography

Books

Agur, C. M. *Church History of Travancore.* New Delhi: Asian Education Service, 1990.

Alter, P. James. *In The Doab and Rohilkhand North Indian Christianity 1815-1915.* Delhi: ISPCK, 1986.

Anchukandam, Thomas. *Roberto De Nobili's Responsio (1610): A Vindication of Inculturation and Adaptation.* Bangalore: Kristu Jyoti Publications, 1996.

Anderson, Allan and Edmond Tang. *Asian and Pentecostal: The Charismatic Face of Christianity in Asia.* Oxford: Regunum, 2005.

Anderson, H. Gerald, ed. *Biographical Dictionary of Christian Missions.* New York: Macmillan Reference, 1998.

Appasamy, P. *The Centenary History of the C.M.S. in Tinnevelly.* Palamcottah, 1923.

Arangaden, A. J. *Church Union in South India: Its Progress and Consummation.* Mangalore: Basel Mission Press, 1947.

Arulraja, M.R. *Jesus the Dalit.* Secunderabad: Jeevan Institute of Printing, 1996.

Ashirvatham, Eddy. *Christianity in the Indian Crucible.* Calcutta: YMCA Publishing House, 1955.

Azariah, Masilamani. *A Pastor's Search for Dalit Theology.* Delhi: ISPCK, 2000.

Azariah, V. S. *India and the Christian Movement.* Madras: CLS, 1936.

Baago, K. *A History of the National Christian Council of India 1914-1964.* Nagpur: NCCI, 1965.

________. *Pioneers of Indigenous Christianity.* Bangalore: CLS, 1969.

________. *The Movement Around Subba Rao: A Study of Hindu-Christian Movement around K. Subba Rao in Andhra Pradesh*. Bangalore: CISRS, 1968.

Bakshi, P. M. *The Constitution of India*. Delhi: Universal Law Publishing Company, 2005.

Banerjee, N. Brojendra. *Religious Conversions in India*. New Delhi: Harnam Publications, 1982.

Barpujari, H. K. *The American Missionaries and North East India: 1836-1900 AD*. Guwahati: Spectrum Publication, 1986.

Barret, B. David. Ed. *World Christian Encyclopedia*. Nairobi: Oxford University Press, 1982.

Bartleman, Frank. *Azusa Street*. New Jersey: Bridge Publishing, 1980.

Basu Durga Das, *Commentary on the Constitution of India* (Nagpur: Lexis Nexis Butterworths Wadhwa, 2008), 132.

Bayne, S. F. *Ceylon, North India and Pakistan*. London: SPCK, 1960.

Becker, C. *History of the Catholic Missions in North East India: 1890-1915*. Shillong: Kerma KLM Pvt. Ltd., 1980.

Bede. *A History of the English Church People*. Translated by Leo Shirley-Price. Harmondsworth: n.p., 1955.

Best, F. Thomas, ed. *Vancouver to Canberra 1983-1990, Report of the Central Committee of the WCC to the Seventh Assembly*. Geneva: WCC Publications, 1990.

Beyreuther, Erich. *Bartholomaeus Ziegenbalg: A Biography of the first Protestant Missionary in India 1682-1719*. Translated by S. G. Lange and H. W. Gensichem. Madras: CLS, 1955.

Bose, Manilal. *Historical and Constitutional Documents of North-Eastern India (1824-1973)*. Delhi: Concept Publishing Company, 1979.

Bowen, Roger. *So I Send You: A Study Guide to Mission*. Delhi: ISPCK, 2004.

Brown L. W. *The Indian Christians of St. Thomas*. Cambridge: Cambridge University Press, 1956. .

Carothers, W. F. *The Baptism with the Holy Ghost and the Speaking in Tongues*. Illinois: Carothers, 1907.

Carroll, Bernice A. ed. *Liberating Women's History: Theoretical and Critical Essays*. Urbana: University of Illinois Press, 1976.

Chandhoke, Neera. *Beyond Secularism: The Rights of Religious Minorities*. New Delhi: Oxford University Press, 1999.

Chandler, S. John. *Seventy-five Years in Madurai Mission*. Madura: n.p., n.d.

Chatterjee, Kumar Sunil. *William Carey and Serampore.* Serampore: Laserplus, 2004.

Chattopadyaya, Kamaladevi. *Tribalism in India.* New Delhi: Vikas Publications, n.d.

Cheriyan, C. V. *A History of Christianity in Kerala.* Kottayam: n.p., 1973.

Christopher, ed. *The Jesuit Tradition in Education and Mission.* Scranton: University of Scranton Press, 1993.

Chute, C. Arthur, *William Carey: A Sketch of Beginning in Modern Missions.* Chicago: Goodman & Dickerson, 1891.

Clark, Sunder. *Let the Indian Church be Indian.* Madras: CLS, 1980.

Clarke, Sathianathan. *Dalits and Christianity: Subaltern Religion and Liberation Theology in India.* Delhi: Oxford University press, 1998.

Costa, R. ed. *One Faith, Many Cultures.* New York: Orbis Book, 1980.

Coward, Harold. *Hindu-Christian Dialogue: Perspectives and Encounters.* Madras: Motilal Banarsidass Publication, 1993.

Cox, Harvey. *Fire from Heaven: The Rise of Pentecostal Spiritually and the Reshaping of Religion in the Twenty-first Century.* Massachusetts: Addison-Wesley Publishing Company, 1995.

Daniel, K. N. *The South Indian Apostolate of St. Thomas.* Serampore: CHAI., n.d.

Das, Somen, ed. *Mission and Evangelism.* Delhi: ISPCK, 1998.

Datta, Swati et. al., eds. *Carey Day Souvenir 2004.* Serampore: Serampore College, 2004.

D.E D.J, *The Constitution of India.* Hyderabad: Asia Law House, 2002.

De Nobili, Roberto. *Dusna Tikkaram.* Tuttukudi: De Nobili Institute, 1964.

________. Ed. *Indian Customs.* Palayamkottai: De Nobili Research Institute, 1972.

Dena, Lal. *Christian Mission and Colonialism.* Shillong: Vendrame Institute, 1988.

Desai, M. *Minority Educational Institutions and Law.* Mumbai: Akshar Prakashan, 1996.

Deshpande, Satish. *Dalits in the Muslim and Christian Communities: a Status Report on Current Social Scientific Knowledge.* Department of Sociology, University of Delhi, 2008.

Devasia, Leelamma, ed. *Women in India: Equality, Social Justice and Developments.* New Delhi: India Social Institute, 1990.

Dewitt, B. Calvin, ed. *The Environment and the Christian - What Can We Learn from the New Testament?* Michigan: Baker Book House, 1991.

Dharmaraj, S. Jacob. *Colonialism and Christian Mission: Postcolonial Reflections*. Delhi: ISPCK, 1993.

Down, F. S. *History of Christianity in North East India*. Guwahati: CLS, 1992.

________. *Essay on Christianity in North East India*. New Delhi: Indus Publishing, 1994.

________. *The Mighty Works of God*. Guwahati: CLC, 1971.

________. *Christianity in North East India: Historical Perspectives*. Guwahati: ISPCK, 1983.

________. *History of Christianity in India: North East India in the Nineteenth and Twentieth Centuries*. Vol. V. Part 5. Bangalore: CHAI, 1992.

Durasoff, Steve. *Bright Wind of the Spirit: Pentecostalism Today*. New Jersey: Logos International, 1972.

Edward, Sir Maclagan. *The Jesuits and the Great Mugal*. London: Burns Oates and Washbourne Ltd., 1932.

Elwin, Verrier. *The Tribal World of Verrier Elwin*. New Delhi: Oxford University Press, 2002.

Estborn, S. *The Church among the Tamils and Telegus*. Nagpur: n.p., 1961.

Farquhar, J. N. *Modern Religious Movements in India*. Delhi: Munshiram Manoharlal, 1967.

Featherstone, Mike, ed. *Global Culture*. New Delhi: SAGE Publications, 1995.

Fenger, J. Fred. *History of the Tranquebar Mission: Worked out from the Original Papers*. Translated by Francke. Madras: Leipzig Evangelical Lutheran Mission, 1906.

Fernandez, Walter. *Caste and Conversion Movements in India*. Bangalore: Indian Social Institute, 1981.

Fiorenza, Elizabeth Schussler. *In Memory of Her: A Feminist Theological Reconstruction of Christian Origins*. New York: Crossroads Publications, 1986.

Firth, C. B. *An Introduction to Indian Church History*. Delhi: ISPCK, 2001.

Forrester, B. Duncan. *Caste and Christianity: Attitudes and Policies on Caste of Anglo-Saxon Protestant Mission in India*. London: Curzon Press, 1980.

Frykenberg, E. Robert, *Christianity in India: From Beginnings to the Present*. New York: Oxford University Press, 2008.

________, ed. *Land Control and Social Structure in Indian History*. London: University of Wisconsin Press, 1969.

Fuller, C. J. *Kerala Christians and Caste System*. N.p.: n.p., 1976.

Gandhi, P. Jegadish and George Cheriyan, eds. *Globalization: A Challenge to the Church*. Bangalore: ACISCA & NCCI-URM, 1998.

George, K. M. *Christianity in India throughout the Centuries*. Hyderabad: Authentic Books, 2009._

________. *Church of South India: Life in Union (1947-1997)*. Delhi: ISPCK, 1999.

Ghose, J. Joseph *The Young Men of India*. Calcutta: n.p., 1908.

Gibbs, M. E. *The Anglican Church in India 1600-1970*. Delhi: ISPCK, 1972.

Gine, Chandra Pratap. *The System of Elementary Education of the Serampore Mission*. Jorhat: ETC, 2001.

Gladstone, J. W. *Protestant Christianity and People's Movements in Kerala: A Study of Christian Mass Movements in Relation to Neo-Hindu, Socio-Religious Movements in Kerala 1850-1936*. Trivandrum: KUTS Publications, 1984.

________, ed. *United to Unite: History of the Church of South India 1947-1997*. Madras: CSI Synod, 1997.

Gnanadason, Aruna, ed. *Ecumenism: Hope in Action*. Nagpur: NCCI, 1990.

Grafe, Hugald. *History of Christianity in India*. Vol. 4. Part. 2. Bangalore: CHAI, 1990.

Guha, Ranajit, ed. *Subaltern Studies I: Writings on South Asian History and Society*. New Delhi: Oxford University Press, 1982.

Guha, Ranajit and G. C. Spivak, eds. *Selected Subaltern Studies*. New York: Oxford University Press, 1988.

Hambye, E. R. *History of Christianity in India*. Vol. III. Bangalore: CHAI, 1997.

Haslam, David. *Caste Out!: The Liberation Struggle of the Dalits in India*. London: CTBI Inter-Church House, 1999.

Hepuni, K. ed. *Manipur North Naga Baptist Association Church History*. Punanamai: MNNBA Golden Jubilee Publication, 1976.

Hewate, E. G. K. *Christ and Western India*. Bombay: J. Kellock, Wilson College, 1950.

Hickey, William. *The Tanjore Maratha Principality in Southern India: The Land of the Cholas: The Eden of the South*. Madras: Foster Press, 1874.

Hogg, Richey William. *Ecumenical Foundations*. New York: Harpers & Brothers, 1952.

Horam, M. *North East India: A Profile*. New Delhi: Cosmo Publications, 1990.

Hough, James. *The History of Christianity in India from the Commencement of the Christian Era*. Vol. I. London: R. B. Seeley and W. Burnside, 1839.

Houghton, Graham. *The Impoverishment of Dependency: A History of the Protestant Church in Madras 1870-1920*. Madras: CLS, 1983.

Hrangkhuma, F. *An Introduction to Church History*. Bangalore: Theological Book Trust, 1999.

Imchen, Panger. *Ancient Ao Naga Religion and Culture*. New Delhi: Har-Anand Publication, 1993.

James, M. Thoburn. *India and Malaysia*. New York: Methodist Book Concern, 1896.

James, Woba. *Revisiting Ecumenical Theological Education in India: With a Special Reference to the Senate of Serampore College*. Delhi: Christian World Imprints, 2016.

________. *Major Issues in the History of Christianity: A Postcolonial Reading*. Jorhat: TDCC Publication, 2013.

Jain, M.P. *Indian Constitutional Law*. Nagpur: Wadhwa and Company, 2003.

Jamir, Menjiwapong, Imsenperong and Walotemjen. *Mapping the Context: An Interdisciplinary Exploration*. Dimapur: Authors, 2011.

Jeyakumar, D. Arthur. *History of Christianity in India: Selected Themes*. Madurai: TTS, 2007.

Jeyaseelan, L. *Impact of the Missionary Movement in Manipur*. New Delhi: Scholar Publishing House, 1996.

Johannes,Van den Berg. *Constrained by Jesus Love*. Rotterdam: J. H. Kok and N. V. Kampen, 1956.

John, E. Clough. *Social Christianity in the Orient*. New York: Macmillan Company, 1914.

Johnstone, Sir James. *My Experience in Manipur and the Naga Hills*. London: 1896.

Joseph, T. K. *The Malabar Christians and their Ancient Documents*. Trivandrum: 1929.

Kadankavil, Thomas, ed. *Religion and Politics from Subaltern Perspective*. Bangalore: Dharmaram Publications, 1999.

Kaye, William John. *Christianity in India: A Historical Narrative*. London: Smith, Elder and Co. 1859.

Keay, F. E. *History of the Syrian Church in India*. Third Edition. Delhi: ISPCK, 1960.

Keitzar, Renthy, ed. *Good News for North East India*. Guwahati: CLC, 1995.

Kellock, James. *Breakthrough for Church Union in North India and Pakistan*. Madras: CLS, 1965.

Kim, C. H. Sebastian. *In Search of Identity: Debates on Religious Conversion in India*. Delhi: Oxford University Press, 2002.

King, A. *The Rites of Eastern Christendom*. Vol. I. N.p.: Burns Oates, 1947.

Kinnamon, Michael, and Brian E. Cope, eds. *The Ecumenical Movement: An Anthology of Key Texts and Voices*. Geneva: WCC Publications, 1997.

Kochupallikunnel, Ipe. *Pentecostal Churches in Kerala and Indigenous Leadership*. Delhi: ISPCK, 2011.

Koodapuzha, Xavier. *Christianity in India*. Kottayam: Oriental Institute of Religious Studies, 1998.

Koshy, Ninan. *Caste in the Kerala Churches*. Bangalore: CISRS, 1968.

Kuriakose, M. K. *History of Christianity in India: Source Materials*. Madras: Christian Literature Society, 1982.

Laird, M. A. *Missionaries and Education in Bengal, 1793-183*. Oxford: n.p., 1972.

Latourette, K. S. *A History of the Expansion of Christianity*. Vol. VI. USA: Harper, 1945.

Lehmann, E. Arno. *It Began at Tranquebar: The story of the Tranquebar Mission and the Beginning of Protestant Christianity in India Published to celebrate the 250th Anniversary of the Landing of the First Protestant Missionaries at Tranquebar in 1706*. Translated by M. Lutz. Madras: CLS, 1056.

Lolly, R. R. *The Baptist Church in Manipur*. Imphal: Modern Printer, 1985.

Longchar, A. Wati. *An Emerging Asian Theology: Tribal Theology: Issues, Methods and Perspectives*. Jorhat: ETC, 2000, 24-25.

Longchar, Wati and Larry E. Davis, eds. *Doing Theology with Tribal Resources*. Jorhat: ETC, 1999.

Luikhan, T., ed. *History of the Manipur Christian*. Ukhrul: NECA, 1948.

Mabry, P. Hunter. *A Manual for Researchers and Writers*. Second edition. Bangalore: BTESSC, 2003.

Marshall, W. J. *A United Church: Faith and Order in the North India/Pakistan Plan*. Delhi: ISPCK, 1987.

Marshman, J. C. *The Life and Times of Carey, Marshman and Ward: Embracing the History of the Serampore Mission*. Vol. I. London: Longmann & Roberts, 1859.

Massey, James. *Indigenous People: Dalits*. Delhi: ISPCK, 1994.

________. Ed. *Towards a Dalit Theology*. Delhi: ISPCK, 1989.

________. *Dalits in India: Religion as a Source of Bondage or Liberation with a Special Reference to Christians*. New Delhi: Manohar Publishers & Distributors, 1995.

________. *Minorities in a Democracy: the Indian Experience*. New Delhi: Manohar Publishers & Distributors, 1999.

Mattam, Joseph and Jacob Kavunkal, eds. *Ecological Concern: An Indian Christian Response*. Bangalore: NBCLC, 1998.

Miller, Basil. *Praying Hyde: The Story of John Hyde: A Man of Prayer*. Belfast, Northern Ireland: Ambassador, 2000.

Mingana, A. *The Early Spread of Christianity in India*. Manchester University: 1926.

Moffet, Hugh, Samuel. *A History of Christianity in Asia*. Vol. 1. Second edition. New York: Orbis Books, 1998.

Moraes, G. M. *A History of Christianity in India from Early Times to St. Francis Xavier: A.D. 52-1542*. Bombay: Manaktalas, 1964.

Morris, H. John. *The History of the Welsh Calvinistic Methodists Foreign Mission: To the End of the Year 1904*. New Delhi: Indus Publishing Company 1996.

Mundadan, A. M. *History of Christianity in India, Vol. I: From the Beginning up to the Middle of the Sixteenth Century*. Revised edition. Bangalore: CHAI, 2001.

________. *Indian Christians Search for Identity and Struggle for Autonomy*. Bangalore: Dharmaram Publications, 1984.

________. *Sixteenth Century Tradition of Thomas Christians*. Bangalore: Dharmaram College, 1970.

Muttumana, Mathew. *Christianity in Assam and Inter-Faith Dialogue: A Study on the Modern Religious Movements in North East India*. Indore: 1984.

Narain, P. Priyanka. *A High Price for Religious Conversion?*. The Wall Street Journal, livemint.com, 12-03-2009.

Narendera, Kumar. *Constitutional Law of India*. Delhi: Pioneer Publications, 997.

Neill, Stephen. *A History of Christianity in India: The Beginning to AD 1707*. Cambridge: Oxford University Press, 1984.

________. *A History of Christianity in India 1707-1858*. Cambridge: Cambridge University Press, 1985.

Newton, Ken. *Glimpses of Indian Church History*. Second edition. Bombay: Living Light Publications, 1975.

Nock, A. D. *Conversion*. London: Oxford University Press, 1961.

Oddie, G. A. *Social Protest in India: British Protestant Missionaries and Social Reforms 1850-1900*. New Delhi: Manohar, 1979.

Orr, Edwin. *Evangelical Awakenings in India in the Early Twentieth Century*. New Delhi: Masihi Sahitya Sanstha, 1970.

Page, Jesse. *Schwartz of Tanjore*. London: SPCK, 1921.

Panikkar, K. M. *The Foundations of New India*. London: 1963.

Panikkar, K. N. *Culture, Ideology, Hegemony: Intellectuals and Social Consciousness in Colonial India*. New Delhi: Tulika, 1998.

Pathak, Madhava, Sushil. *American Missionaries and Hinduism*. Delhi: Munshiram Manoharlal, 1967.

Paul, D. Rajaiah. *Ecumenism in Action: Church of South India and Assessment.* Madras: CLS, 1972.

________. *The Cross Over India*. London: SCM Press, 1952.

________. *The First Decade: An Account of the Church of South India*. Madras: CLS, 1956.

Paul, D. Rajaiah and J. Kumarsan. *Church of South India-Lutheran Conversations: A Historical Sketch*. Madras: CLS, 1970.

Paul, Khrishna Amar. *Northeast A-Z General Knowledge*. Panbazar, Guwahati: Good Books Distributors Pub., 2003.

Perumalil, A. C. *The Apostles in India*. Allepy: Prakasm Publication, 1971.

Perumalil, H. C., ed. *History of Christianity in India: A History in Ecumenical Perspective*. Alleppey: Prakasan, 1972.

Philip, E. M. *The Indian Church of St. Thomas*. Nagercoil: L.M. Press, 1950.

Philip, Mammen. *Robert F. Cook*. Vennikulam: Deepam Book Club, 1992.

Philip, P. T. *The Growth of Baptist Churches in Nagaland*. Guwahati: CLC, 1976.

Pickett, J. Waskom. *Christian Mass Movements in India*. New York: The Abingdon Press, 1933.

Pillay, K. K. *Studies in the History of India with Special Reference to Tamil Nadu.* Madras: Rathnam Press, 1979.

Pongener, Mar. *Key Issues in the History of Christianity in India 19th through 20th Centuries*. Jorhat: Barkataki & Co. Ltd., 2000.

Pothen, S. G. *The Syrian Christians of Kerala*. Fourth edition. Madras: K. M. Cherian, 1968.

Prabhakar, M. E., ed. *Towards a Dalit Theology*. Delhi: ISPCK, 1988.

Purkait, A. B. *Indian Renaissance and Education: From Ram Mohan to Vivekananda*. Calcutta: Firma K.L.M. Ltd, 1992.

Puthenpurakal, Joseph. *Baptist Mission in Nagaland.* Shillong: Vendrame Missiological Institute, 1984.

________. *Impact of Christianity on North East India*. Shillong: Vendrame Institute Publication, 1996.

Pylee, M. V. *India's Constitution*. Bombay: Asia Publishing House, 1962.

Raiser, Konrad. *For a Culture of Life: Transforming Globalization and Violence.* Thiruvalla: CSS, 2002.

Rajamanickam, S., ed. *His Star in the East.* Madras: De Nobili Institute, 1995.

________. *The First Oriental Scholar.* Tirunelveli: De Nobili Research Institute, 1972.

Ramabai, Pandita. *A Testimony.* Pune: Ramabai Mukti Mission, 1917.

Ray, B. Datta. *Tribal Identity and Tension in North East India.* New Delhi: Omsons Publications, 1989.

________, ed. *The Emergence and Role of Middle Class in North East India.* New Delhi: Uppal, 1983.

Reid, Robert. *Years of Change in Bengal and Assam.* London: 1966.

Richter, Julius. *A History of Mission in India.* Translated by Sidney Moore. London: Oliphant Anderson and Ferrier, 1908.

Robert, M. Cecil. *The Azusa Street Mission and Revival: The Birth Place of Global Pentecostals in India.* Tennessee: Thomas Nelson, 2006.

Rosaldo, M. Z. and L. Lamphere, eds. *Women, Culture and Society.* Stanford: Stanford University Press, 1974.

Rosemary Radford Ruether, *Womanguide.* Boston: Beacon Press, 1985.

Rouse, Ruth and Stephen Charles Neill, eds. *A History of the Ecumenical Movement: 1517-1948.* Geneva: WCC, 1986.

Russel, Letty M., ed. *Feminist Interpretation of the Bible.* Philadelphia: Westminster, 1985.

Russel. J., ed. *The Joint Council of the CNI, CSI and Malankar Mar Thoma Syrian Church: A Brief History and Interpretation.* Delhi: ISPCK, 1984.

Sahu, D. K. *United and Uniting: A History of the Church of North India.* Delhi: ISPCK, 2001.

Said, W. Edward. *Orientalism: Western Conception of the Orient.* New Delhi: Penguin Books, 2001.

Sangma, Milton. *American Baptist Mission in North East India.* Dibrugarh: NEIHA, 1981.

Sastry, K. A. Nilakanta and G. Srinivasachari. *India: A Historical Survey.* Bombay: Allied Publishers, 1970.

Seamands, J. T. *Tell It Well: Communicating Gospel Across Cultures.* Missouri: Beacon Hill Press of Kansas City, 1981.

Senate of Serampore College Regulations for Internal and External Candidate: Relating to the Bachelor of Divinity Degree. December, 1962.

Shah, Abid. Ed. *Indian People's Tribunal on Untouchability: Untouchability on Trial.* New Delhi: Human Rights Law Network (HRLN), 2008.

Sherring, M. A. *The History of Protestant Mission in India from their Commencement in 1706-1871.* London: Trubner and Co., 1975.

Shiri, Godwin. *The Plight of Christian Dalits: a South Indian Case Study.* Bangalore: Asian Trading Corporation, 1997.

Shiva, Vandana. *Staying Alive: Women, Ecology and Survival in India.* New Delhi: Kali for Women, 1998.

Shukla, V.N. *Constitution of India.* Lucknow: Eastern Book Company, 2001.

Sietzema-Riemer, Elze. *Christian Dalits: A Research on Christian Dalits in India.* Germany: Universiteit Utrecht, 2009.

Singh, K. M. *History of Christian Missions in Manipur and other Neighboring States.* New Delhi: Mittal Publications, 1991.

Singh, K. Suresh, ed. *Tribal Situation.* Shimla: n.p., 1972.

Smith, George. *Life of William Carey, Shoemaker & Missionary.* London: n.p., 1909.

________. *The Life of Alexander Duff.* New York: A. C. Armstrong & Sons, 1879.

Snaitang, O. L. *Christianity and Social Change in North East India.* Shillong: Vendrame Institute, 1993.

Solo M. Johnah and K. Mahengthei, eds. *William Pettigrew 40 years in Manipur and Assam.* Imphal: Modern Press, 1986.

Sreenivas, H. V. Murthy and S. U. Kamath. *Studies in Indian Culture.* Madras: Asia Publication House, 1973.

Srivastana, K. Dhirendra. *Religious Freedom in India: A Historical and Constitutional Study.* New Delhi: Deep & Deep Publications, 1982.

Stewart, S. Wilma, ed. *The Story of Serampore and Its College.* Serampore: The Council of Serampore College, 1961.

Sundkler, Bengt. *Church of South India: The Movement towards Union 1900-1947.* London: Lutterworth Press, 1954.

Sutharalingam, R. *Politics and National Awakening in South India 1852-1891.* Arizona: The University of Arizona Press, 1974.

Syemlieh, David. *A Brief History of the Catholic Church in Nagaland.* Nagaland: n.p., 1990.

Synan, Vinson, ed. *Aspects of Pentecostal Charismatic Origins.* New Jersey: Logos International, 1975.

Talibuddin, W. Ernest. *An Introduction to the History of the Anglican Church in North East India (1841-1970).* Delhi: ISPCK, 2009.

Tauli-Corpus, Victori. *Globalization and its Impacts on Indigenous Women: The Philippines Experience*. Malaysia: Third World Network, 2001.

Thaliath, Jonas. *The Synod of Diamper*. Rome: n.p., 1958.

Thanzauva, K. *Theology of Community: Tribal Theology in the Making*. Aizawl: Mizo Theological Conference, 1997.

Thekedathu, Joseph. *The Troubled Days of Francis Garcia S.J.: Archbishop of Cranganore (1641-1659)*. Rome: n.p., 1972.

The Preamble to the Constitution of India.

Thekkedath, Joseph. *History of Christianity in India*. Vol. II (Bangalore: Church History Association of India, 1982.

Thomas, M. M. *Recalling the Ecumenical Beginnings*. Delhi: ISPCK, 1987.

Thomas, P. *Christianity in India and Pakistan: A General Survey of the Progress of Christianity in India from Apostolic Times to the Present Day*. London: George Allen and Unwin Ltd., 1954.

Tillich, Paul. *Christianity and the Religions of the World.* New York: Columbia University Press, 1963.

Tisserant, E. *Eastern Christianity in India*. Translated by E. R. Hambaye, S.J. Bombay: Orient Longmans, 1957.

Toynbee, George. *A Sketch of the Administration of the Hooghly District from 1795-1845*. Calcutta: 1888.

Tracy, Joseph. *History of the American Board of Commissioners for Foreign Missions*. New York: M.W. Doddm, 1842.

Varghese V. Titus and P. P. Philip. *Glimpses of the History of the Christian Churches in India*. Madras: CLS, 1983.

Verma, R. C. *Indian Tribes through the Ages*. New Delhi: Patiala House, 1990.

Victor, Vinod, Leslie Nathaniel and P. Surya Prakash, eds. *Ecumenism, Prospects and Challenges*. Delhi: ISPCK, 2001.

Vidyarthi, L. P. and B. K. Rai. *The Tribal Culture of India*. New Delhi: Concept Publishing Company, 1985.

Walsh, W. P. *Heroes of the Mission Field*. London: Hodder and Stoughton, 1883.

Webster, C. B. John. *The Christian Community and Change in Nineteenth Century North India*. Delhi: The Macmillan Company of India Ltd, 1976.

________. *Religion and Dalit Liberation: an Examination of Perspectives*. Delhi: Manohar, 1999.

Young, G. William. *Handbook of Source-Materials for Students of Church History, Indian Theological Library*, No. 28. Madras, 1969.

________. *Patriarch, Shah and Caliph: A Study of the Relationships of the Church of the East with the Sassanid Empire and the Early Caliphates up to 820 A.D with Special Reference to Available Syriac Sources*. Rawalpindi: n.p., 1974.

Young, Pamela Dickey. *Feminist Theology/Christian Theology: In Search of Method.* Eugene: Wipf & Stock Publishers, 2000.

Zachariah, Aleyamma. *Modern Religious and Secular Movements in India.* Bangalore: Theological Book Trust, 1998.

Zachariah, Mathai. *Beyond Ecumenism: A Journey in Light.* Thiruvalla: CSS, 2002.

________. Ed. *Freedom of Religion in India.* Nagpur: NCCI, 1979.

Articles/Journals/Periodicals/Unpublished Materials etc.

Adhikari, Prabhudan. "Episcopacy in the CNI." *The North Indian Churchman* (June, 1979): 1-5.

Anderson, H. Allan. "Signs and Blunders: Pentecostal Mission Issues at Home and Abroad in the Twentieth Century." *JAM* 2 (2000): 193-210.

Ariarajah, S. Wesley. "Socio-Political Issues and the Credibility of Dialogue." *NCCR* 120/4 (May, 2000): 424-530.

Burgess, M. Stanley. "Pentecostalism in India: An Overview." *AJPS* 4/1 (July, 2001): 86-87.

Chitnis, Varsh. "The Legacy of Colonialism: Law and Women's Rights in India." *Washington and Lee Law Review* 64/4 (Sept-December, 2007): 1310- 1315.

Cronin, V. "Roberto De Nobili." *New Catholic Encyclopedia* X.

Downs, F. S. "Origin of Christianity in the Garo Hills of Meghalaya." *ICHR* 1 (June, 1972): 1-3.

________. "Rangamati: A Christian Community in North East India during the Seventeenth and Eighteenth Centuries." *ICHR* XII/2 (Dec, 1978): 85-89.

Farquhar, J. N. "The Apostle Thomas in North India." *Bulletin of the John Rhylands Library* 10 (1926): 80-90.

________. "The Apostle Thomas in South India." *Bulletin of the John Rhylands Library* 10/1 (January, 1927): 21.

Fernando, S. Vanatius. "Portuguese Patronage (Padroado) and the Evangelization of the Pearl fishery Coast." *ICHR* XVIII (December, 1984): 91-98.

Gensichen, D. H. W. "Daring, in order to know the contribution of Christian Missionaries to the Understanding of Hinduism, 1550-1850." *ICHR* (December 1986): 92-95.

Gensichen, H. W. "Abominable Hinduism: A Rediscovered Tract by Bartholomaeus Ziegenbalg." *ICHR* 1 (June 1967): 35-40.

________. "Imitating the wisdom of the Almighty." *Concordia Theological Monthly* 28 (September 1957): 834-840.

________. "Tranquebar Then and Now." *The Indian Journal of Theology* V (October 1956): 21-27.

George, A. C. "Pentecostal Beginnings in India." *DD* (2002), 41-43.

________. "Pentecostal Beginnings in Travancore, South India." *AJPS* 5/1 (2002): 24-26.

Gladstone, J. W. "Historical Development of the Indian Ecumenical Movement and its Implications for the Future." *NCCR* 114/6 (July, 1994): 449-456.

Grafe, Hugald. "Hindu Apologetics at the Beginning of the Protestant Mission Era in India." *ICHR* VI (June 1972): 43.

________. "The Relation between the Tranquebar Lutheran and the Tanjore Catholics." *ICHR* I (June 1967): 43.

________. "Tranquebar Lutherans and Tanjore Catholics." *ICHR* 1 (June, 1967): 54.

Gregson, J. "Benares Missionary Conference." *Calcutta Christian Observer* 18/2 (December, 1857): 114-116.

Jeyakumar, D. Arthur. "Methodological Issues in the History of Christianity." A Paper Presented at the Doctoral Research Methodology Seminar. Bangalore: UTC, 2007.

Justus, M. "Schwartz: A Missionary in Politics 1750-1798." *ICHR* XXVI (June 1992): 38-43.

Kaserow, M. John. "Christian Evaluation of Buddhism from Clement of Alexandria to the Renaissance." Doctoral Dissertation, University of St. Michael's College, Toronto: 1976, 49.

Kennedy, D. M. "The CNI History." *ICHR* 6/2 (December, 1972): 108-113.

________. "Work in Progress: The CNI History." *ICHR* 8/1 (June, 1973): 11-16.

Ka Pateng Khristan (KPK) 3/9 (Shillong: September, 1939): 131-132.

Lehmann, E. Arno. "August Hermann Francke and the Beginning of the Tranquebar Mission." *Lutheran World* X (July 1963): 310

Letter of Nobili to Provincial Laerzio January, 15, 1609.

Longchar, Wati. "Tribal Theology: Development, Issues and Challenges." *Journal of Tribal Studies* XVII/1 (January-June 2012): 1-7.

Massey, James. "Christian Dalits in India: An Analysis." *RS* XXXVII/3 (September, 1990).

________. "The Role of Partner Churches in the Whole Dalit Issue." *NCCR* CXII/7 (September, 1992): 504-505.

________. "The Role of the Churches in the Whole Dalit Issue." *NCCR* CXVI/5 (May-June, 1996): 396-397.

Mathew, P. "C.N.I.-C.S.I.-Mar Thoma Church Union." *NCCI* CXIII/7 (August, 1993): 404-410.

Meersman, Schilles. "The Catholic Church in Tranquebar and Tanjore during the Formative Years of the Lutheran Mission." *ICHR* I (December 1967): 96.

McGee, B. Gary. "'Latter Rain' Falling in the East: Early Twentieth-Century Pentecostalism in India and the Debate over Speaking in Tongues." *Church History: Studies in Christianity and Culture* 68/3 (Sept. 1999): 658-65.

________. "The Calcutta Revival of 1907 and the Reformulation of Charles Parharm's Bible Evidence Doctrine." *AJPS* 5/1 (2002): 123-43.

Mingana, A. "The Spread of Christianity in India." *Bulletin of the John Rhylands Library* 2 (Manchester, July 1926): 437-442.

Minz, Nirmal. "Mission in the Context of Diversity: Mission in Tribal Context." *RS* 36/1 (March, 1989): 10-15.

Mundadan, A. M. "Changing Approaches to Historiography." *ICHR* XXXV/1 (June, 2001): 43-49.

Oddie, G. A. "Indian Christians and the National Congress, 1885-1910." *ICHR* 8/2 (December, 1968): 46-50.

Oommen, George. "A Commentary on Subaltern Studies Collective: Methodological Implications for Theological Research." *A Paper Presented during D.Th. Colloquium Program at UTC (Bangalore)*, 12th May 2003.

________. "Historiography of Indian Christianity and Challenges of Subaltern Methodology." *Journal of Dharma* XXVIII/2 (April-June 2003): 211-219.

Philip, T. V. "Christianity in India during Western Colonialism: Conflicts, Reconciliation or Adjustment." *ICHR* XXI/1 (June 1987): 13-19.

Pulikottil, Paulson. "As East and West Met in God's Own Country: Encounter of Western Pentecostalism with Native Pentecostalism in Kerala." *AJPS* 5/1 (2002): 34-39.

________. "Emergence of Indian Pentecostalism." *DD* (2002): 51-54.

Rajamanickam, A. "Roberto de Nobili and Adaptation." *ICHR* 1 (December 1967): 83-91.

Rajamanickam, S. "De Nobili in the Madurai Jail: a letter of Sebastian de Maya." *ICHR* 18 (December 1984): 87-93.

Rivenburg, S. W. "Historical Sketch of the Angami Naga Mission." *The Assam Mission of the ABMU* (December, 1886): 85-90.

Scherer, A. James. "Bartholomew Ziegenbalg." *Missiology: An international Review* XXVI (October, 1999): 482-490.

SC/ST Commissioner's Report, Extracts. *Dalit Voice* (December, 1989): 17-19.

Singson, D. "The Baptist Involvement in the Church Union Movement in India." M.Th, Thesis, Senate of Serampore College, 1975.

Snaitang, O. L. "The Indigenous Pentecostal Movement." *Dharma Deepika* 6/2 (2002): 6-16.

Stafford, E. "A Brief Report of the Church Union Consultation." Manuscript CBCNEI Office, 1971. Stafford Papers. CBCNEI Office Archives, Guwahati.

Sunderaraj, T. "Establishment of the old Jesuit Mission of Madurai." *ICHR* XV (December, 1981): 114-122.

Victor, Henry. "Tamil Translation of the Bible by the Danish-Halle Mission during the Eighteen Century." *ICHR* XVI (June 1982): 74-80.

Weber, Edmund. "Religion: A Source of Oppression and Liberation." *Bulletin of the Christian Institute for Religious Studies* 23/2 (July, 1994): 4-8.

Webster, C. B. John. "The History of Christianity in India: Aims and Methods." *ICHR* XIII/2 (December, 1979): 87-95.

Wright, D. I. "Schwartz of Thanjavur: Rajaguru?" *ICHR* XV (December 1981): 128-132.

Yesudas, D. "Indigenisation or Adaptation? A Brief Study of Robert de Nobili's Attitude to Hinduism." *Bangalore Theological Forum* I (April 1967): 50-53.

Reports/Meeting Minutes/Dictionaries/Letters/News Papers etc.

"A Glimpse of Nagaland Churches." *Nagaland Celebrates Quasqui Centennial.* Kohima, Nagaland: NBCC, 1997.

A Statement from the Workshop of Sustainable Mobility, July 14-16 2000. Bangalore: ECC, 2000.

Assam Christian Council, 3rd Annual Conference. Minutes of the Meeting of the Committee, 29-31 March 1940.

Assam Christian Council, 5th Annual Conference. Minutes of the Meeting of the Committee, 1942.

Assam Christian Council, 7th Annual Conference. Minutes of the Meeting of the Committee, 1944.

Assam Christian Council, 10th Annual Conference. Minutes of the Meeting of the Committee, 1947.

Assam Christian Council, 12th Annual Conference. Minutes of the Meeting of the Committee, 1949.

CSI-CNI-MTC. Minutes of the Executive Meeting of the Joint Council, 25-26 June 1982. (Cyclostyled).

CSI-CNI-MT Churches. Minutes of the First Meeting of the Joint Theological Commission, 16 January 1975. (Cyclostyled).

CSI-CNI-MTC Churches. Minutes of the Second Meeting of the Joint Theological Commission, 3-4 June 1975. (Cyclostyled).

Lutheran and Church Union Symposium (Madras: TPH, 1989).

Laerzio, Provincial. Letter to the General, 8th December 1610.

Marthoma Church Constitution. Chapter 16, Section 388.

Minutes of the Meetings of the NCCI 1989-91 (Nagpur: NCCI, 1991). (Cyclostyled).

Minutes of the Meetings of the National Council of Churches in India, July 1991 (Nagpur: NCCI, 1992). (Cyclostyled).

Oxford Advanced Learner's Dictionary of Current English (2003), 234.

Report of the General Secretary of Manipur Baptist Convention for the year 2011 Presented at the Annual Meeting of CBCNEI held at Hamren Town Baptist Church, Karbi Anglong from April 27-29, 2012.

Report of the General Secretary of Nagaland Baptist Church Council for the year 2011 Presented at the Annual Meeting of CBCNEI held at Hamren Town Baptist Church, Karbi Anglong from April 27-29, 2012.

Report of the Punjab Missionary Conference held at Lahore in December and January 1862-63 on the Communion Service, 1863.

Report of the Regional Secretary of the Garo Baptist Convention Presented at the Annual Meeting of CBCNEI held at Hamren Town Baptist Church, Karbi Anglong from April 27-29, 2012.

Report on the General Missionary Conference, held at Allahabad on Dec. 26, 1872, to January 1, 1873.

The Annual Report of the General Secretary, Assam Baptist Convention Presented at the 62nd CBCNEI AGM held at Hamrem Town Baptist Church, 27-29 April, 2012.

The Annual Report of the General Secretary, Karbi Anglong Baptist Convention Presented at the 62nd CBCNEI AGM held at Hamrem Town Baptist Church, 27-29 April, 2012.

The Constitution of the Church of South India. Madras: CLS, 1982.

The Constitution of the Church of South India Chapter II, Section 2. Madras: CLS, 1952.

The Constitution of the Church of the South India Chapter II, Section 21. Madras: CLS, 1952.

The Constitution of the Joint Council of the CNI, CSI and MTC. Delhi: ISPCK, 1981.

The CSI after 30 Years. Report of the Special Committee appointed by the CSI Synod to Study the Life and Work of the Church. Madras: CLS, 1978.

The Hindu (Kochi), 20 January 2004.

http://www.utc.edu.in/